How to use this book

Let's Begin - Gather Your Materials

Grab your "Creative Kids' Step-by-Step Sketchbook" and your favourite drawing tools. Pencils, erasers, and colored markers or crayons are perfect for this artistic journey!

☆ **Start your drawing here**

☆ **Follow the Steps**

Take your time and follow the instructions carefully, adding one element at a time.

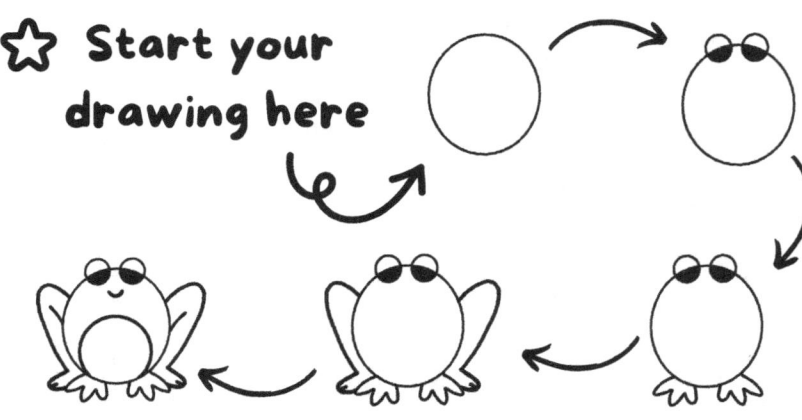

Trace the provided outline to set up your drawing

Space provided for your own drawing

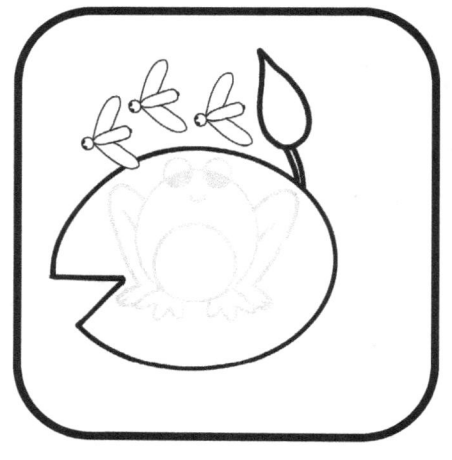

Add your creative touch with colors and details

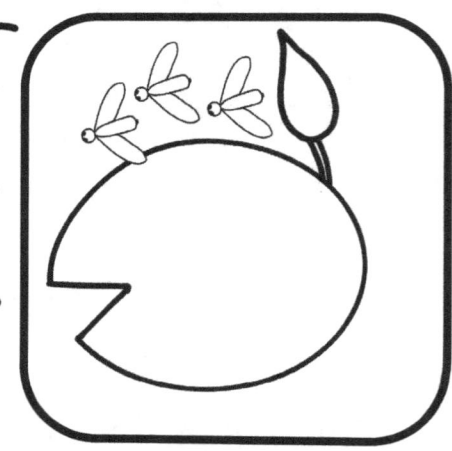

Show off your masterpieces and have fun creating!

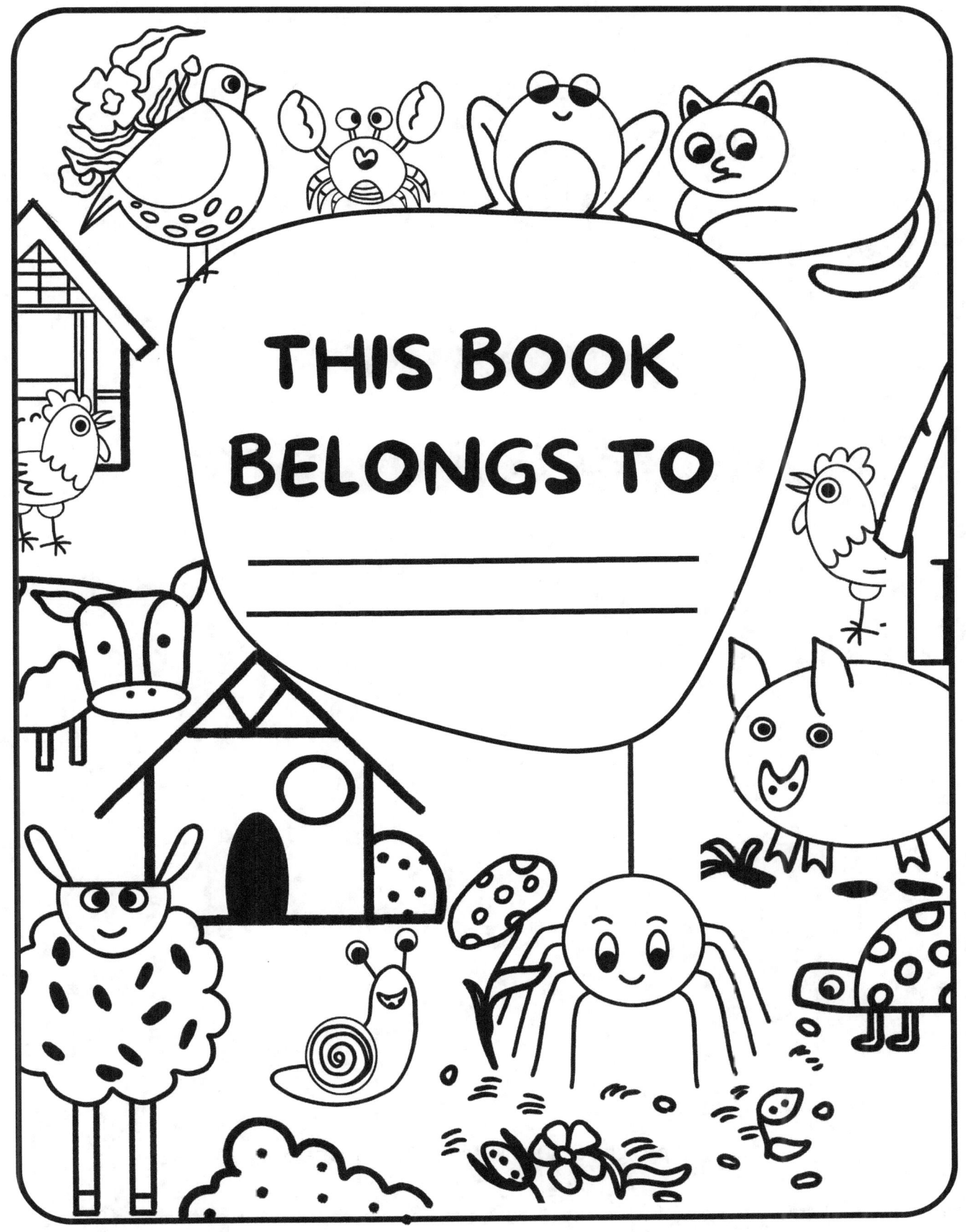

THIS BOOK BELONGS TO

_____

_____

Tortoise

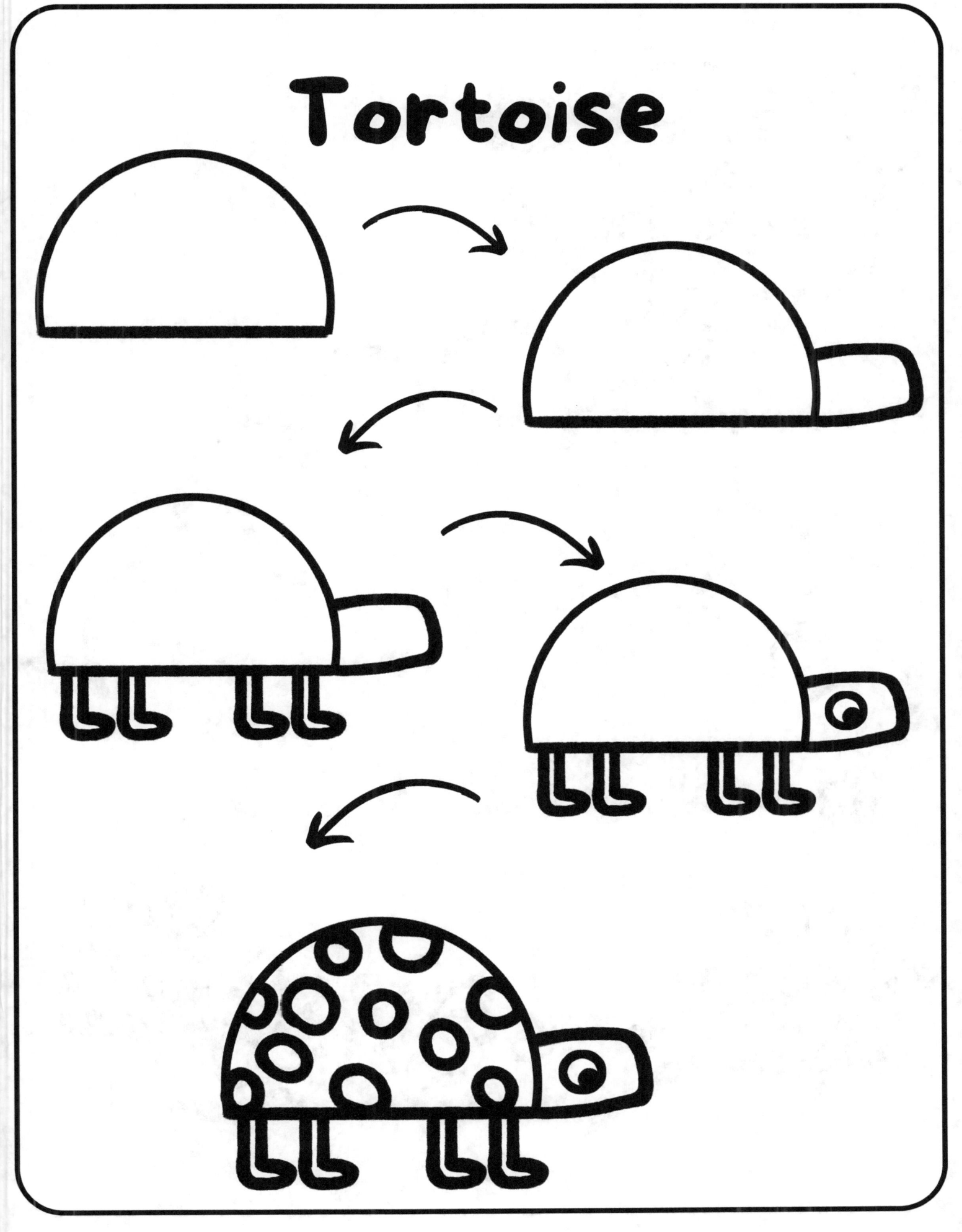

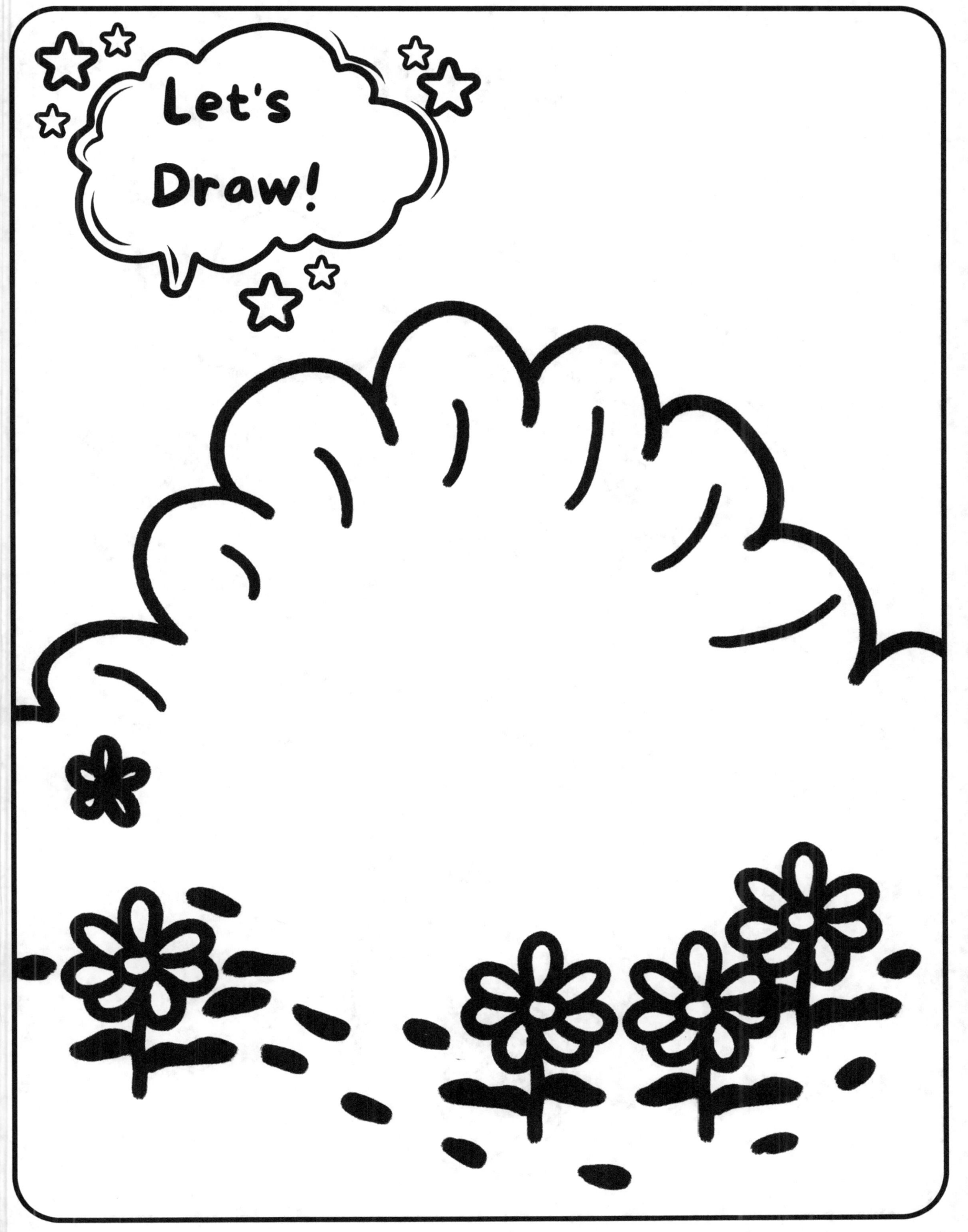

Snail

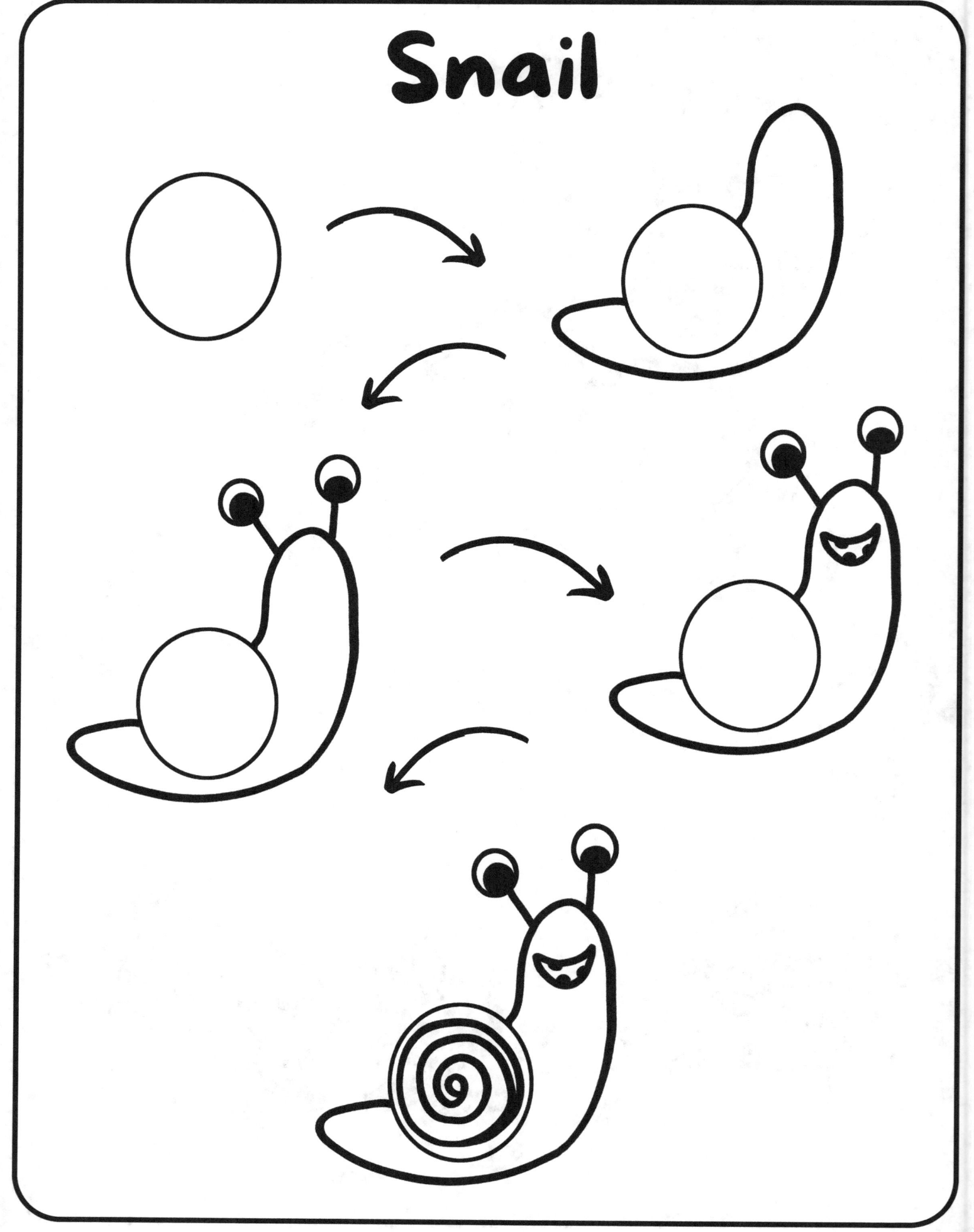

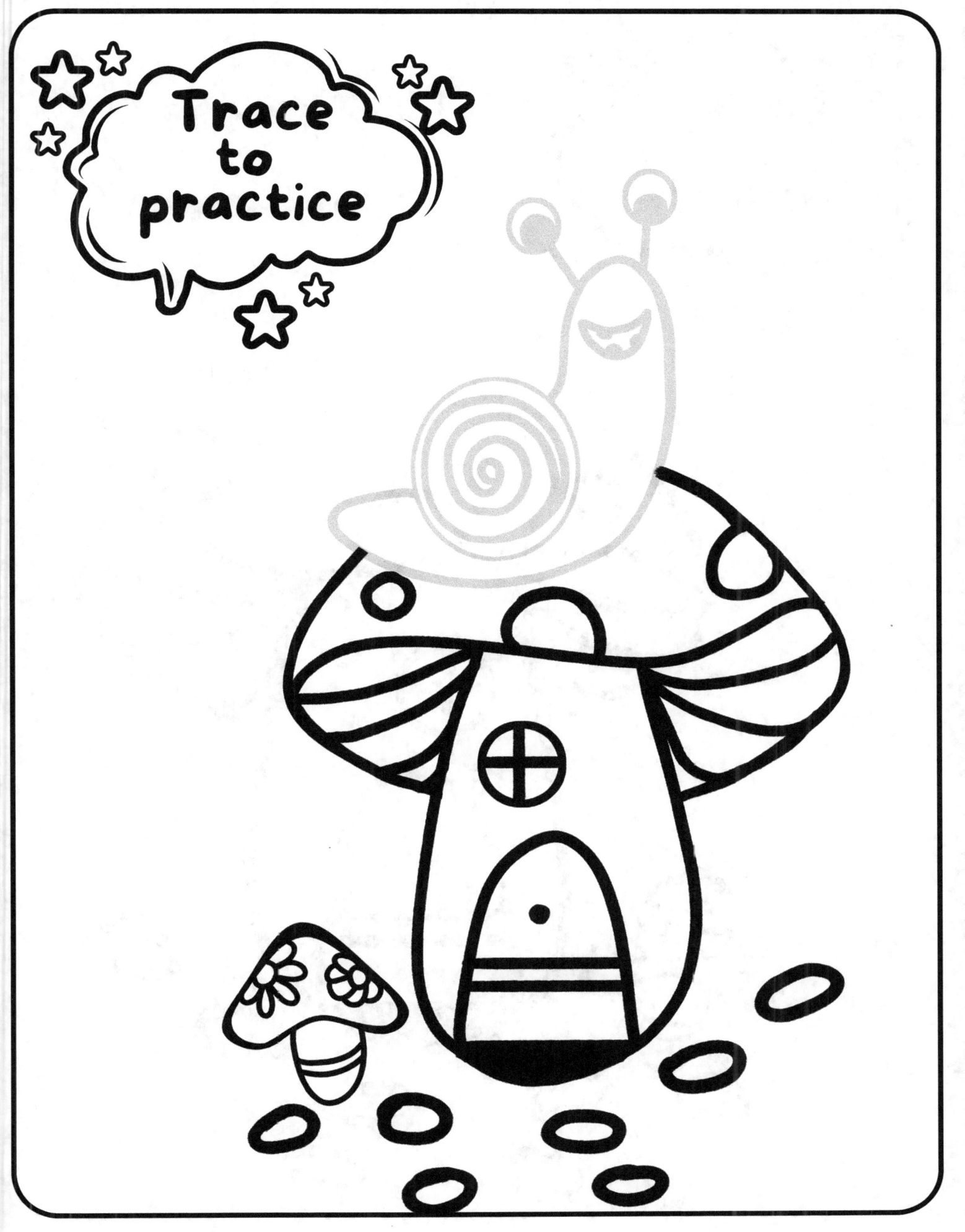

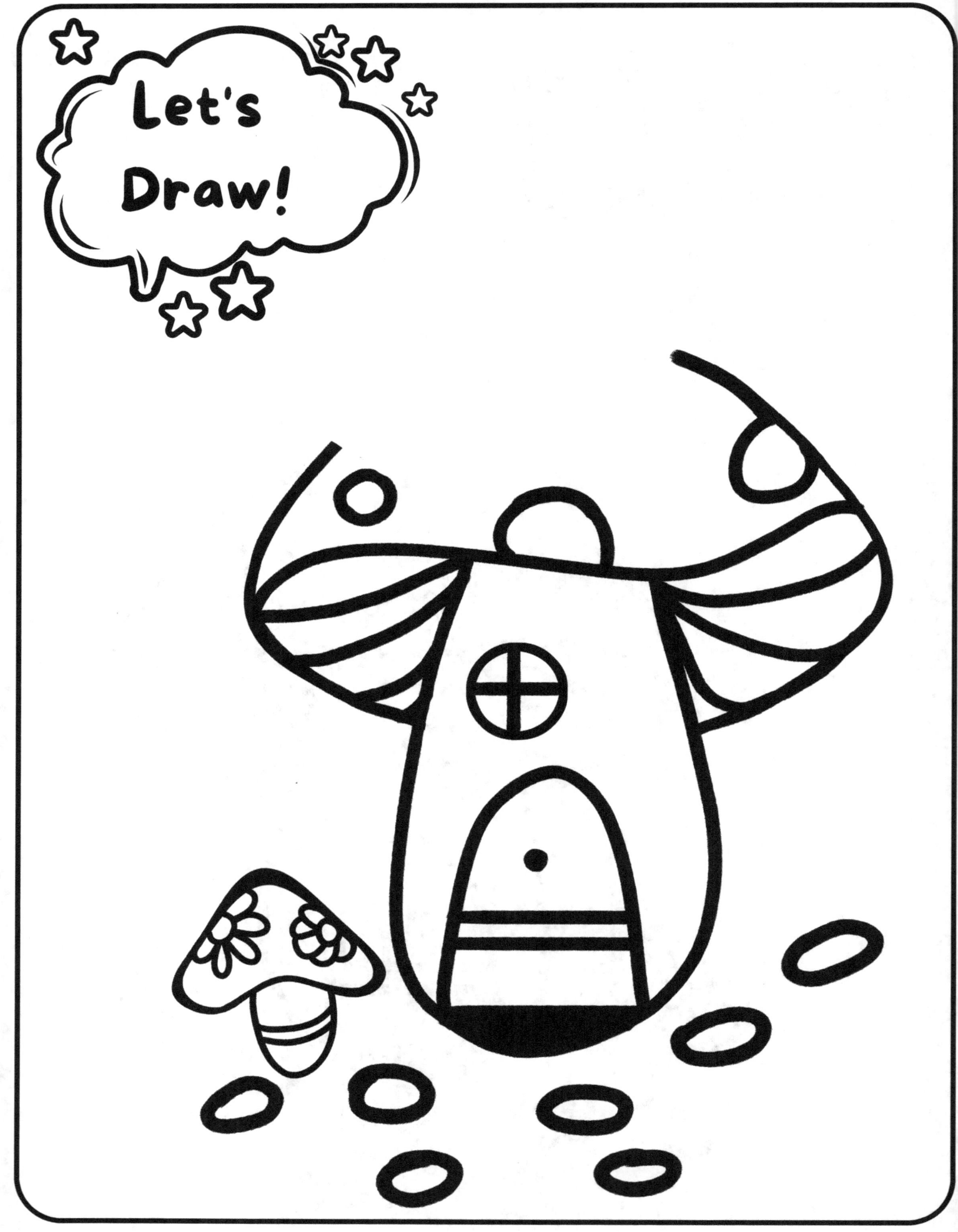

Breakfast

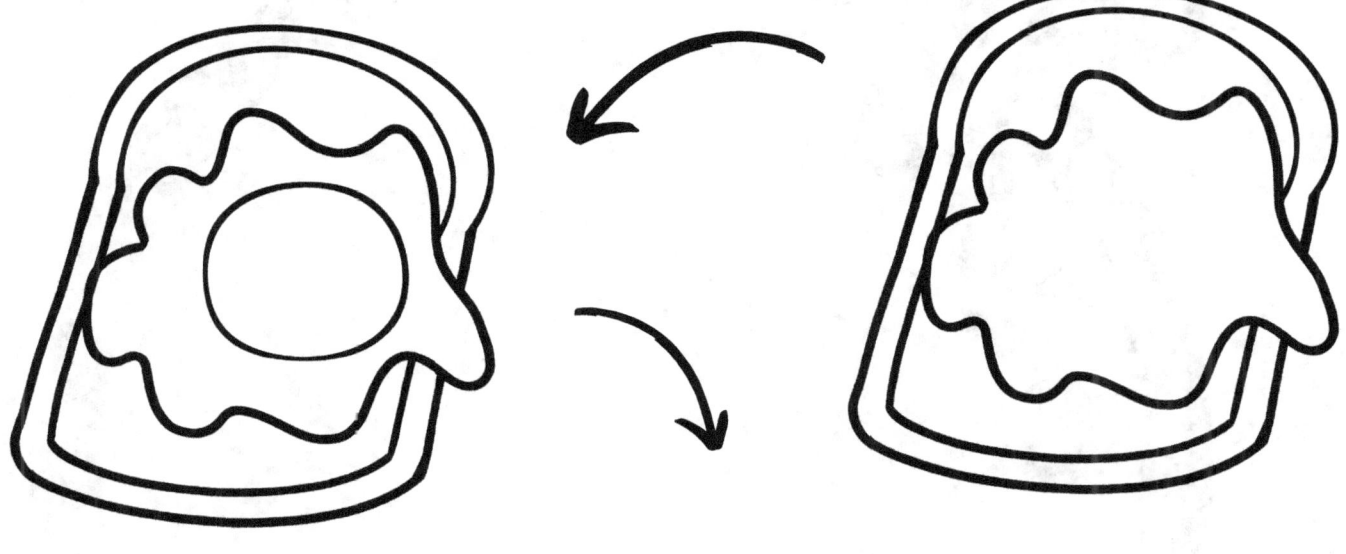

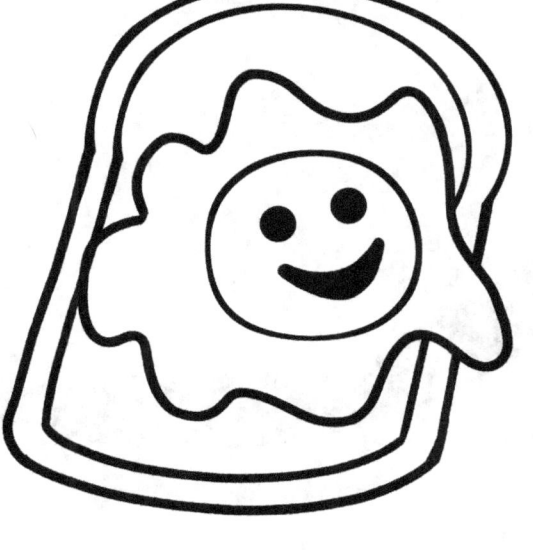

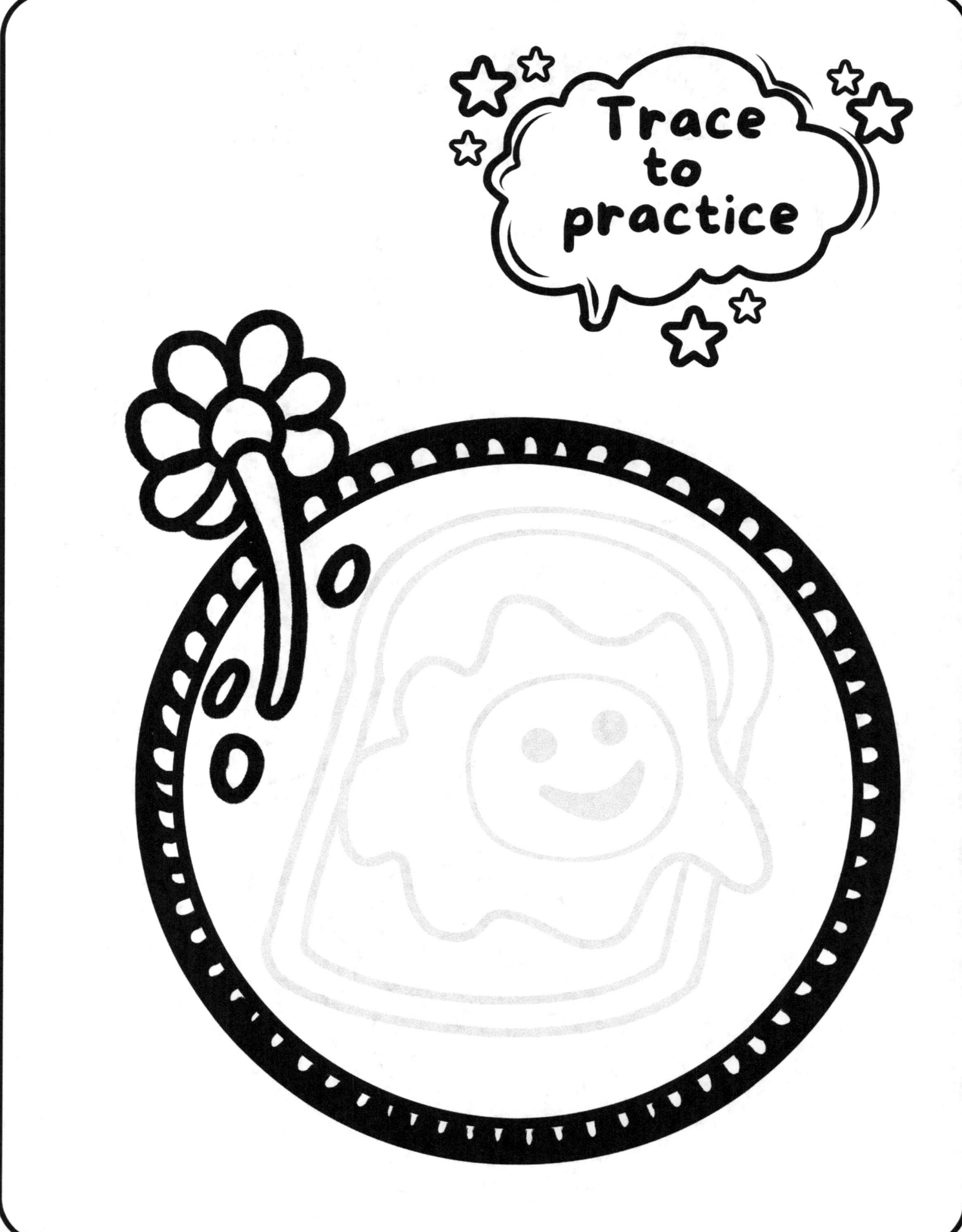

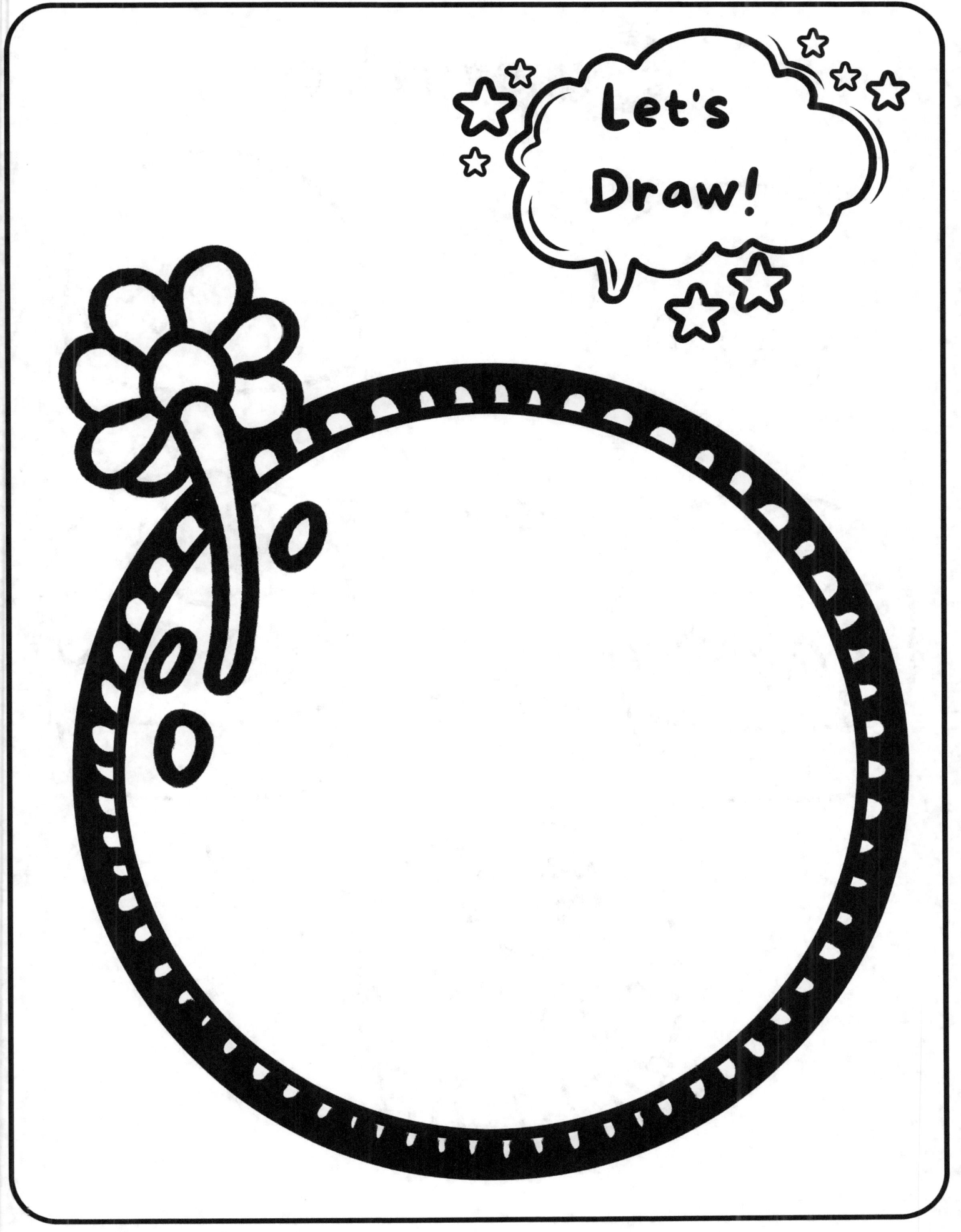

Cupcake

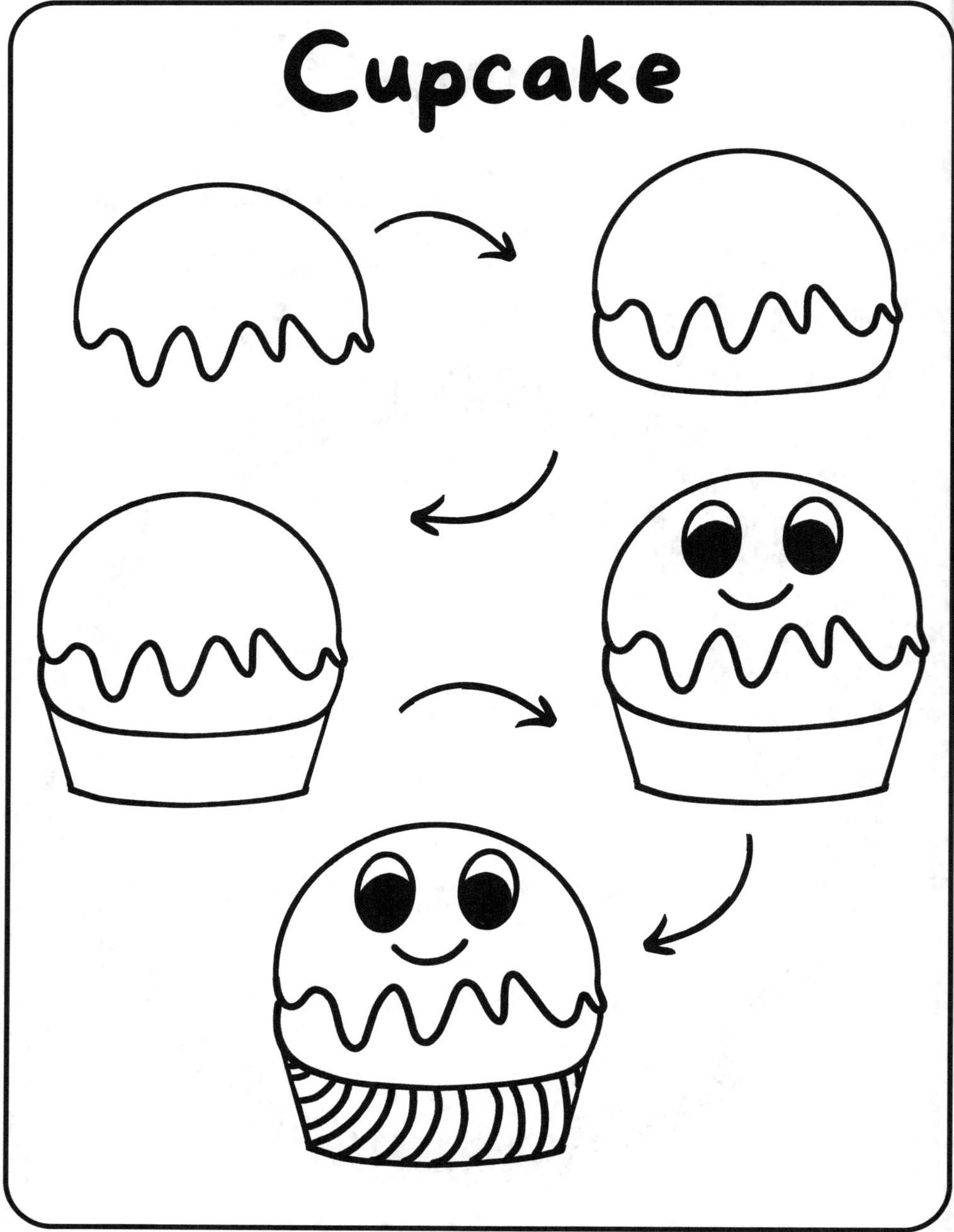

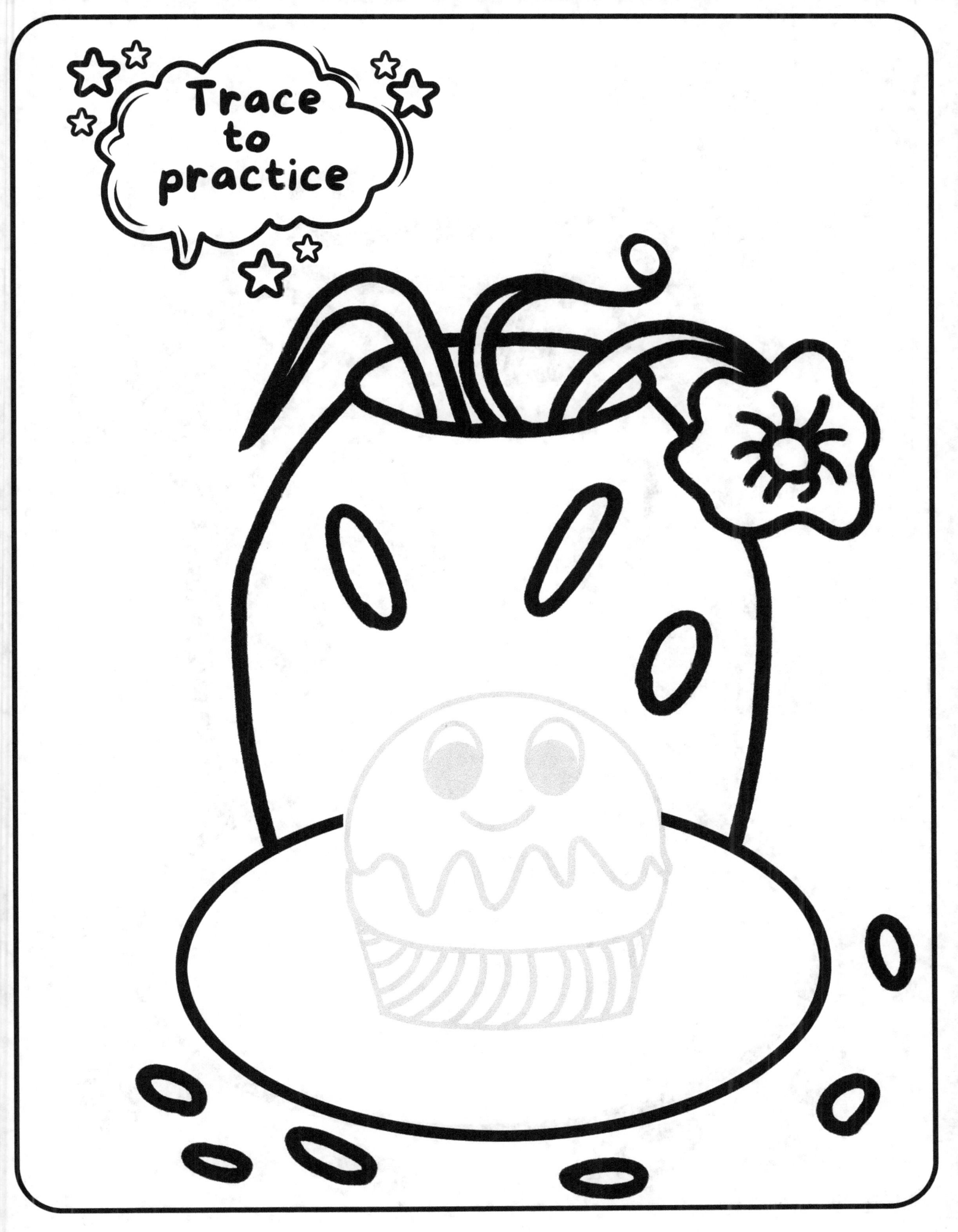

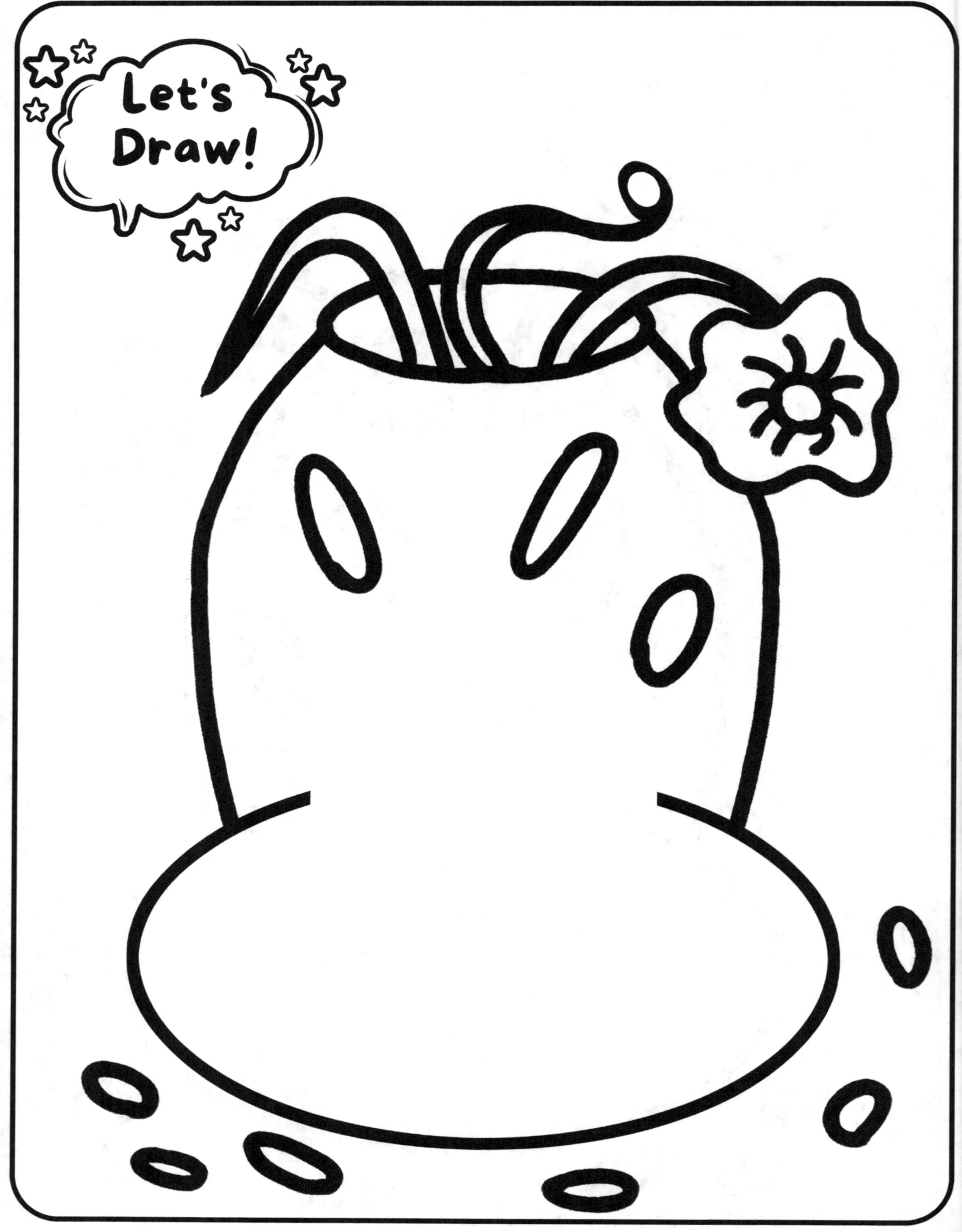

Car

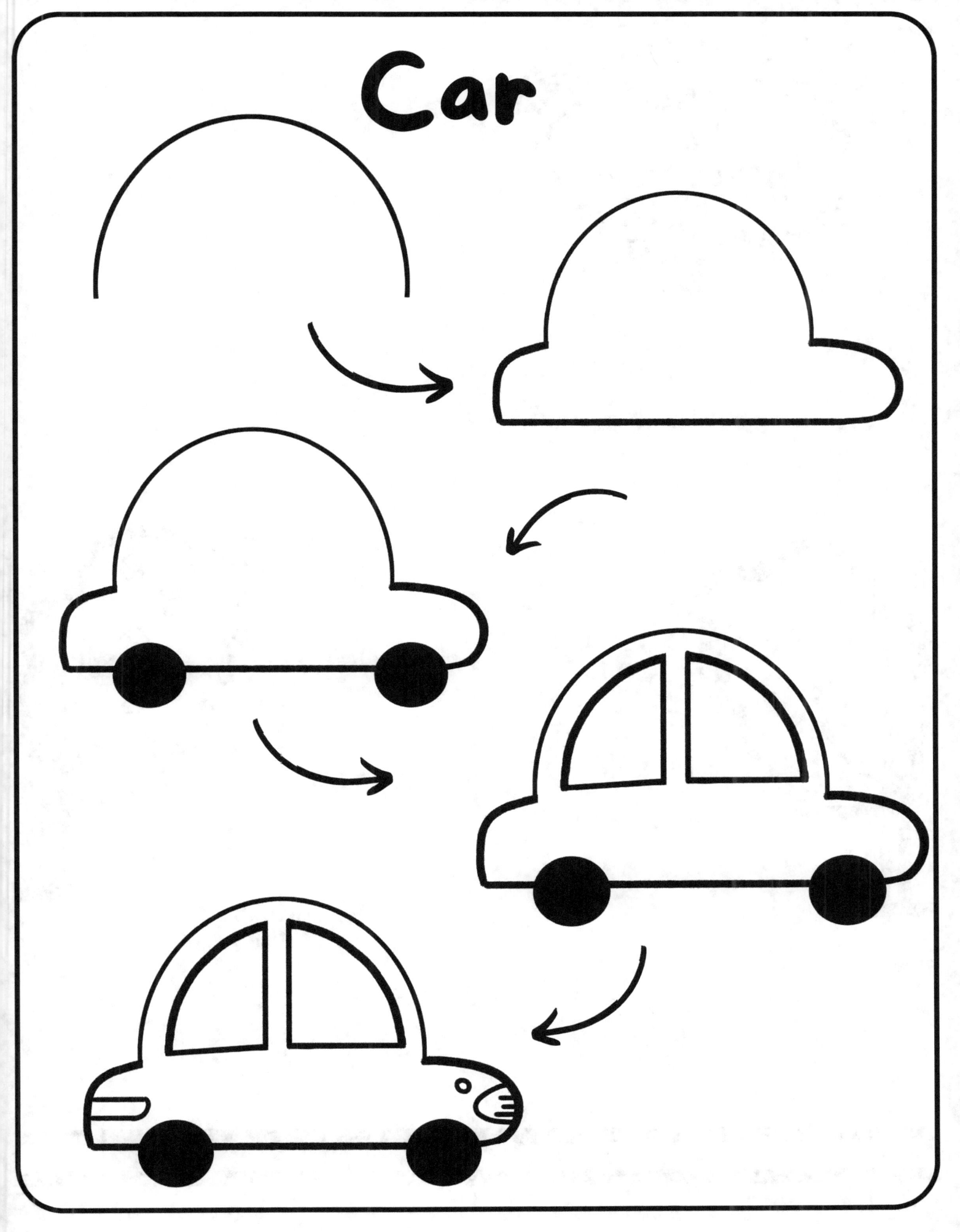

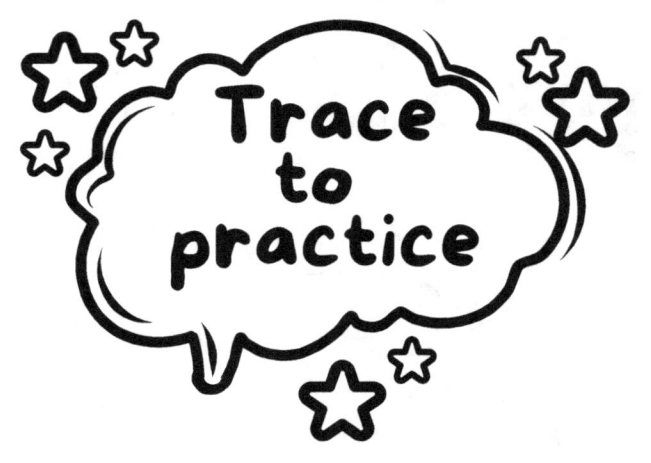

Trace
to
practice

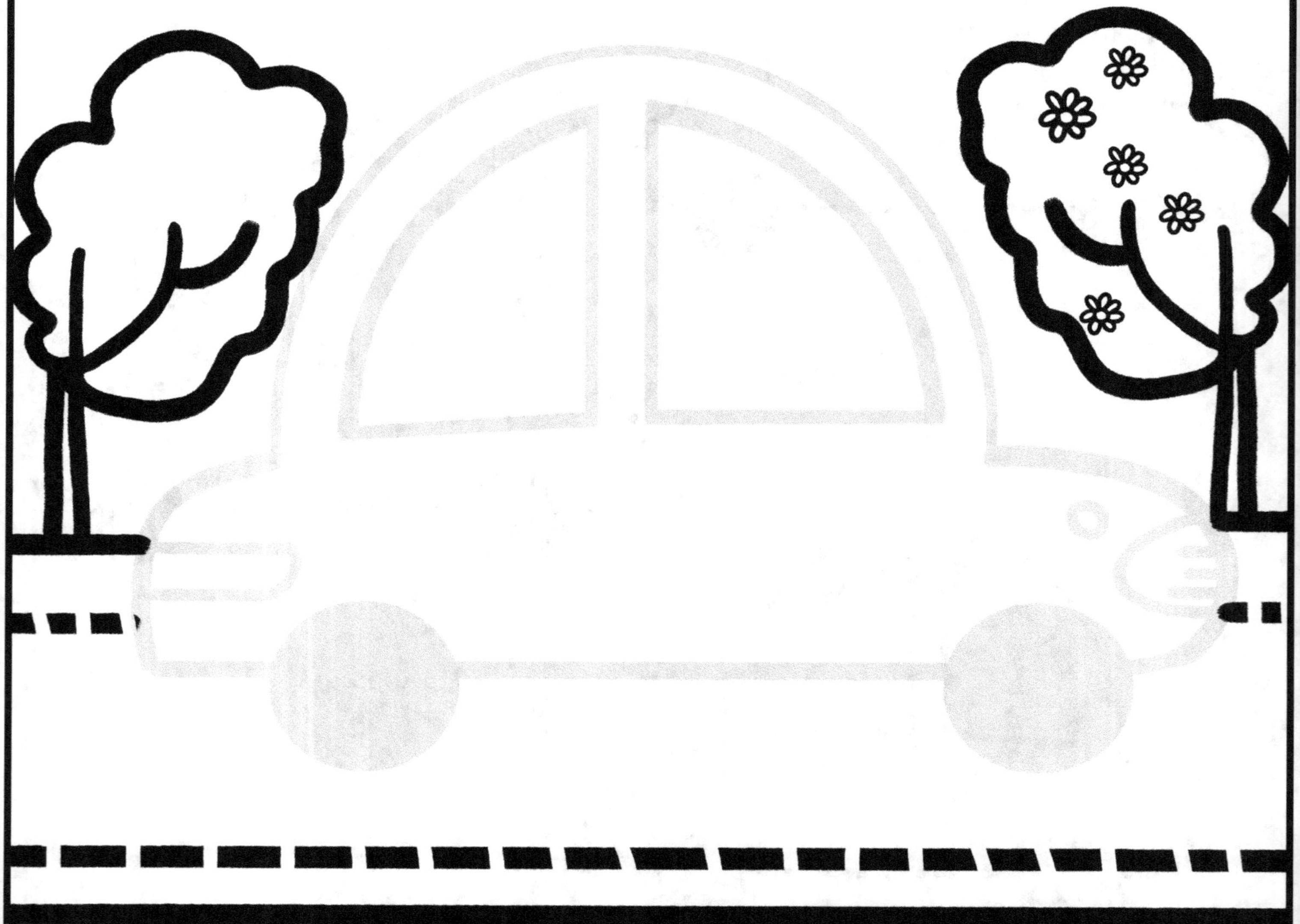

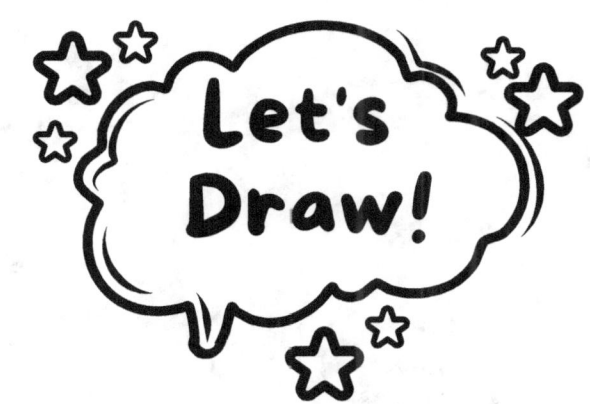

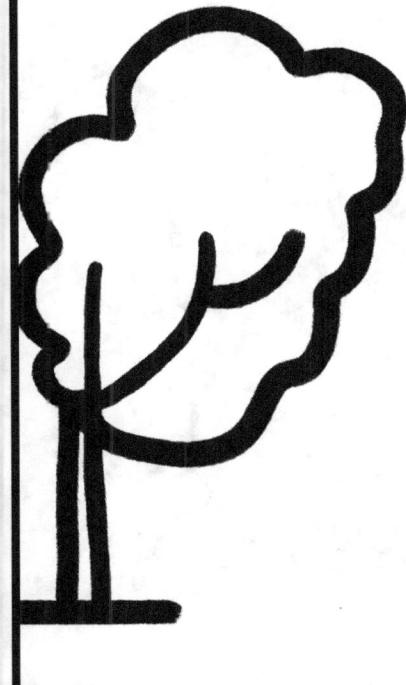

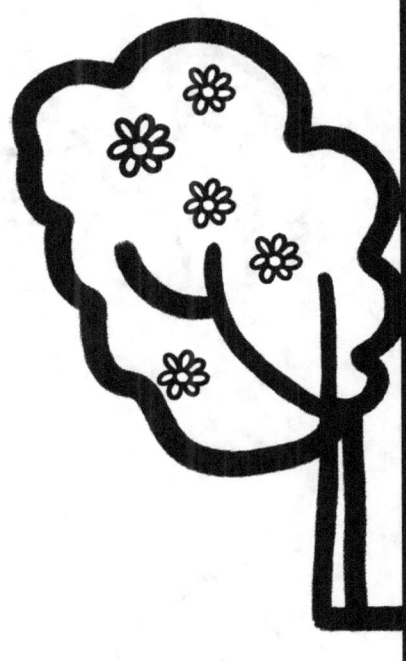

Crab

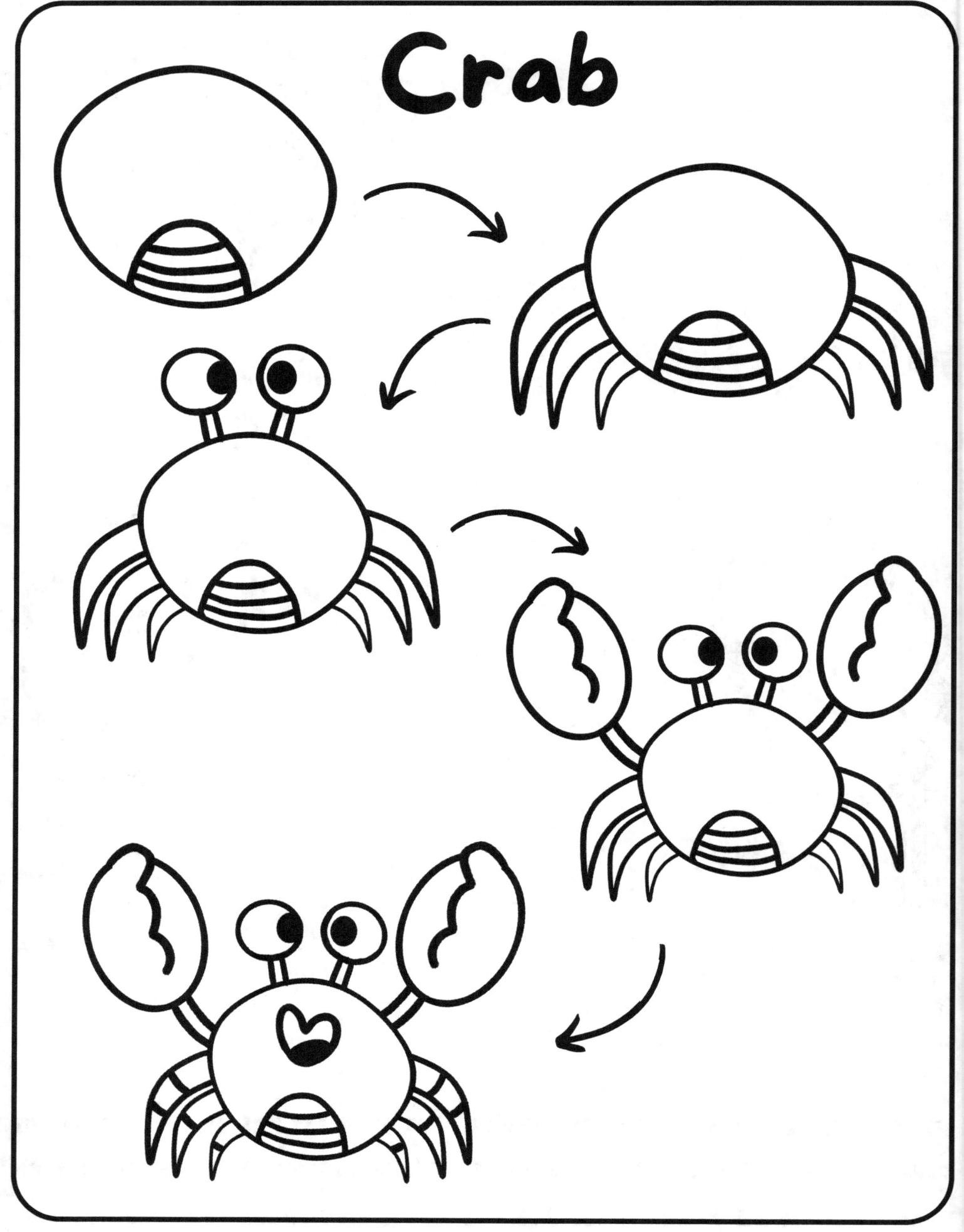

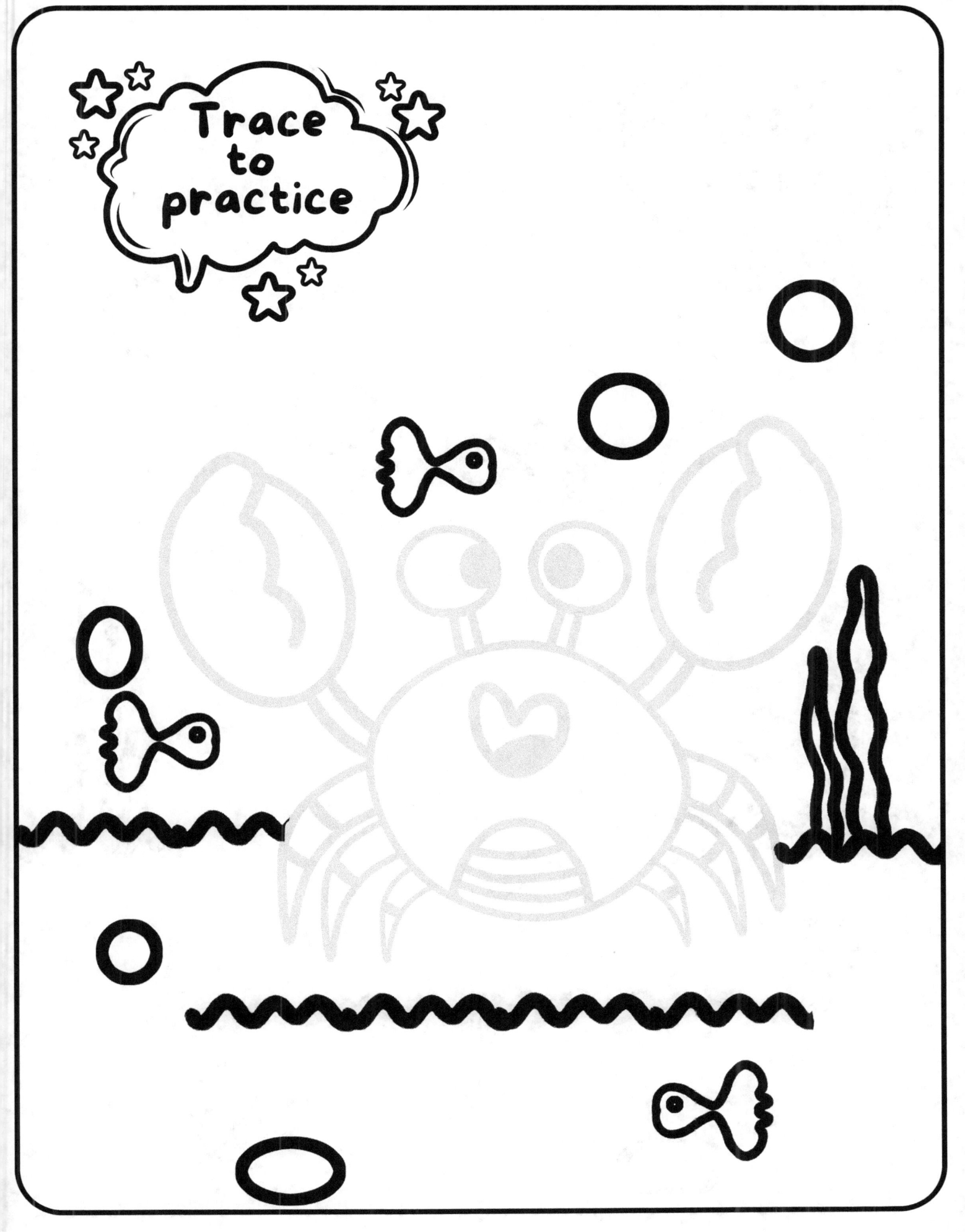

Trace
to
practice

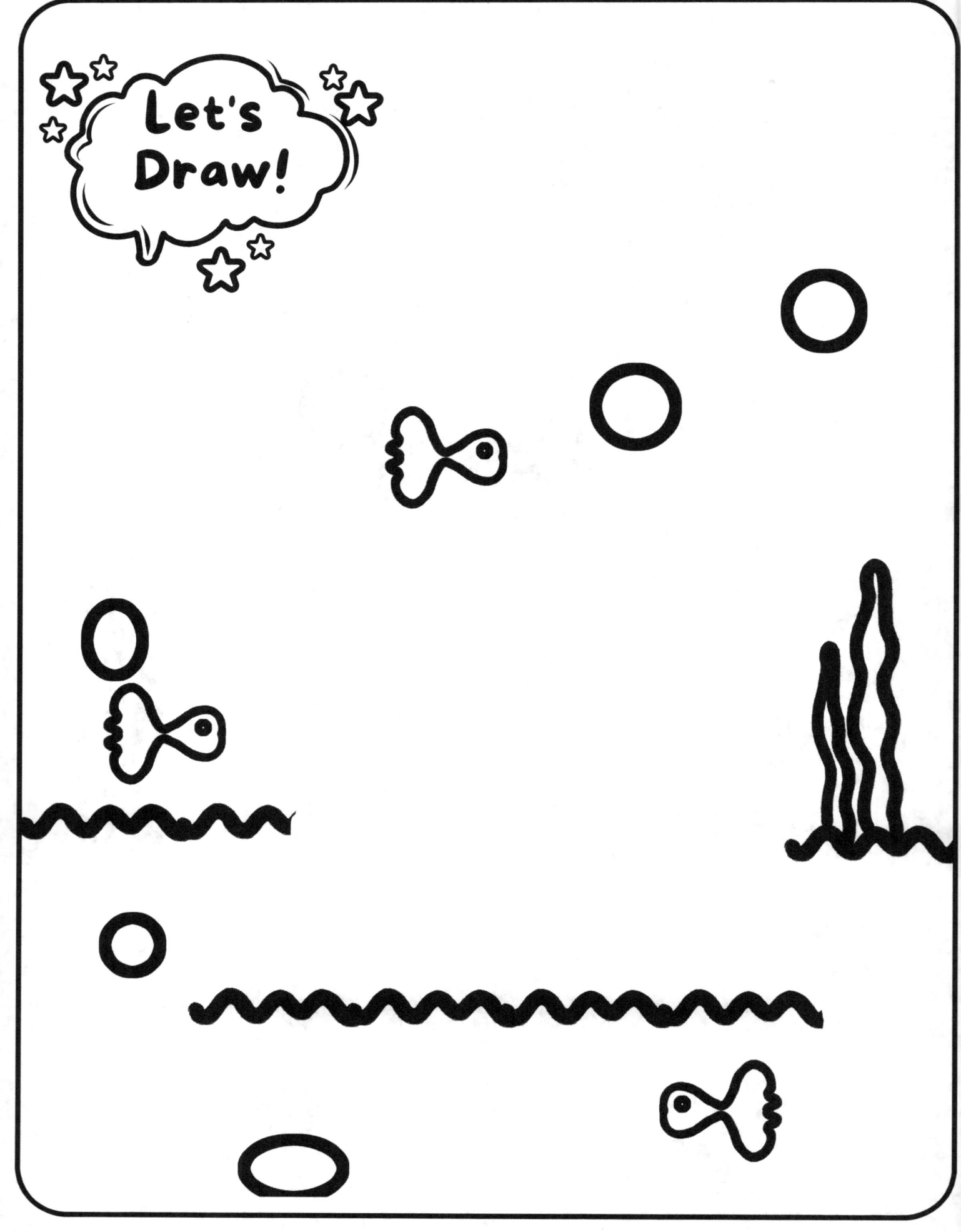

Sheep

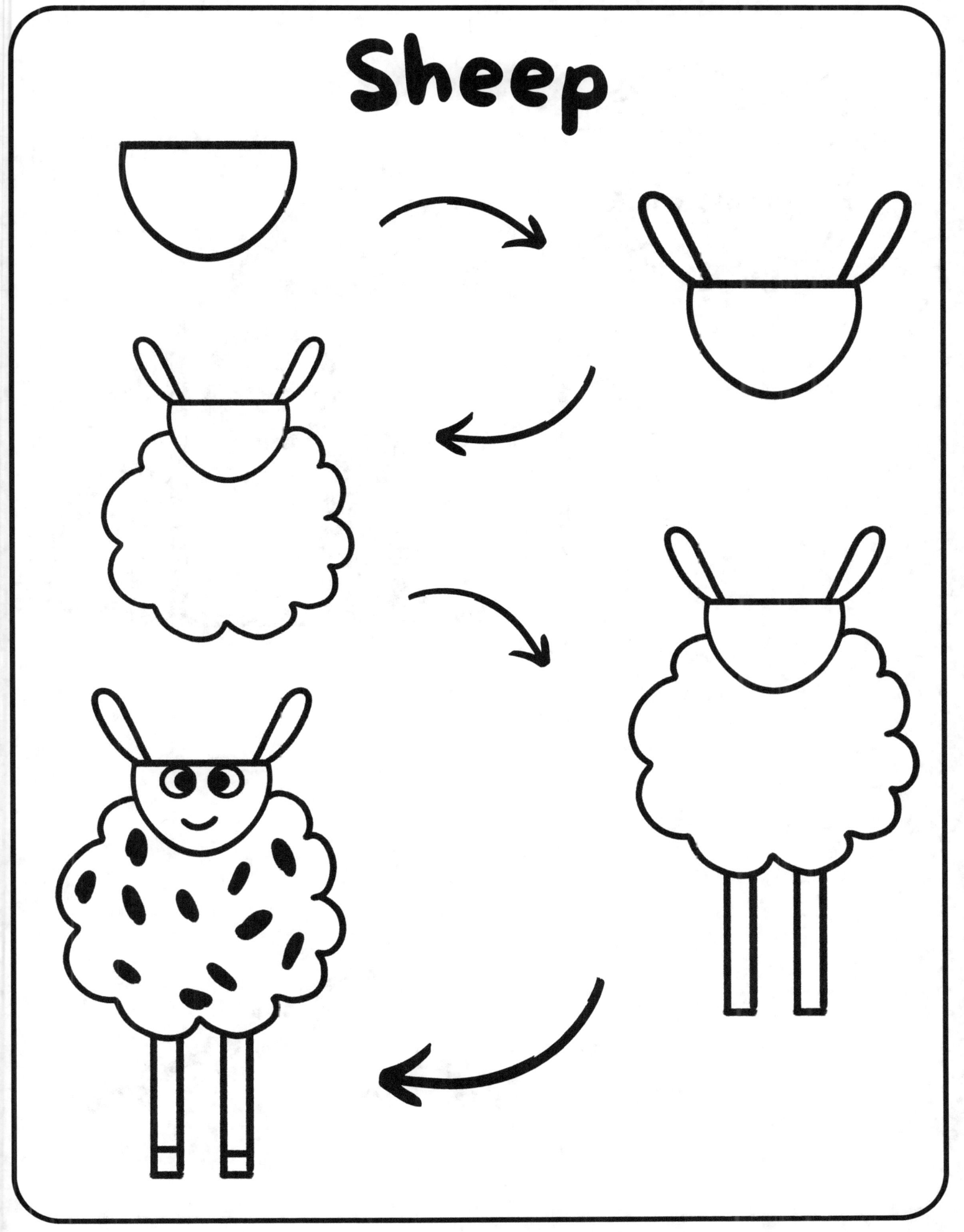

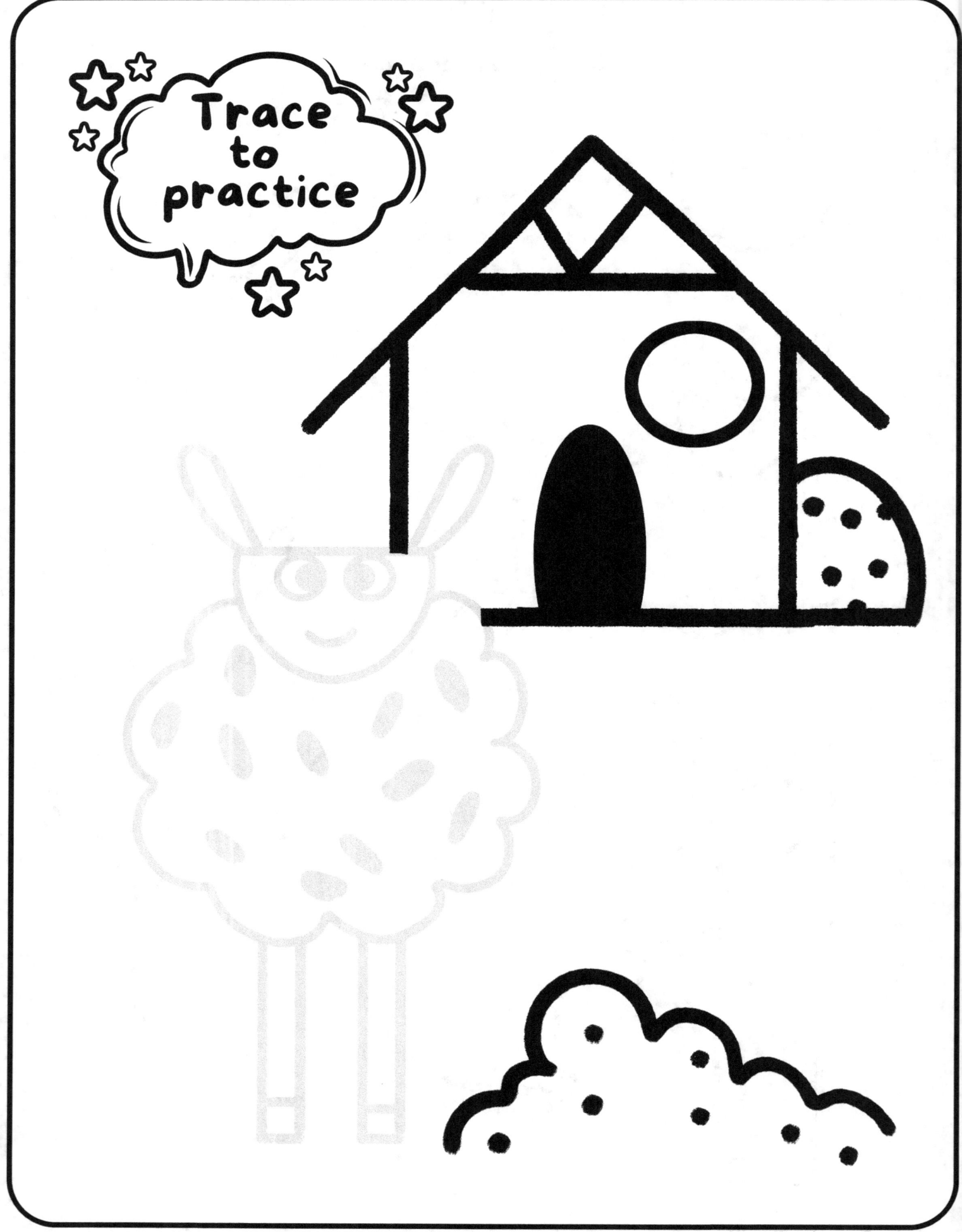

Trace
to
practice

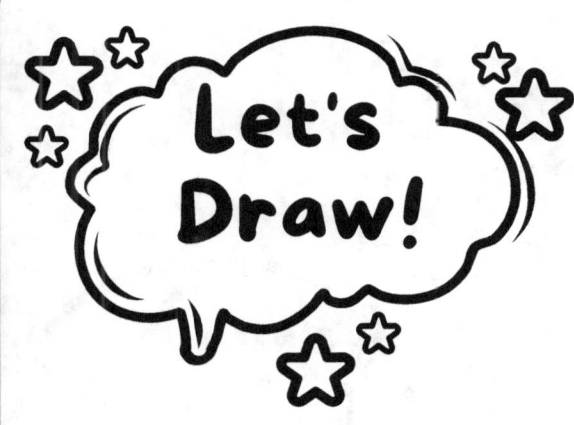

Let's Draw!

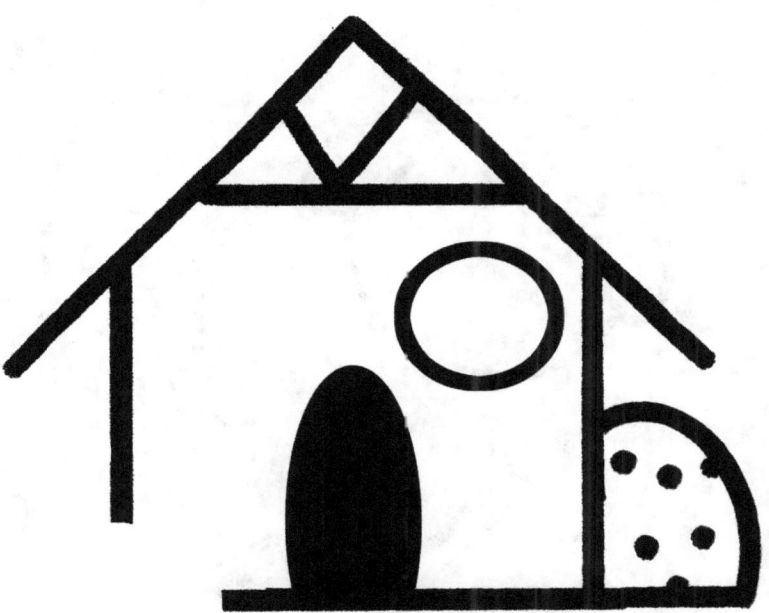

Puppy

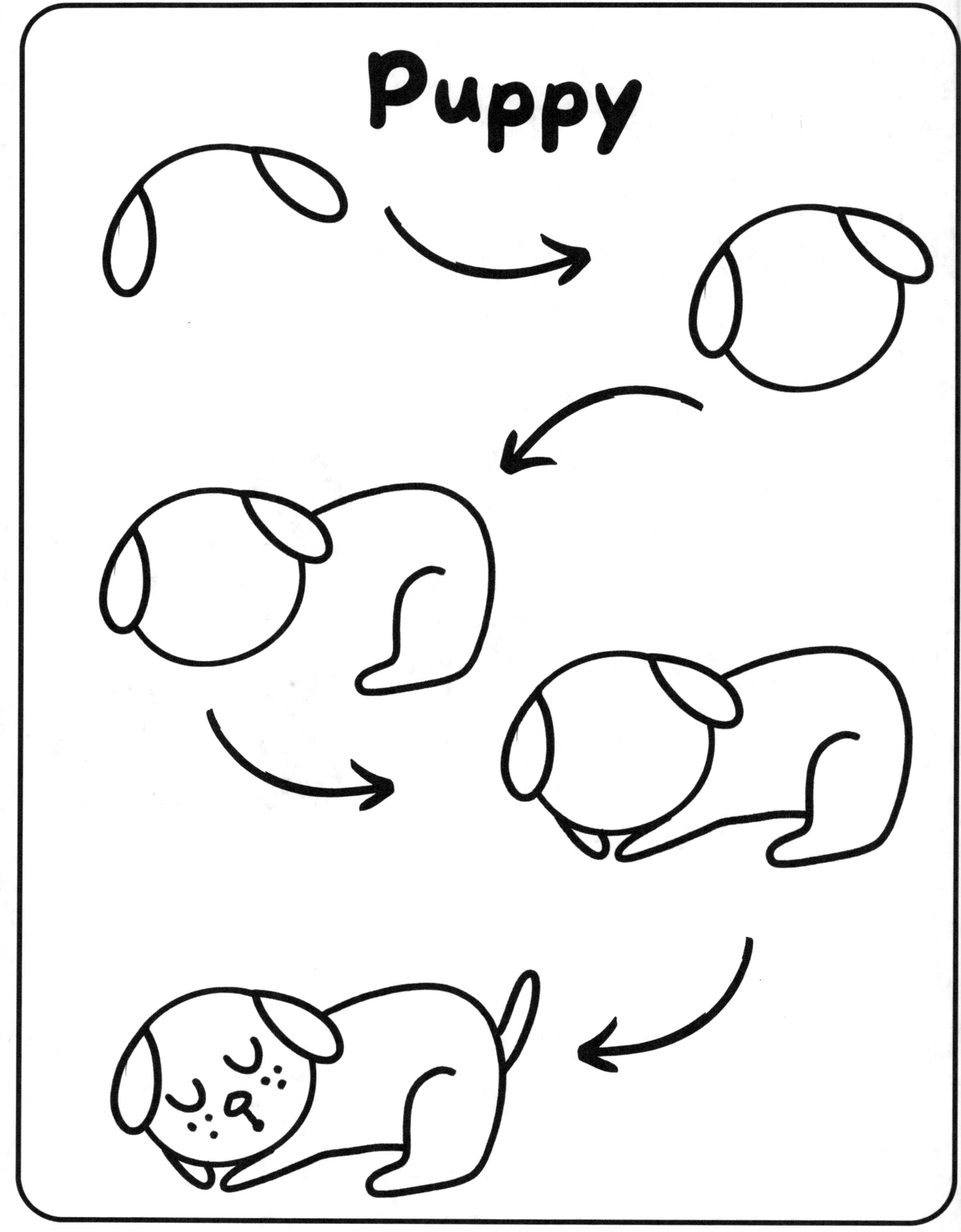

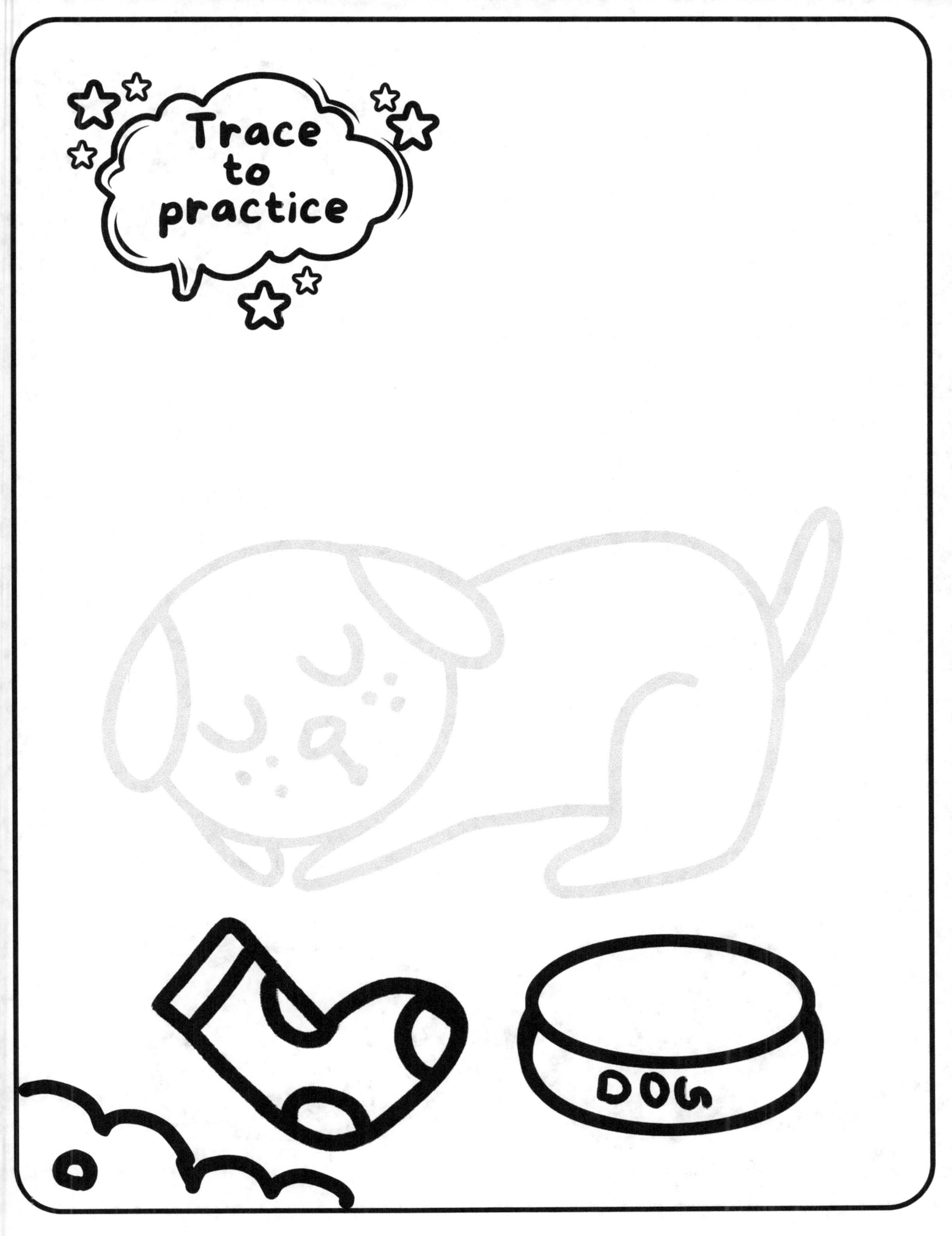

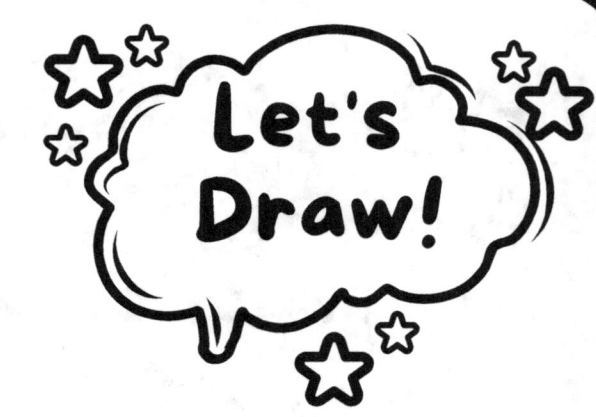

Let's Draw!

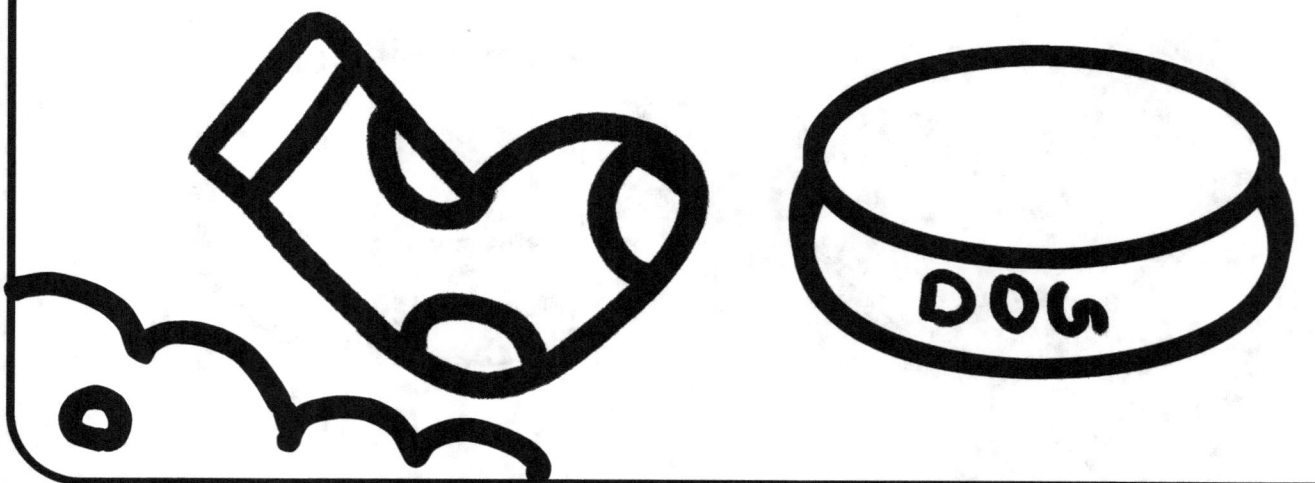

Helicopter

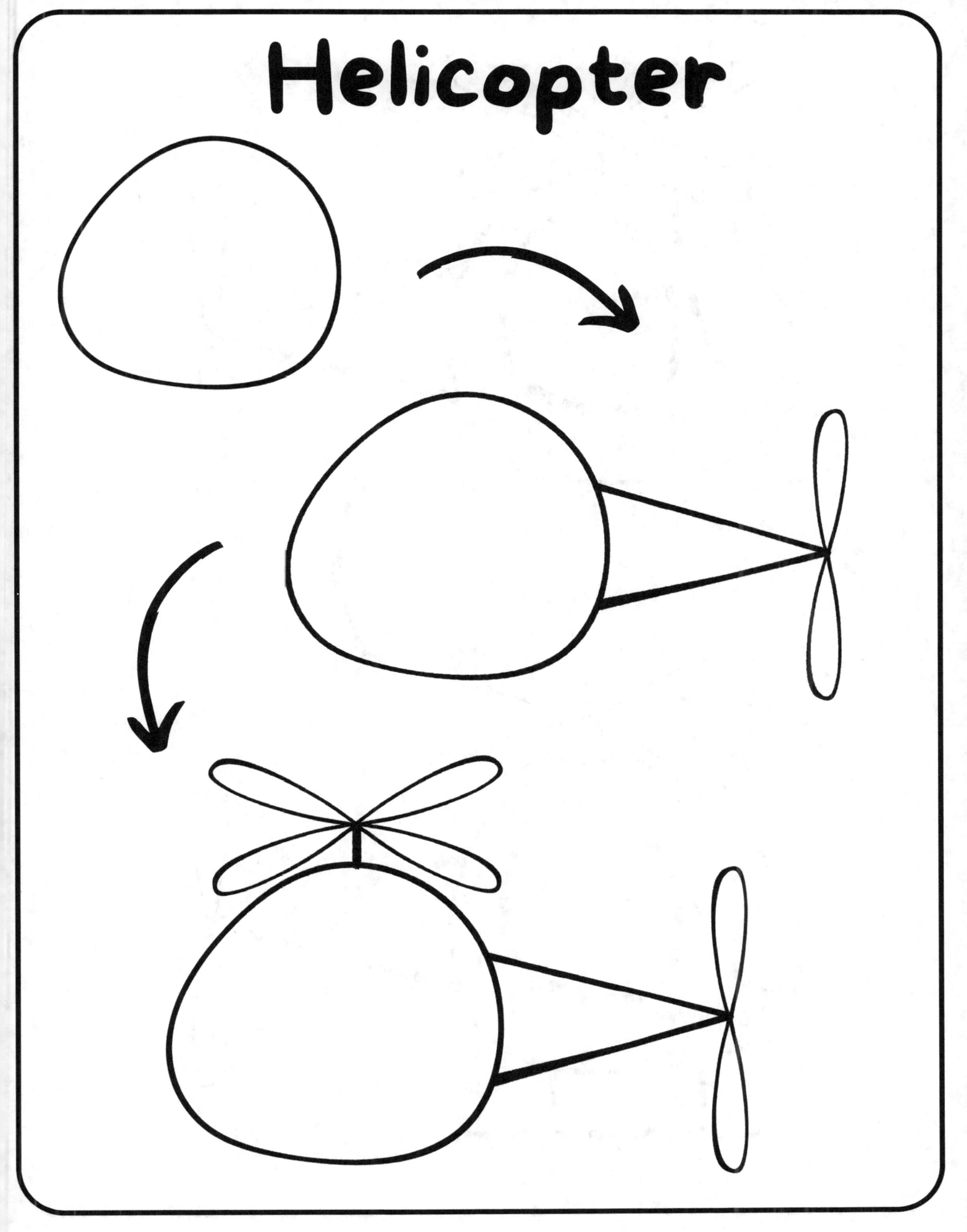

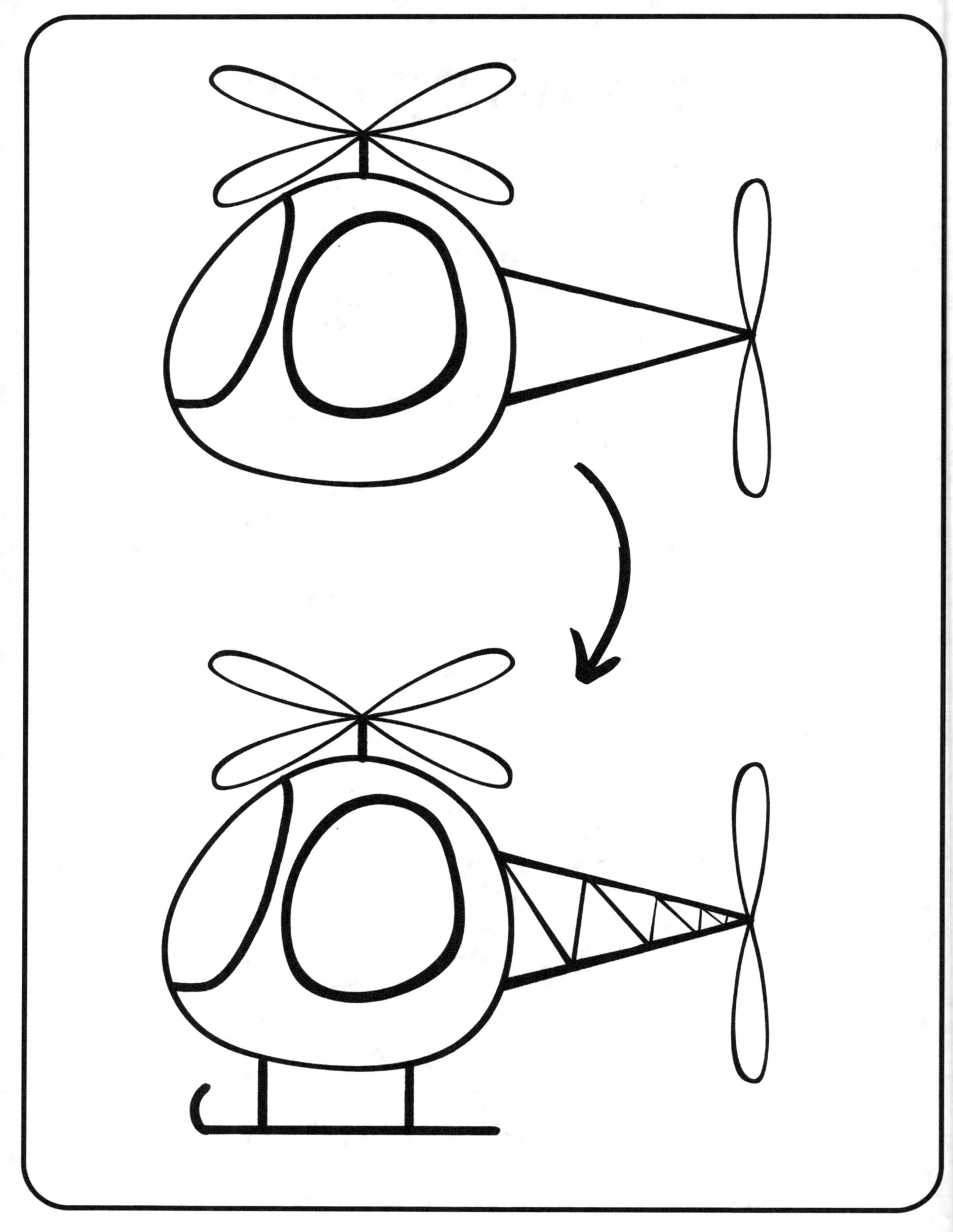

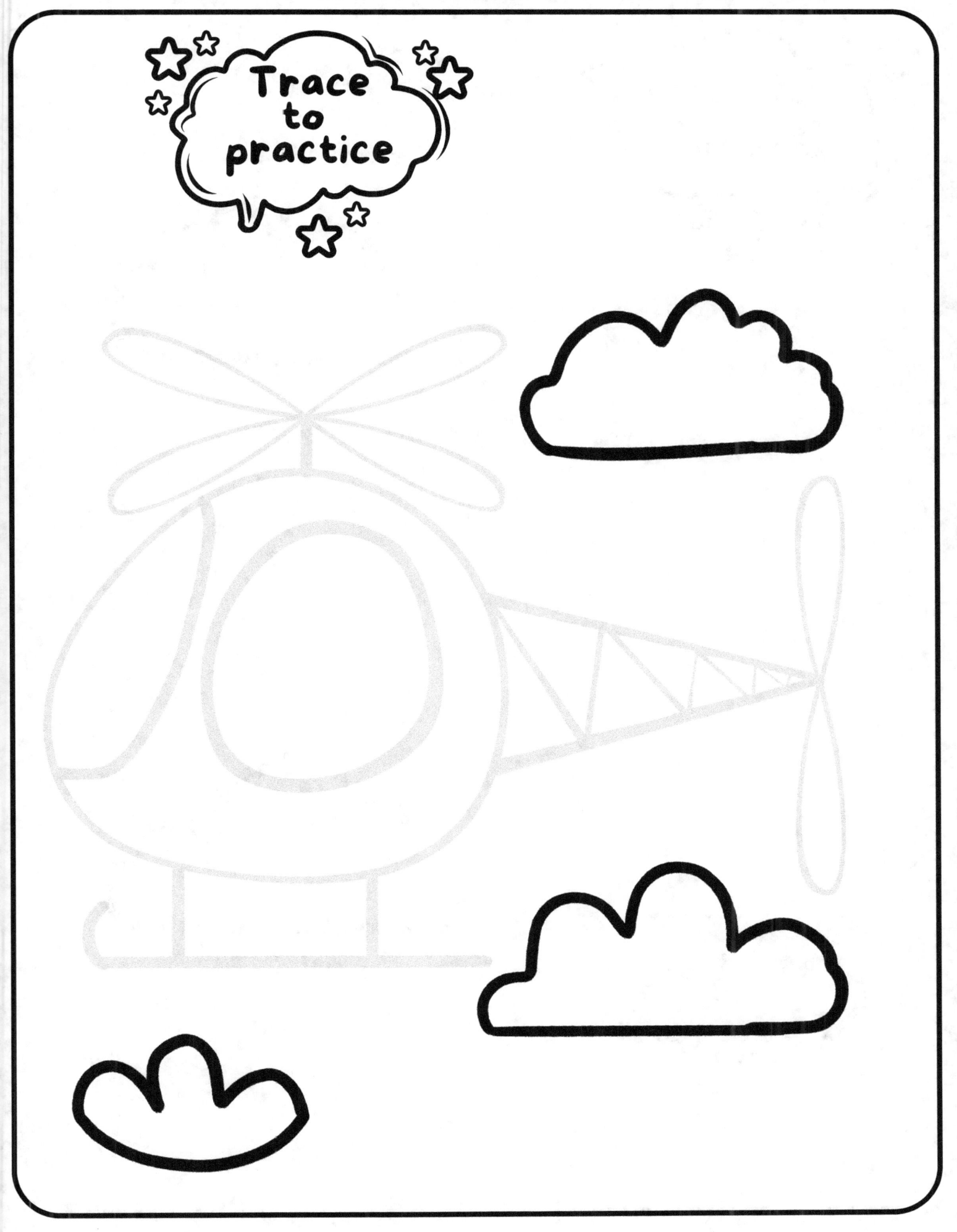

Trace
to
practice

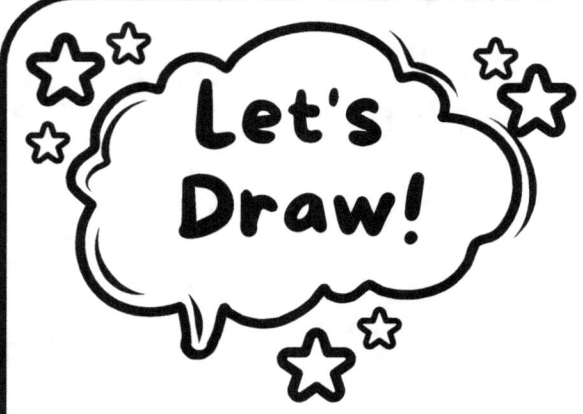

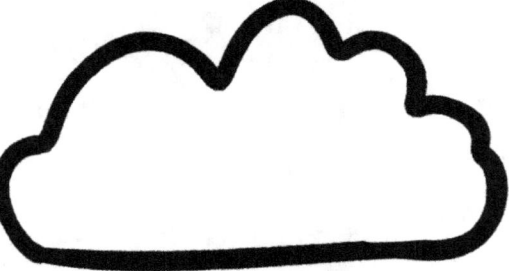

Penguin

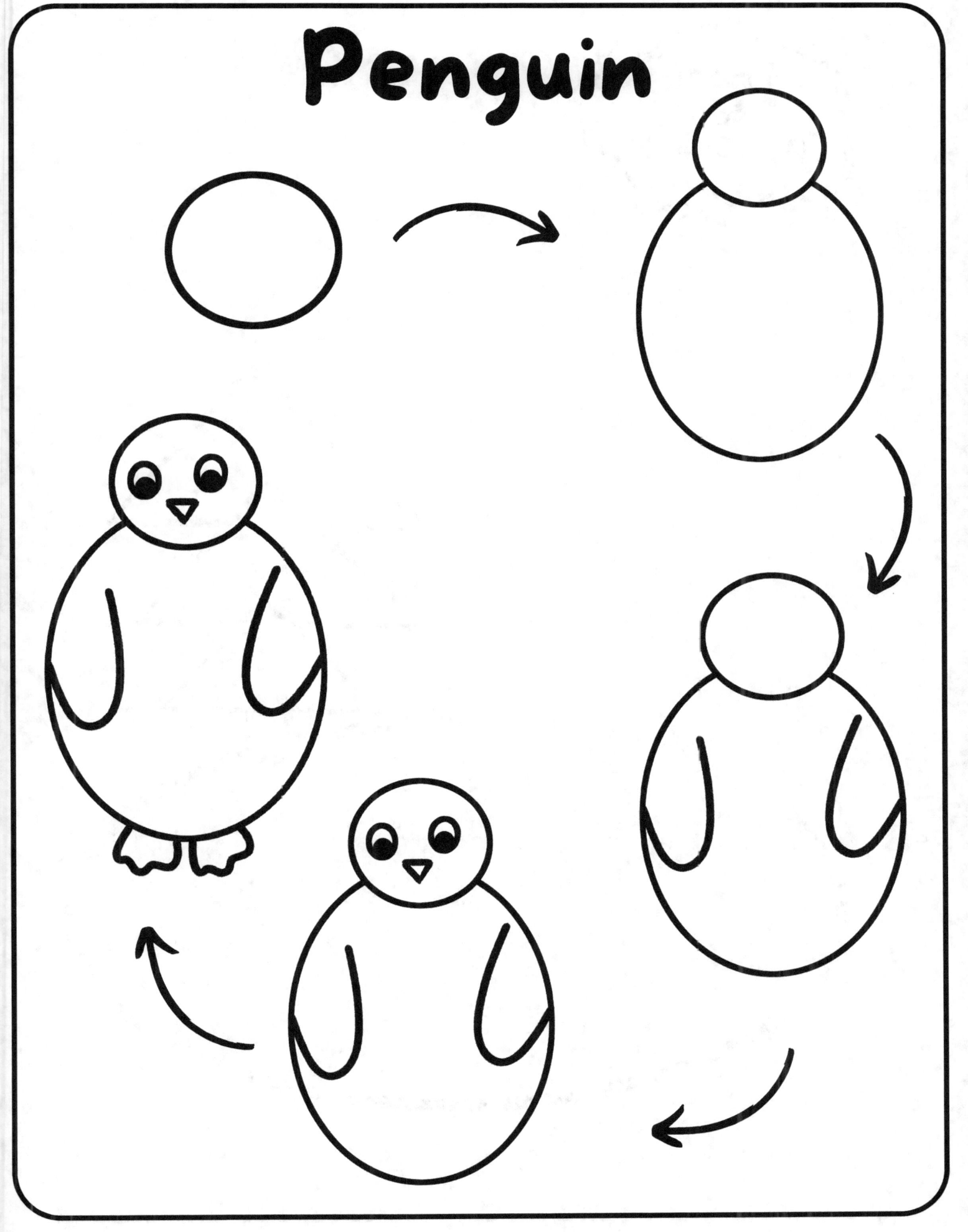

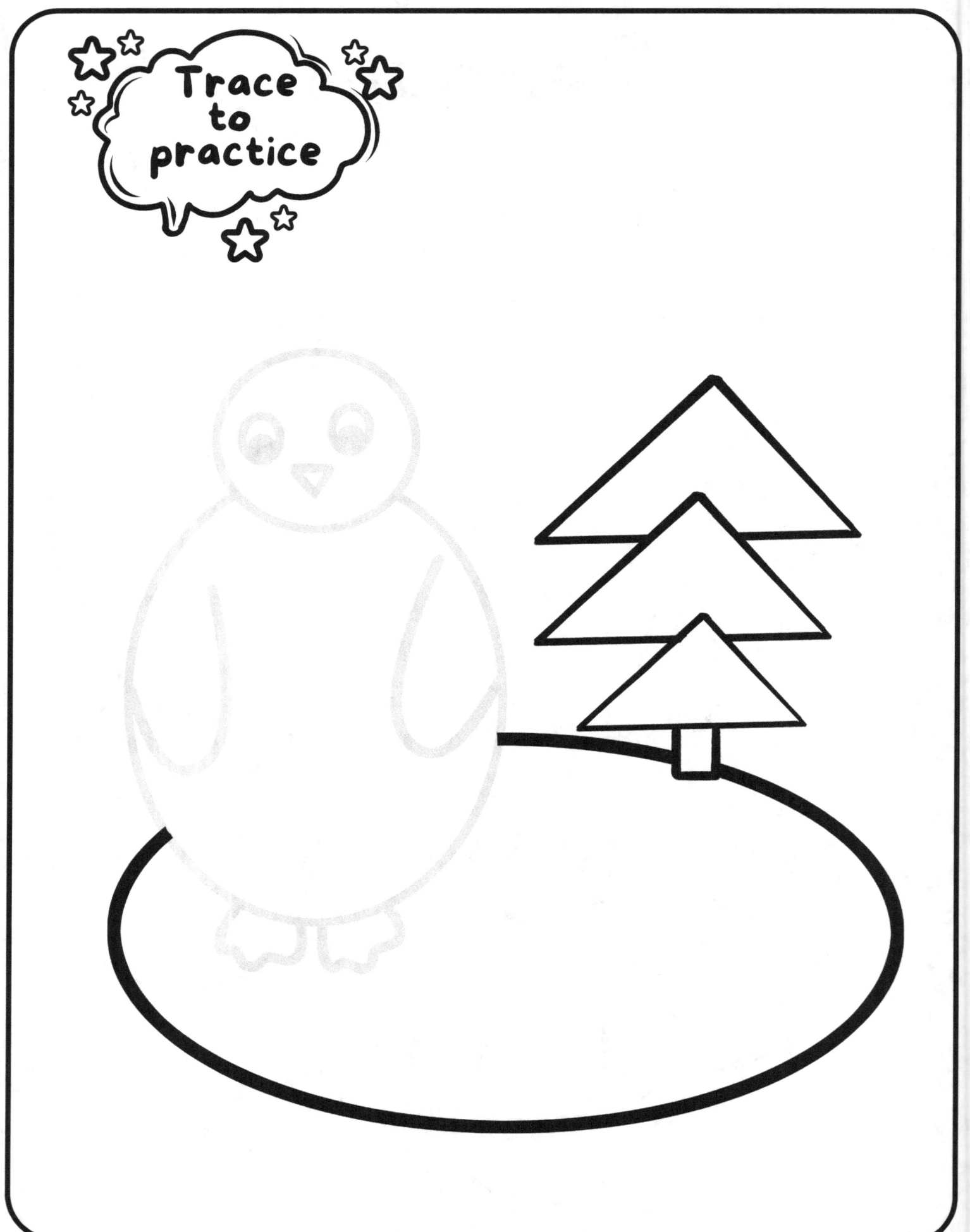

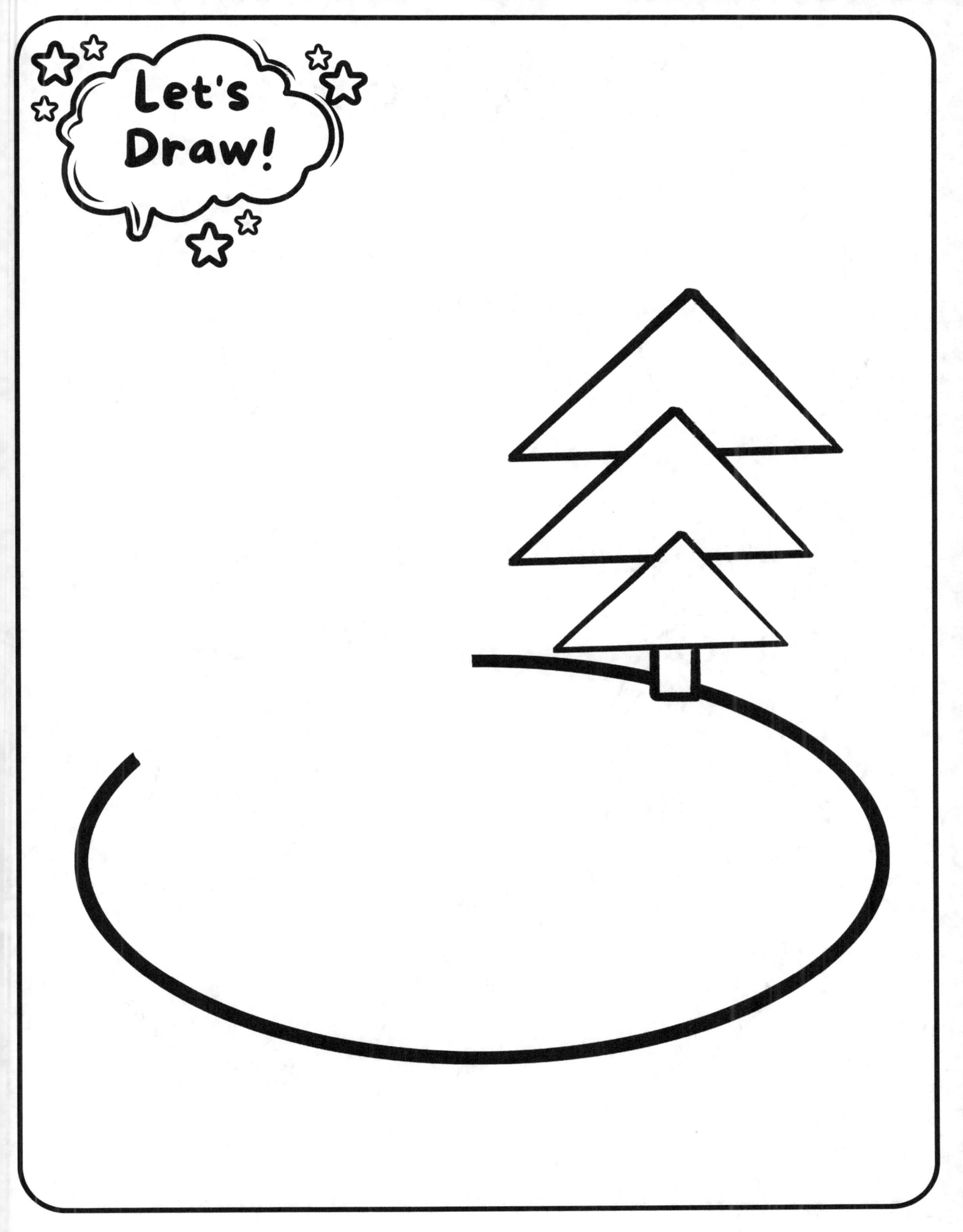

Ladybug

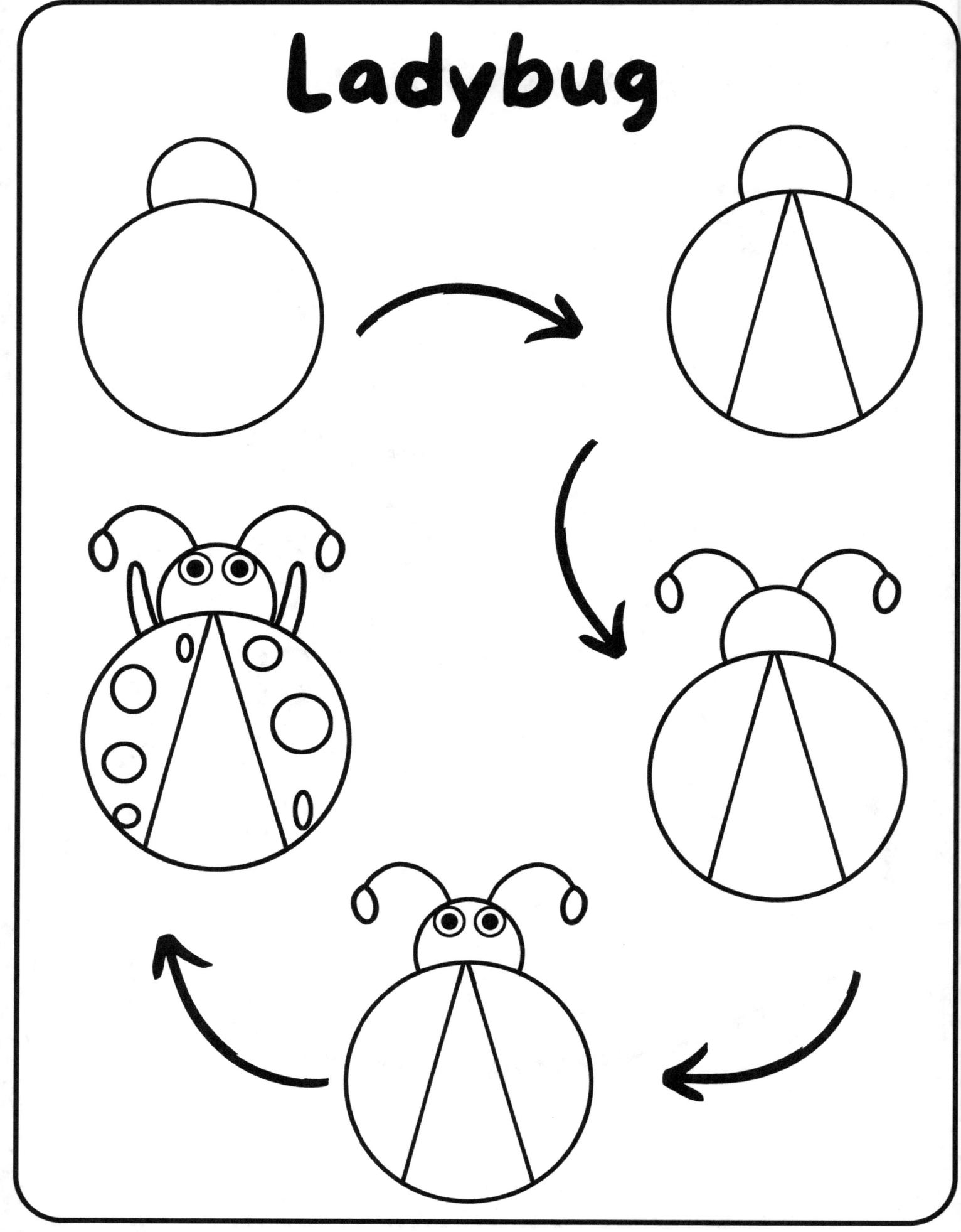

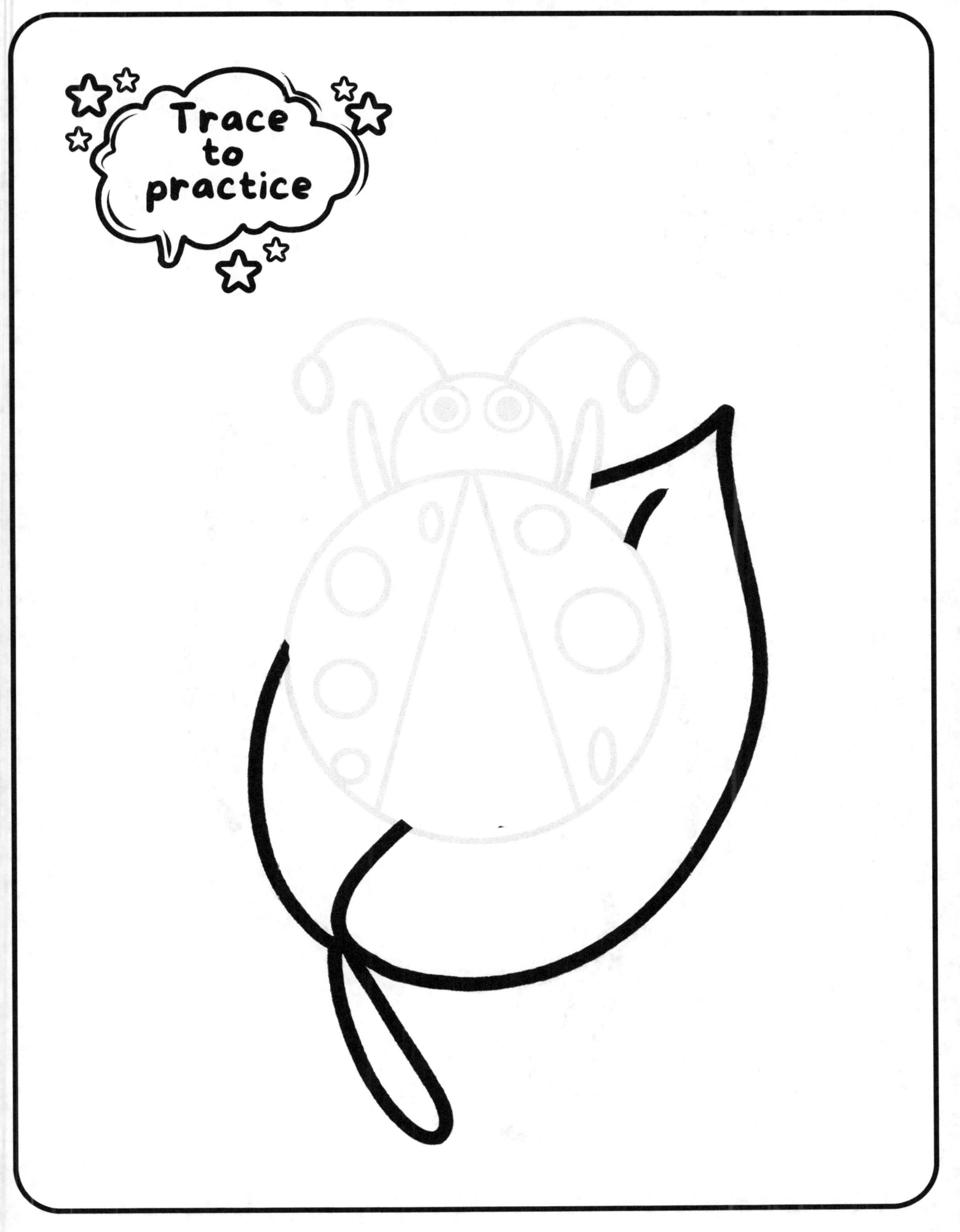

Trace
to
practice

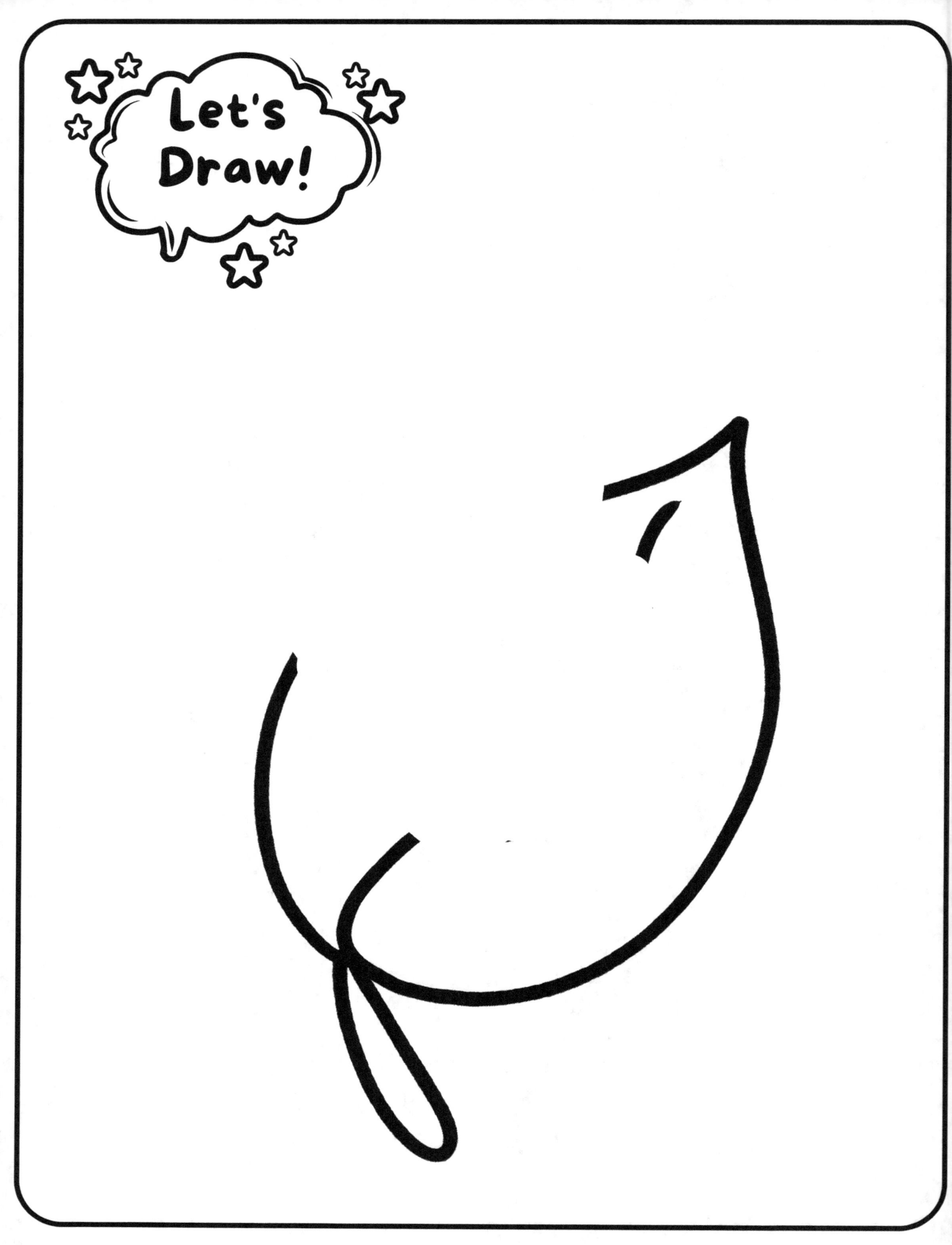

Chameleon

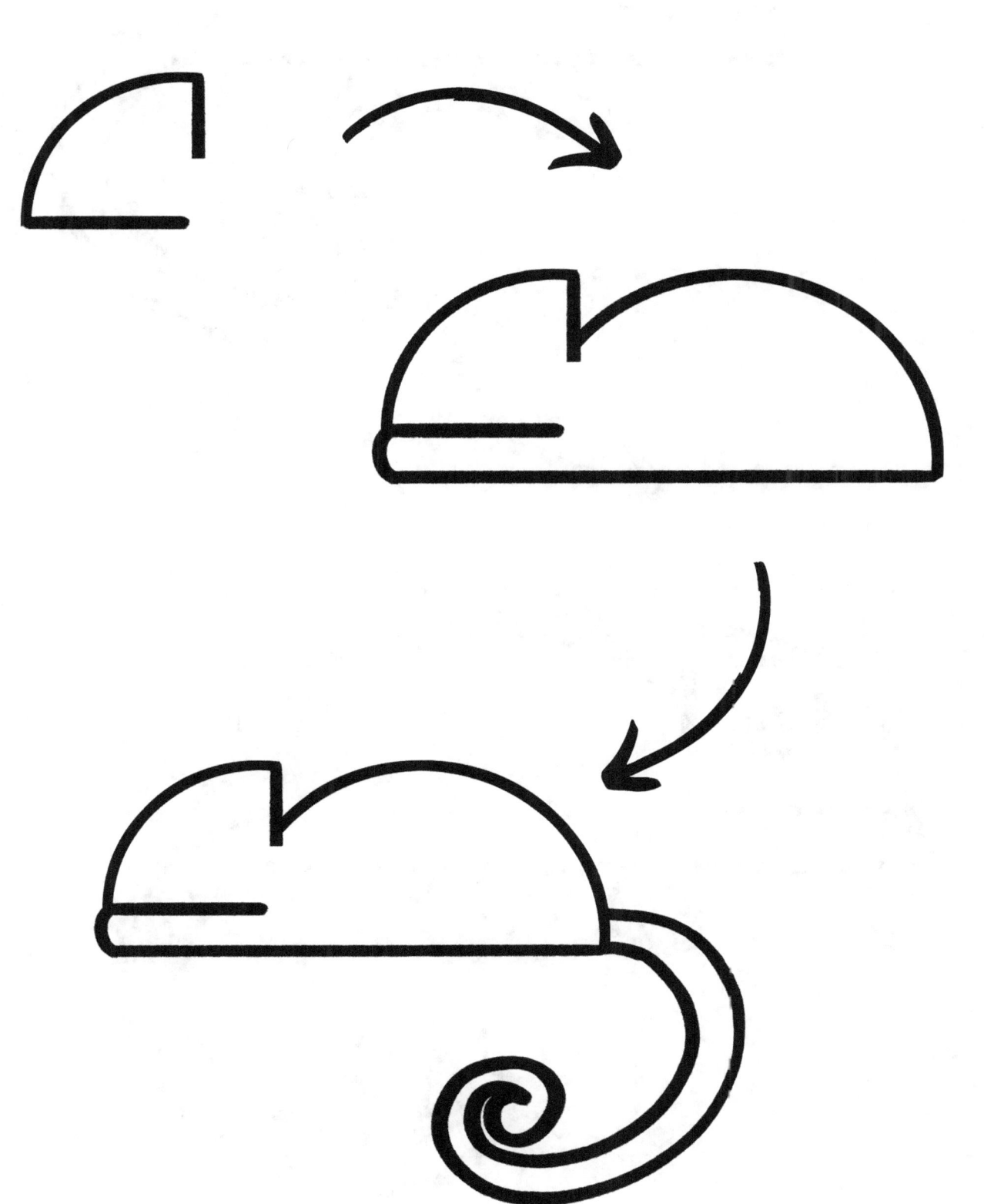

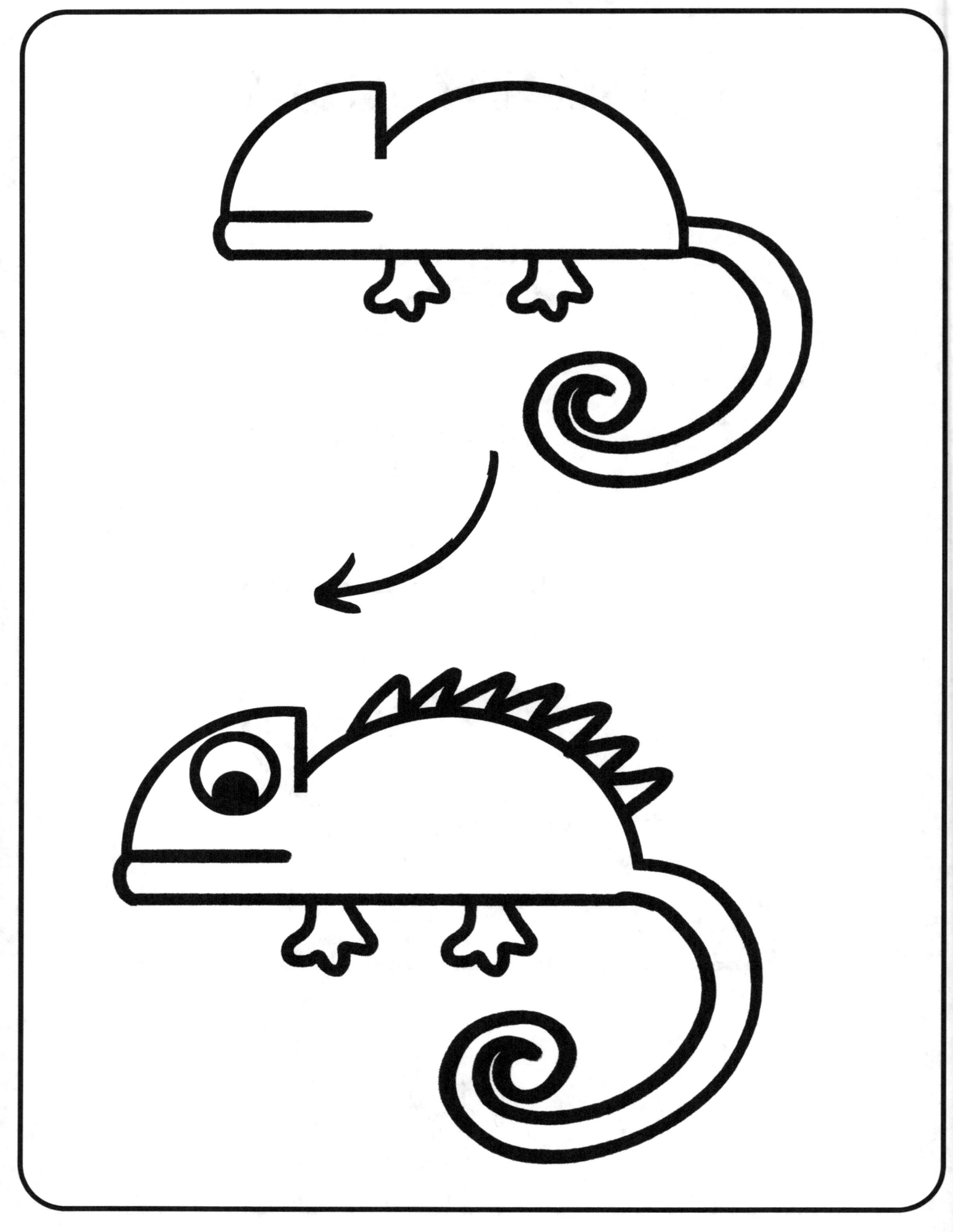

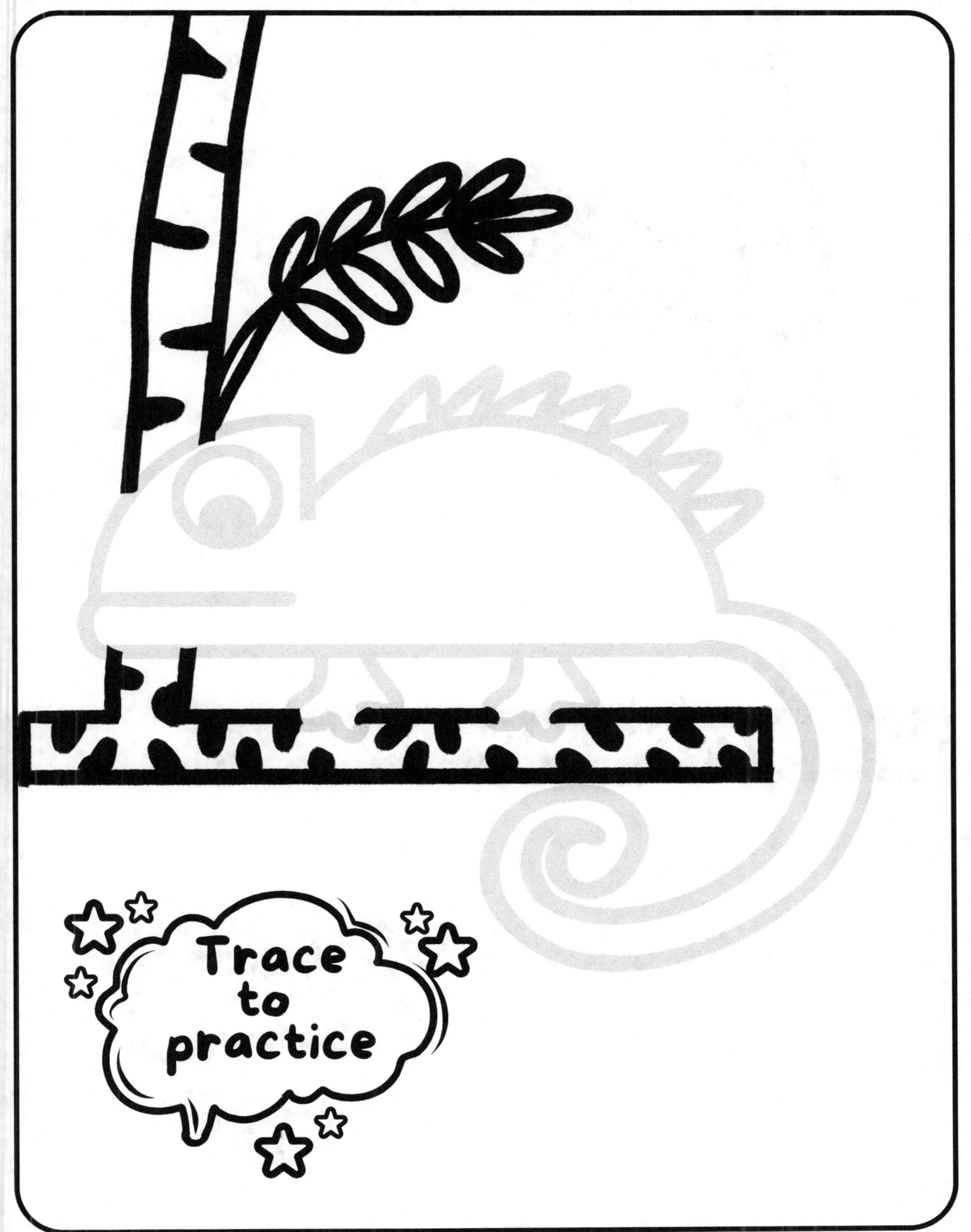

Trace
to
practice

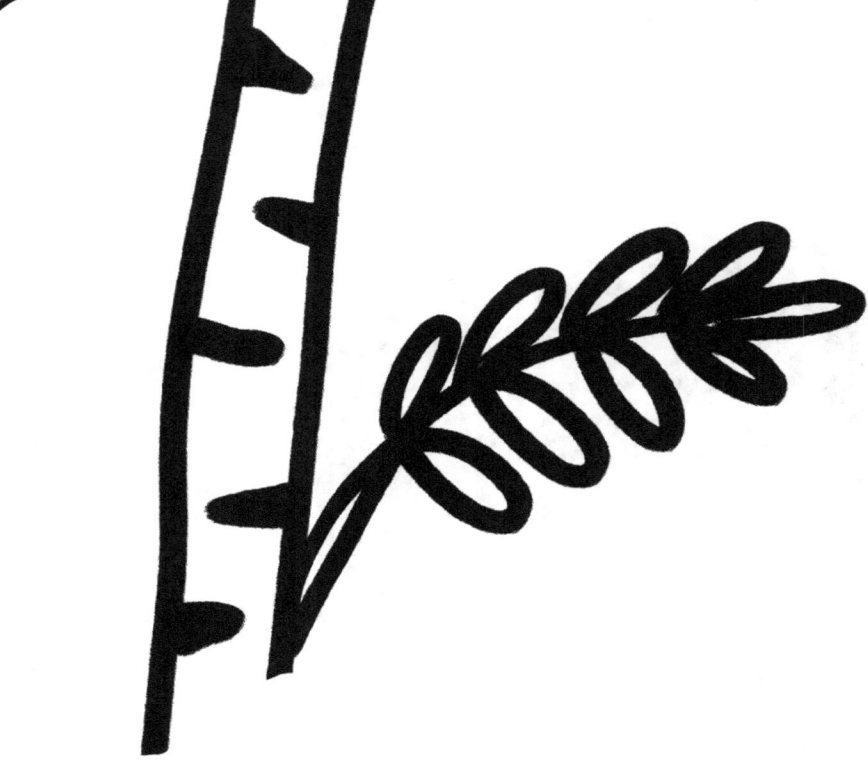

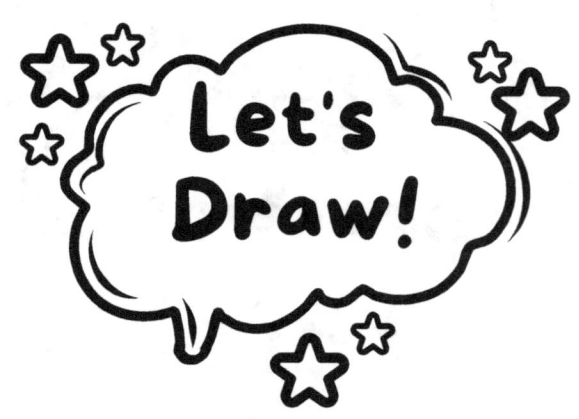

Let's Draw!

Pig

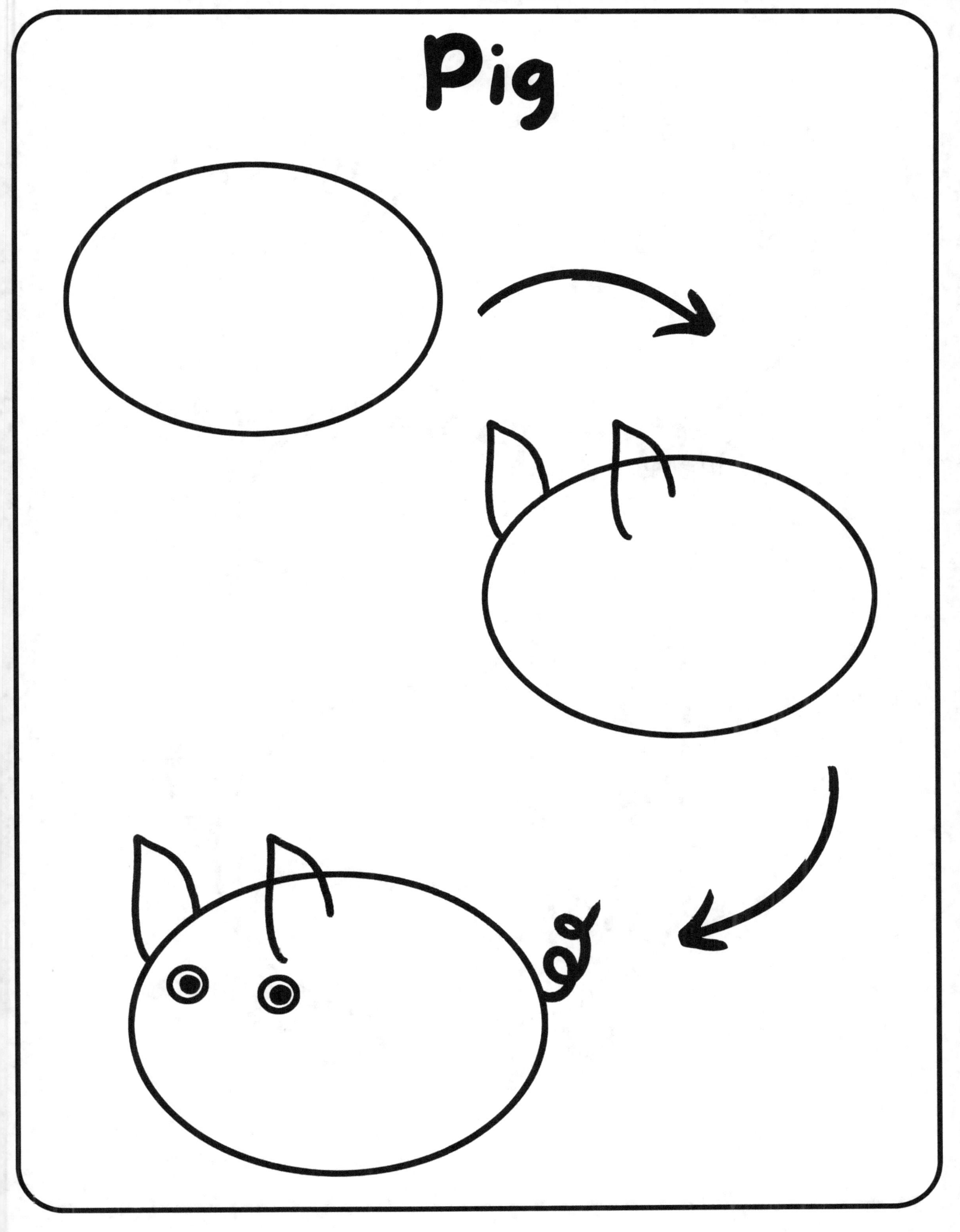

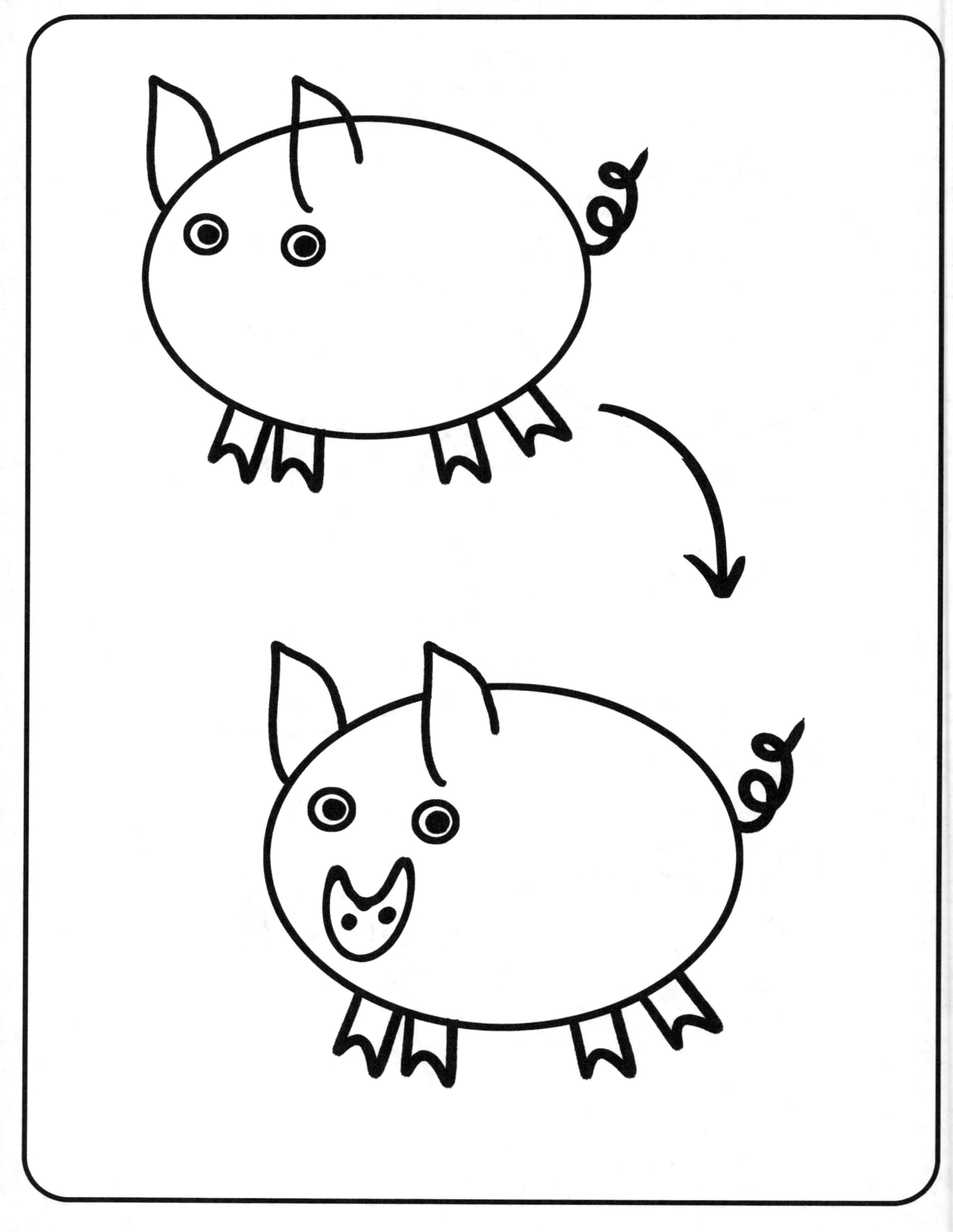

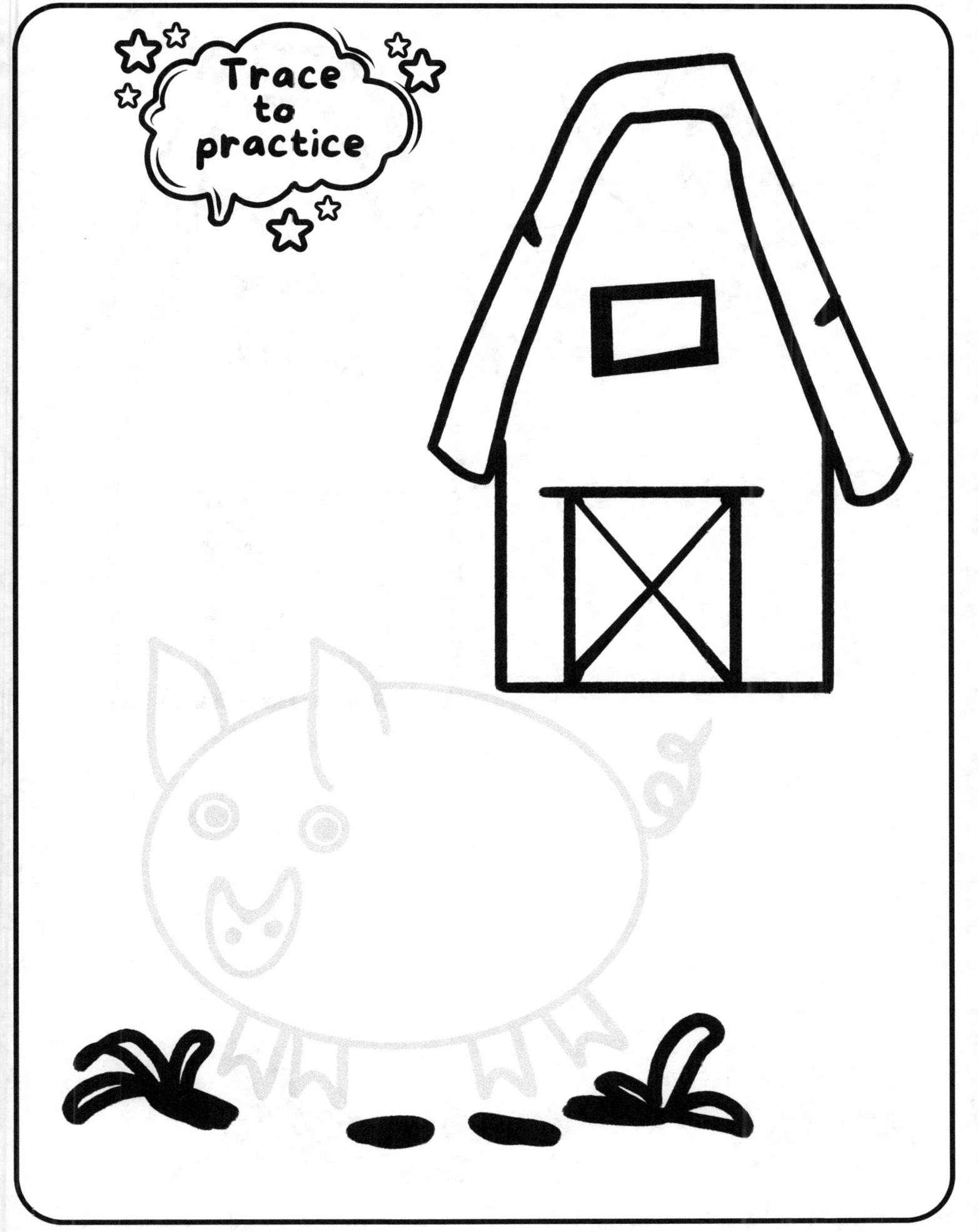

Let's
Draw!

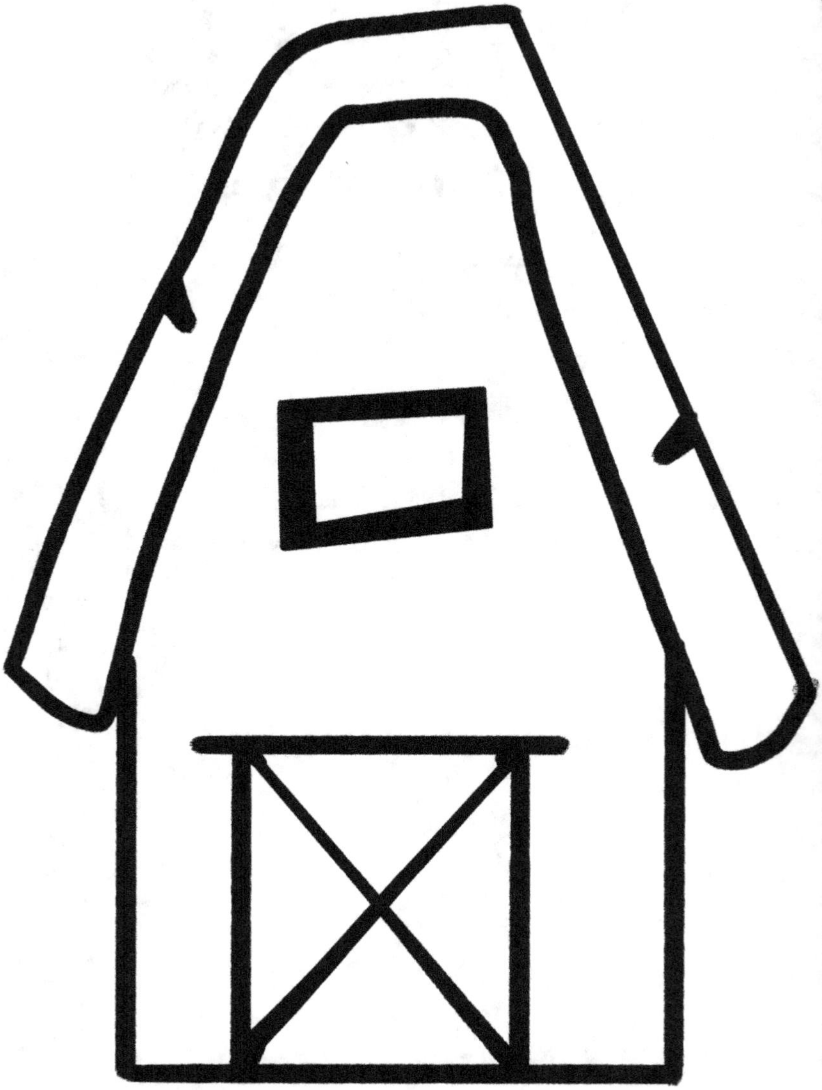

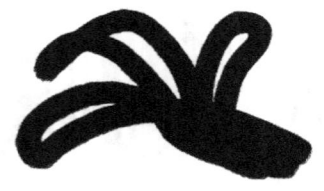
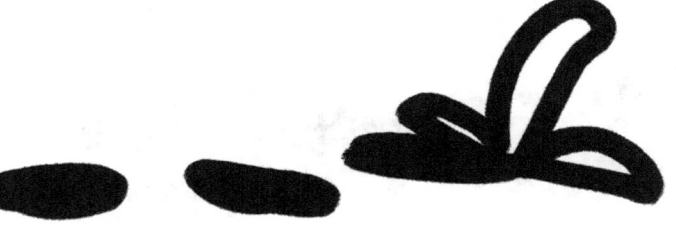

Guitar

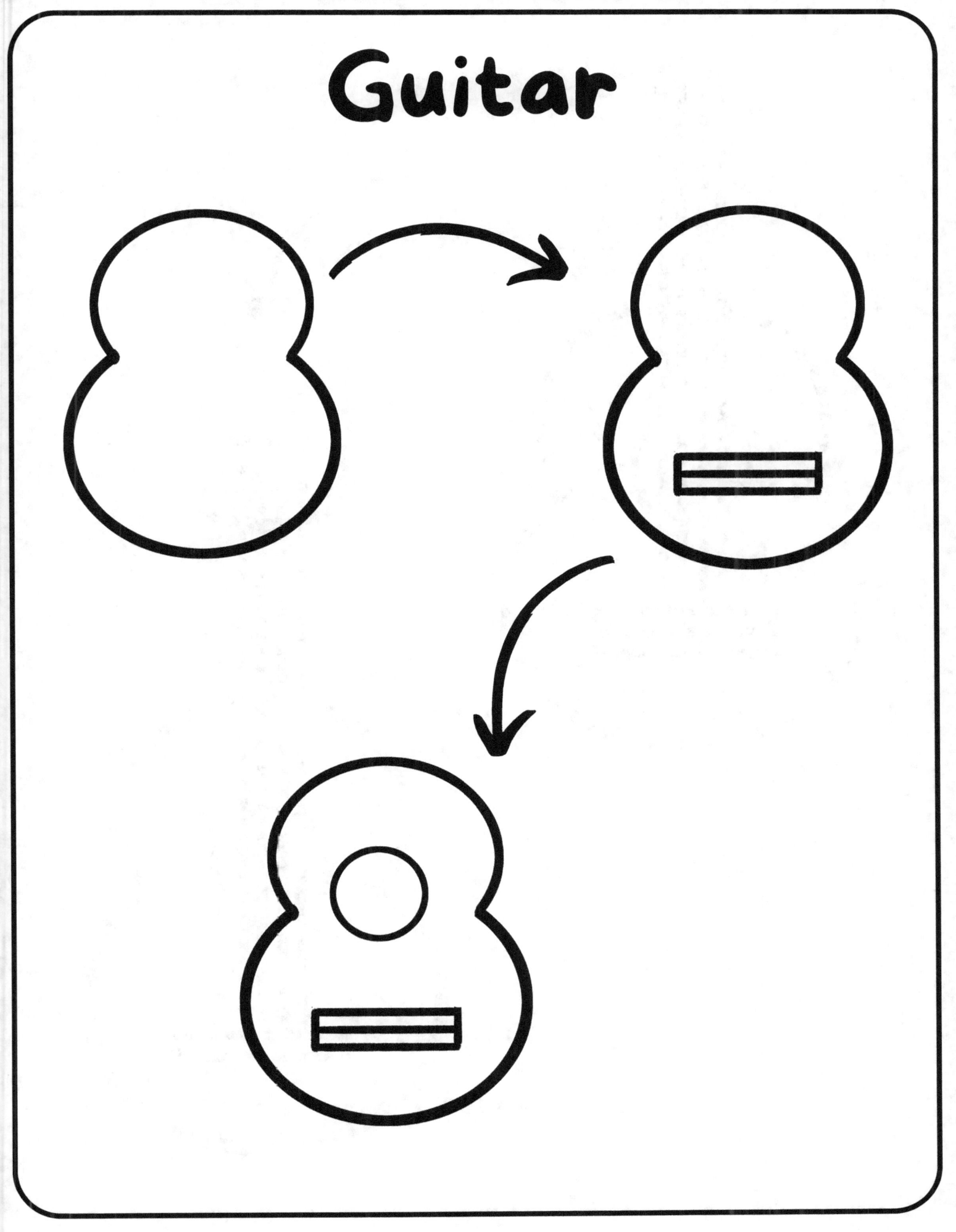

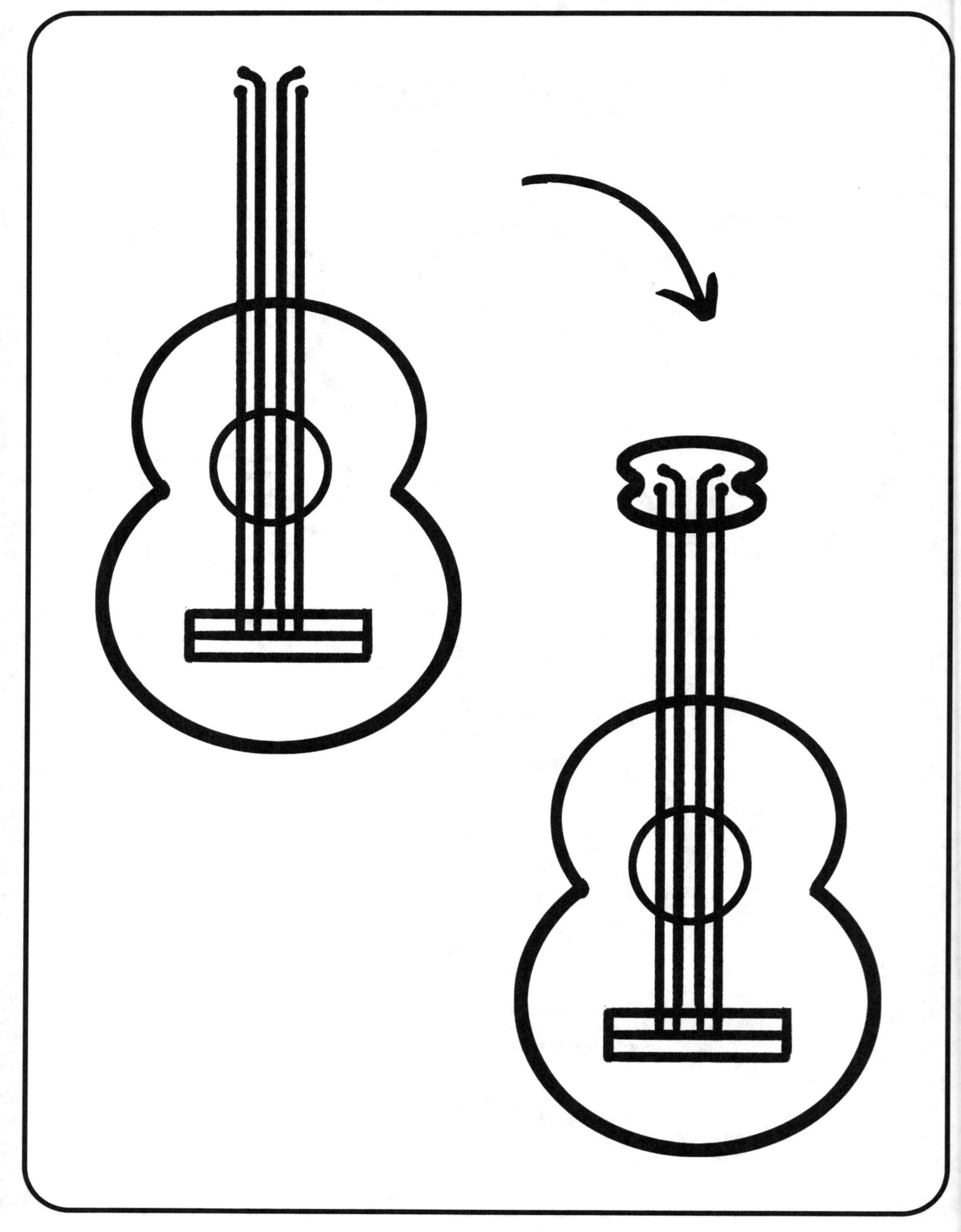

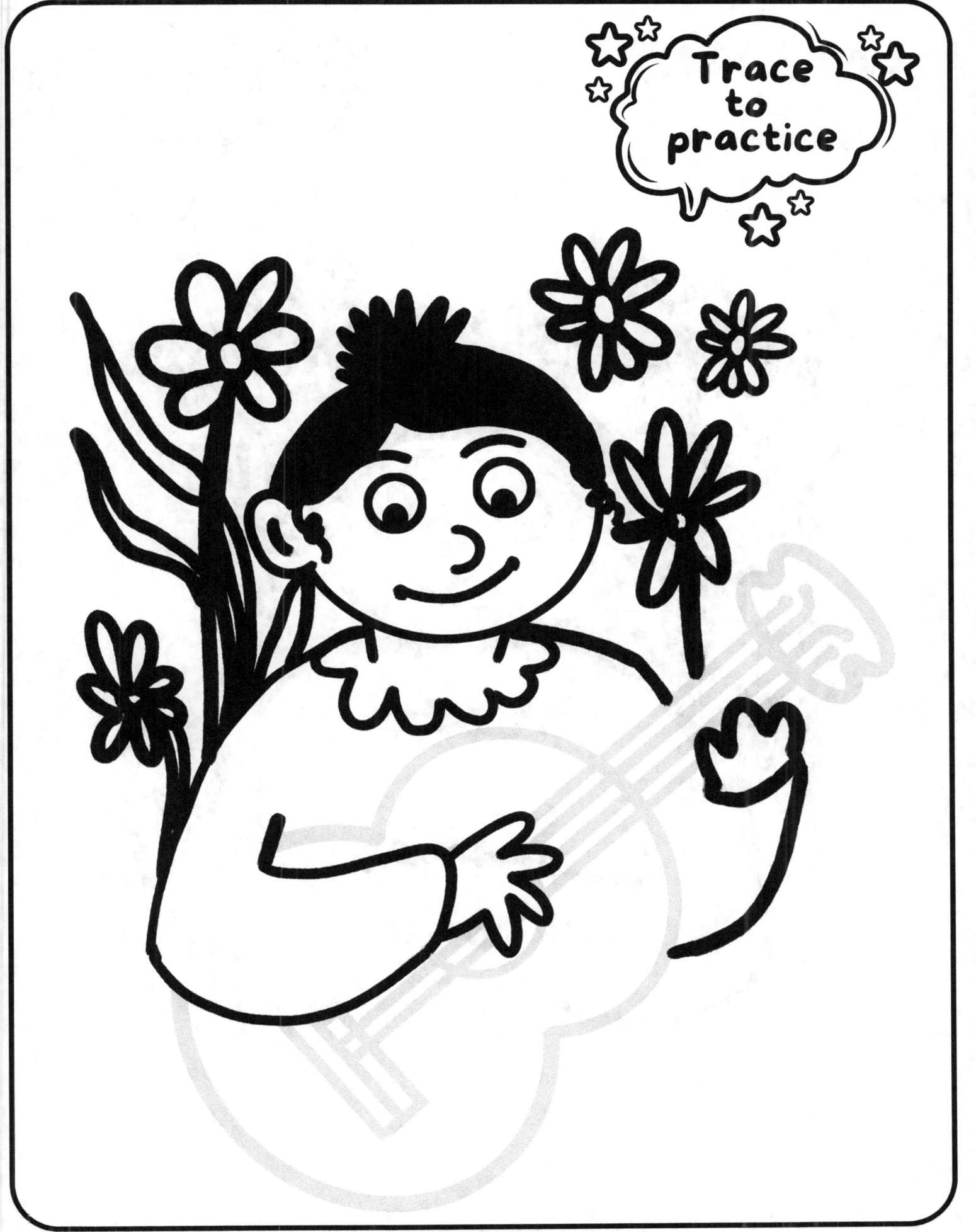

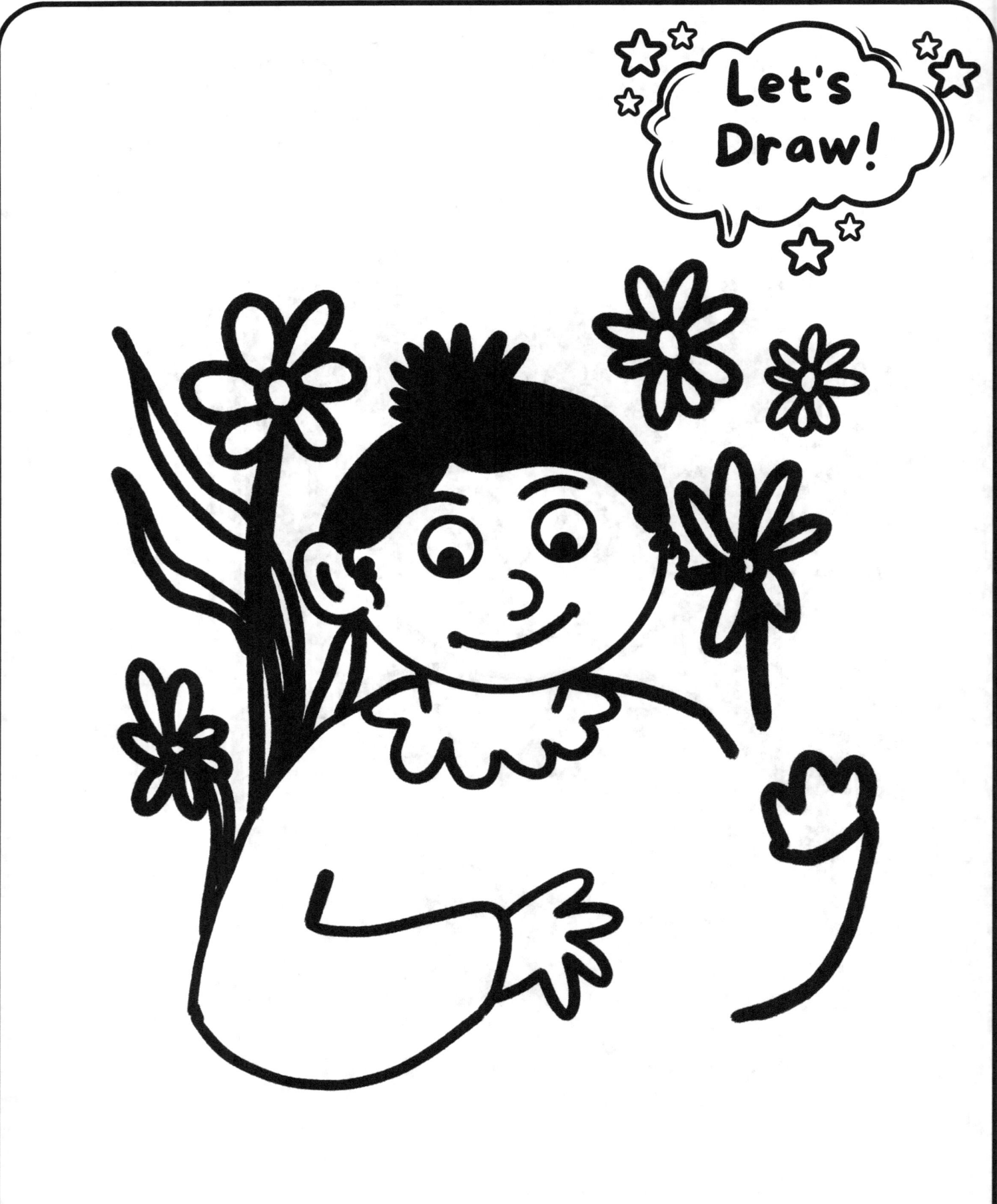

Cow

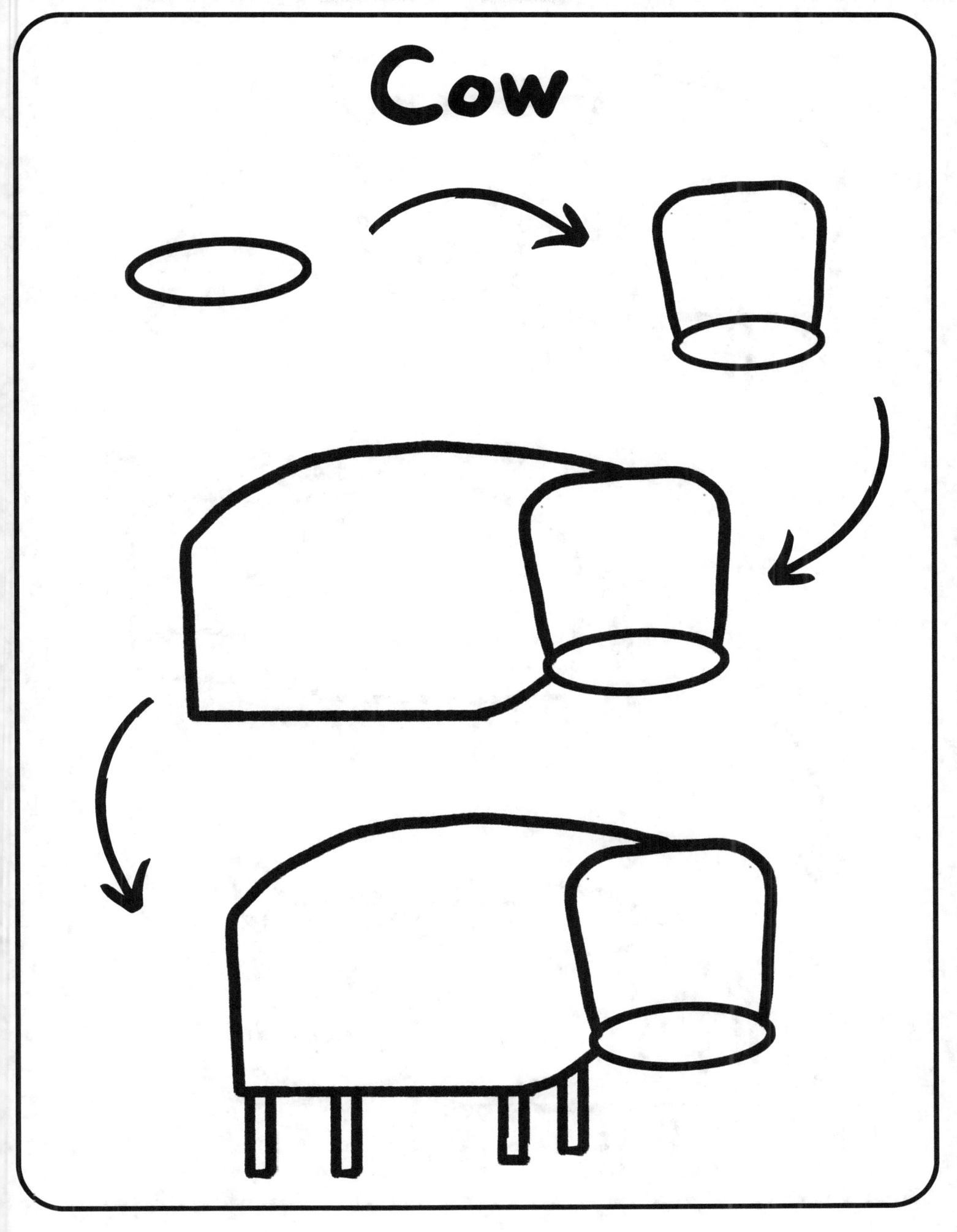

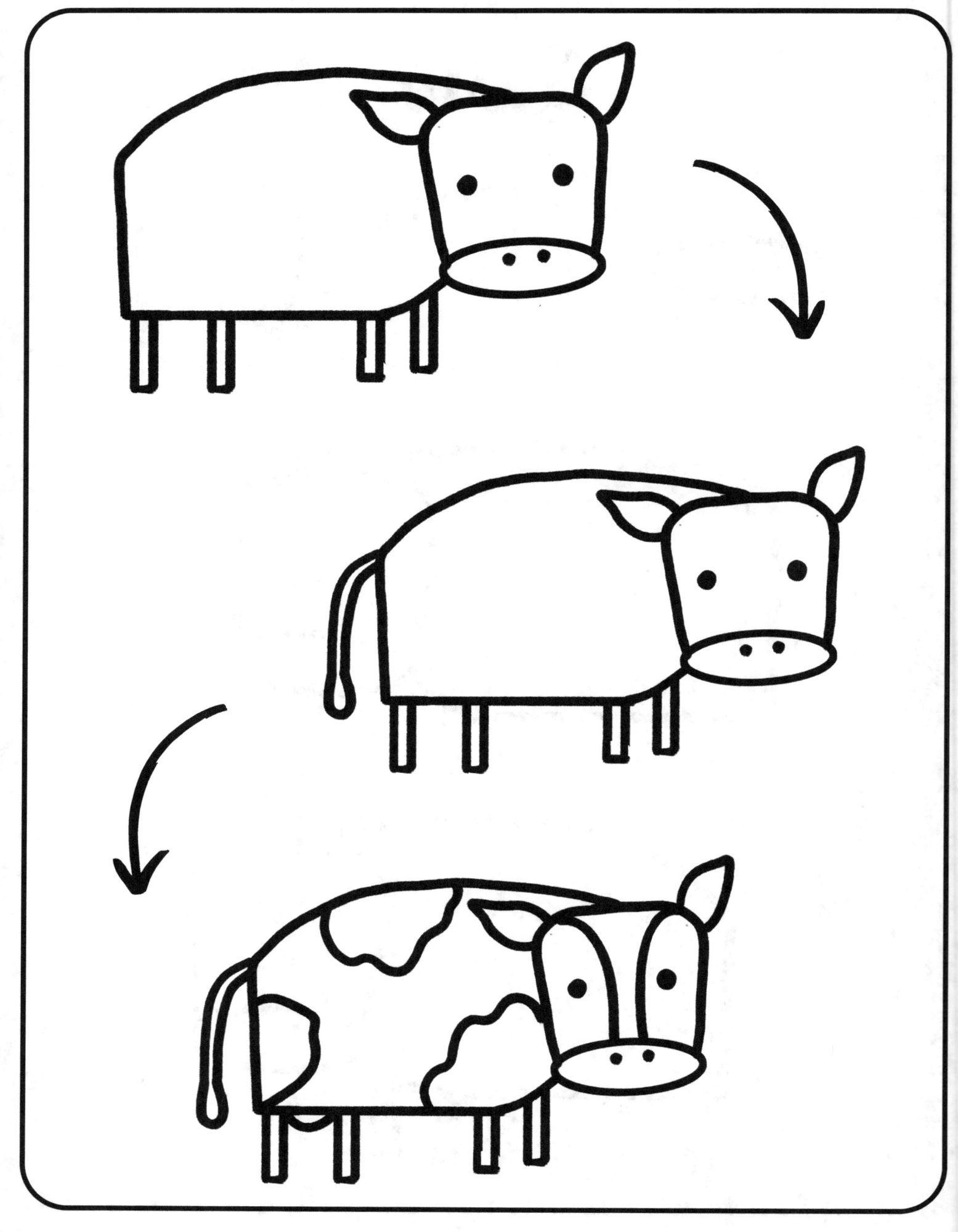

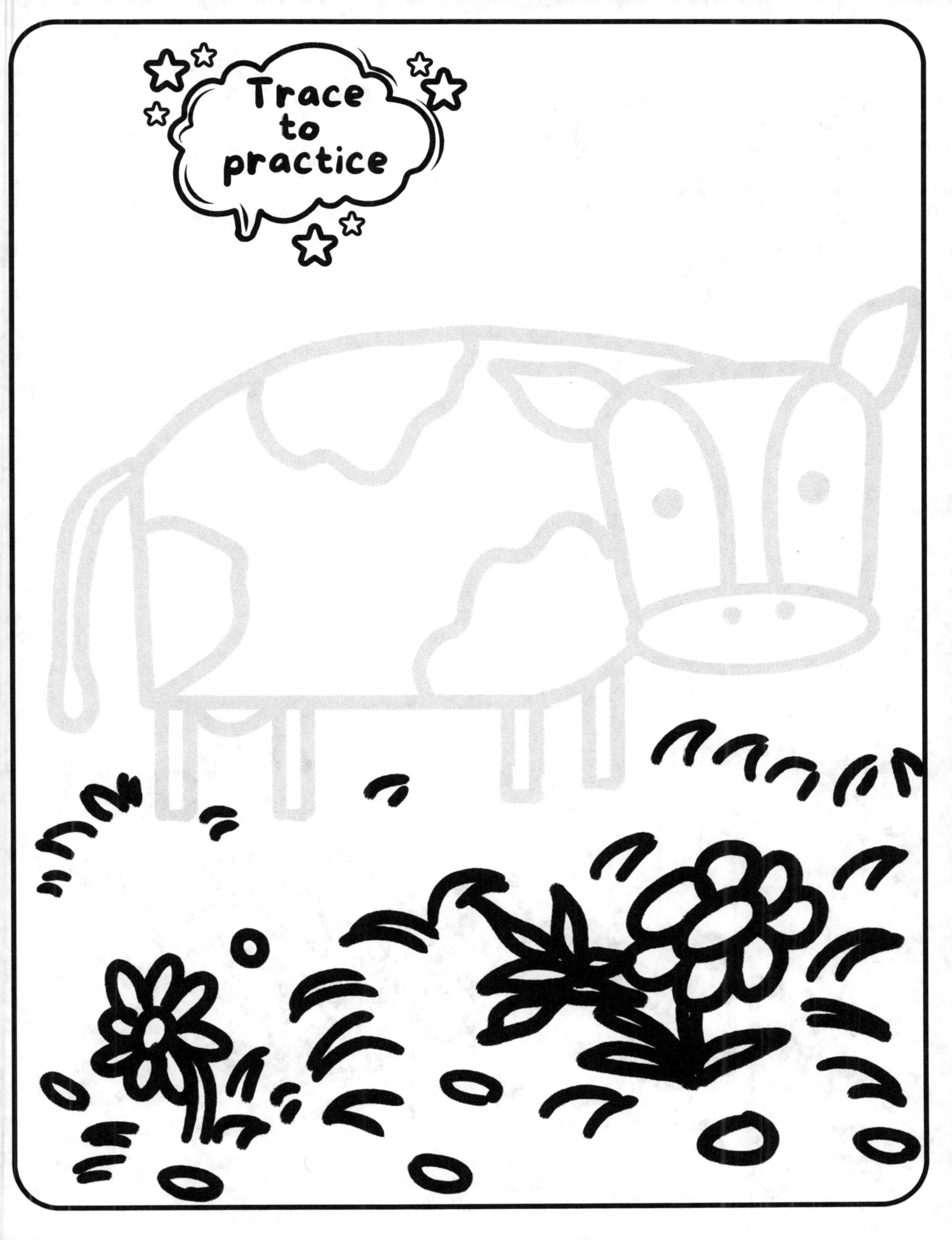

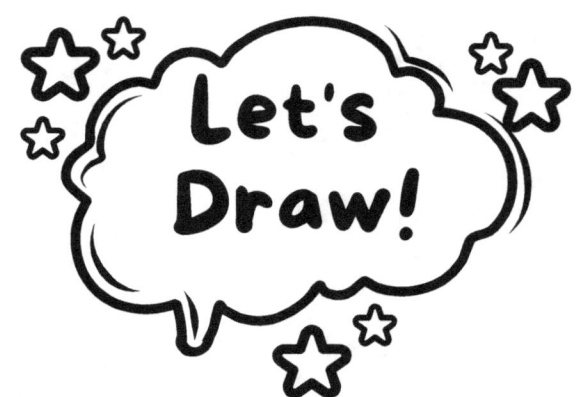

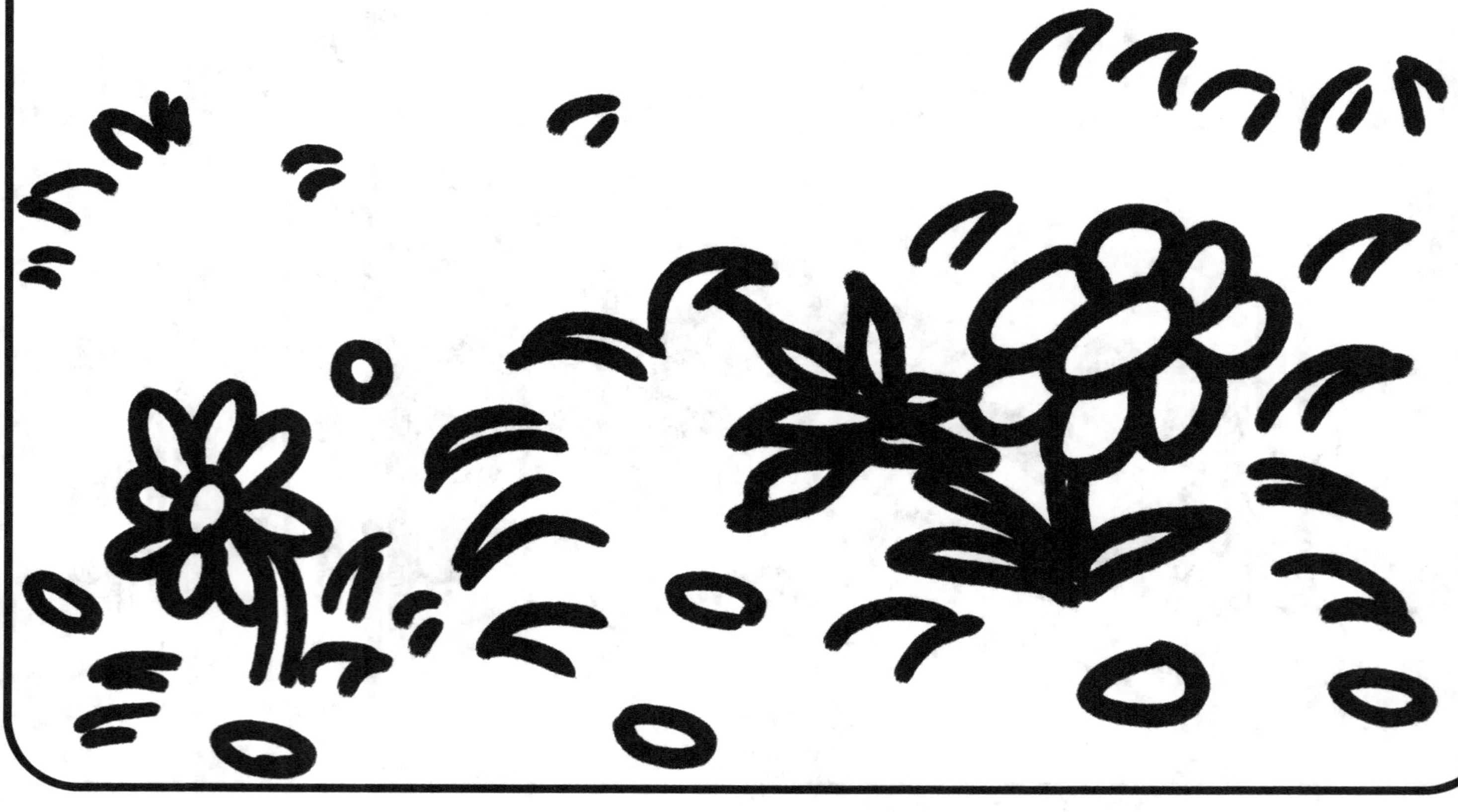

Girl

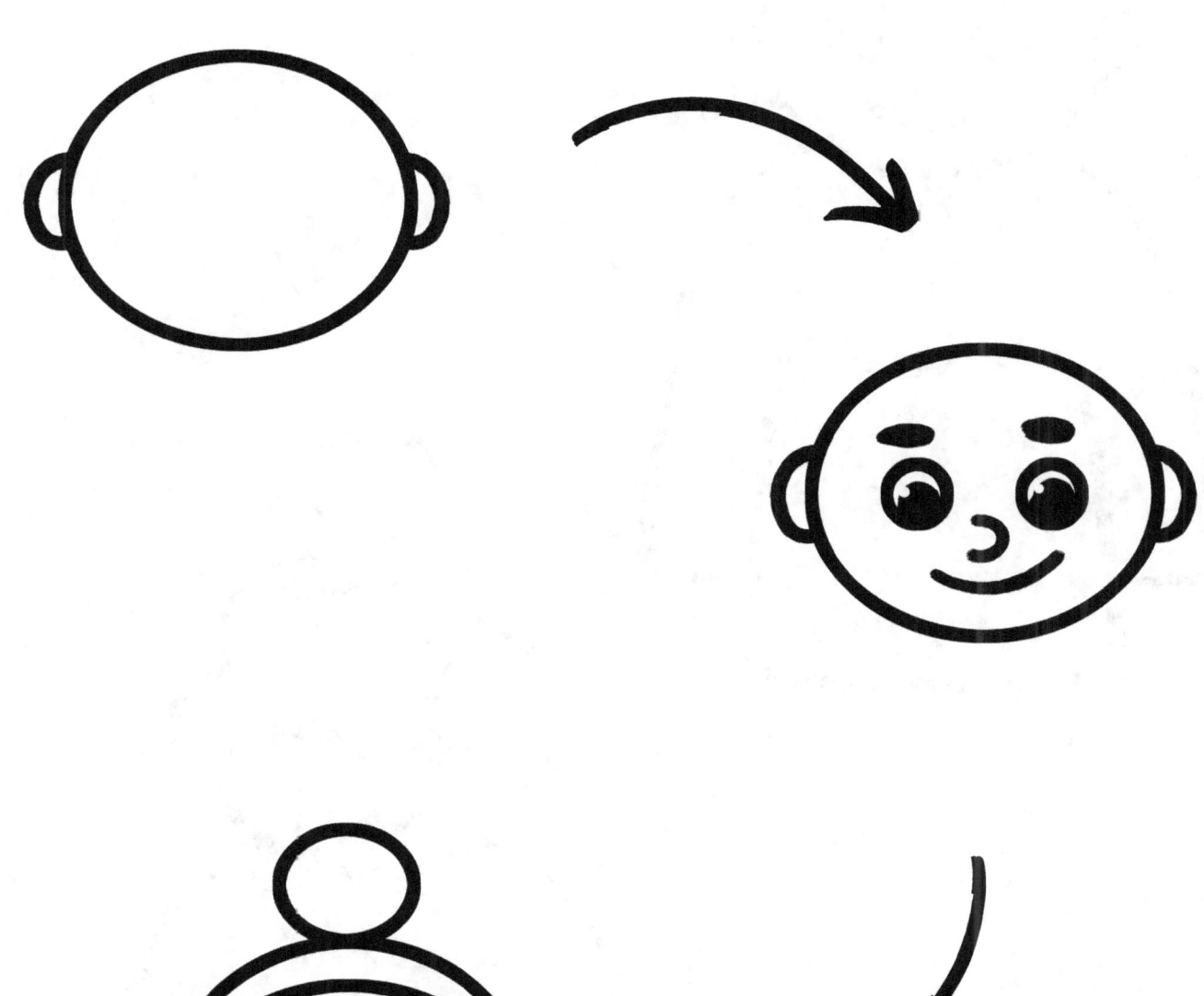

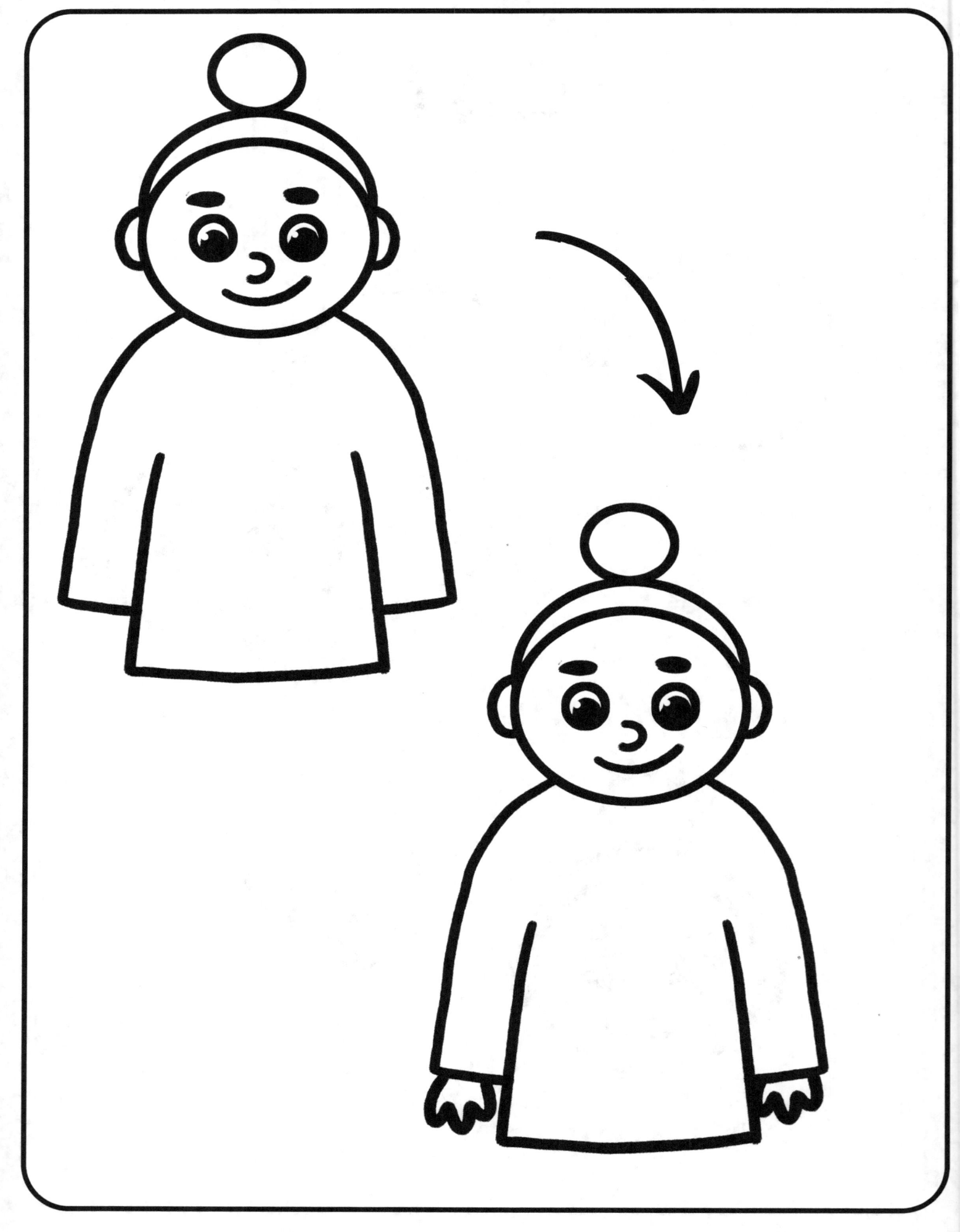

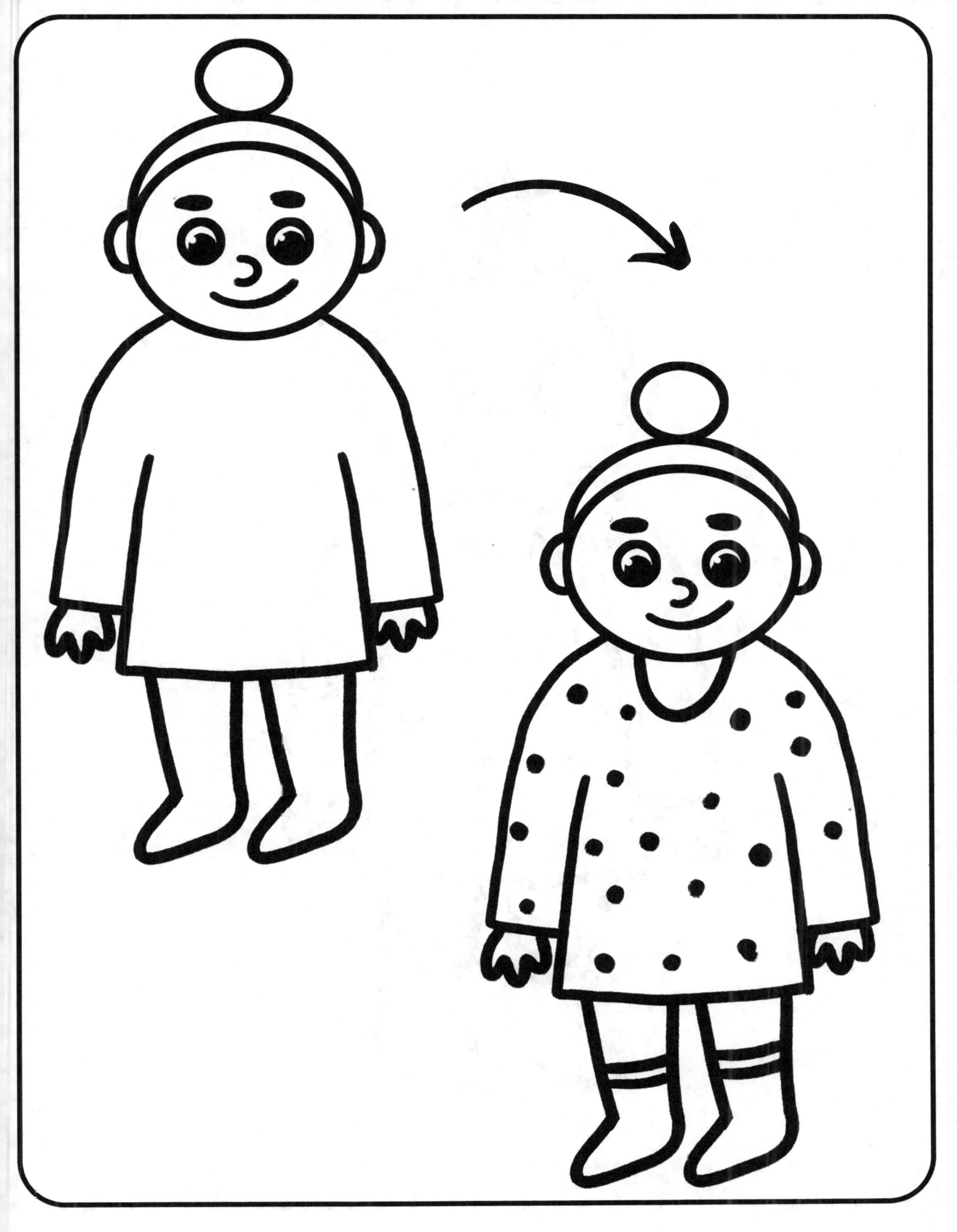

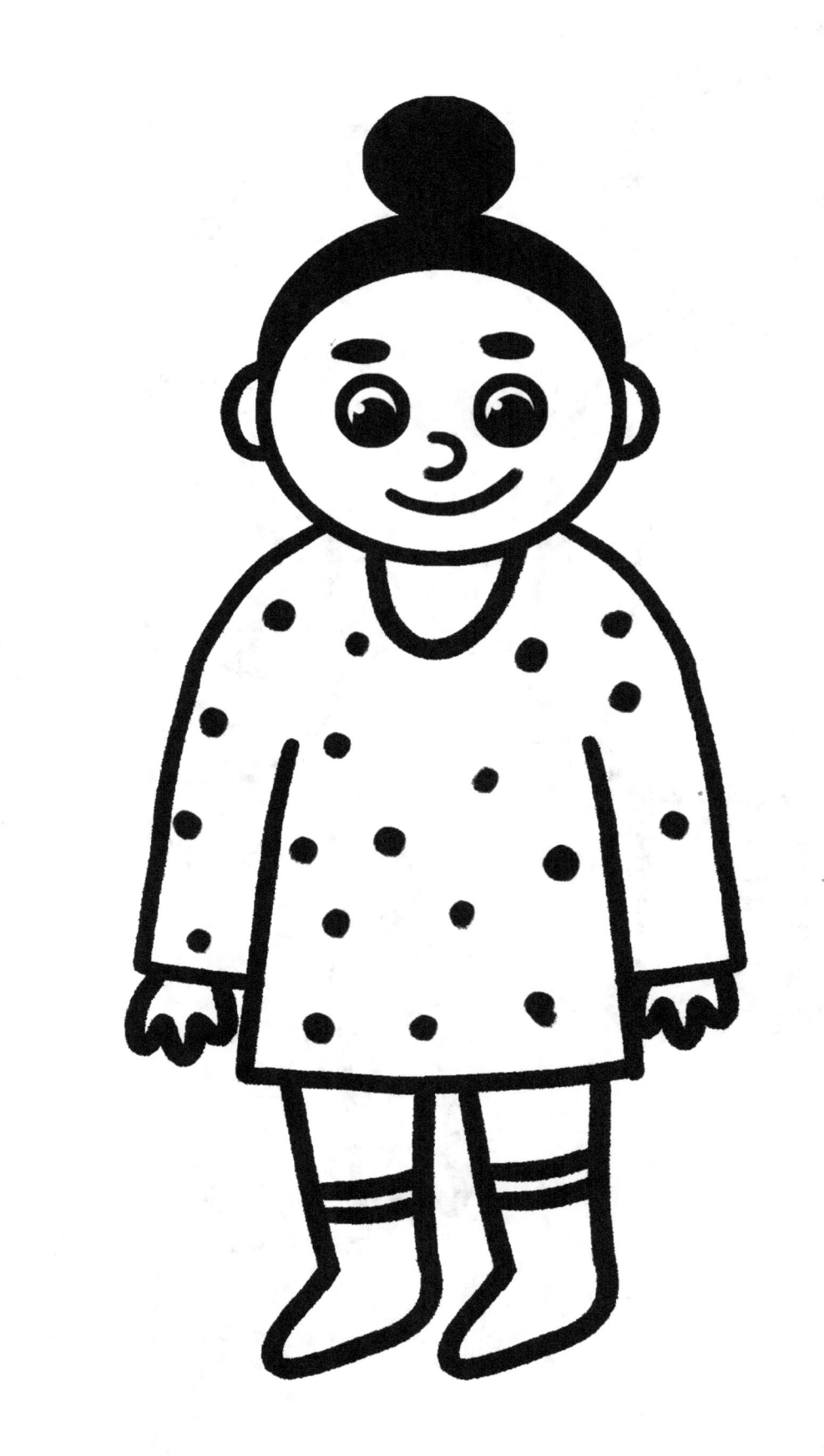

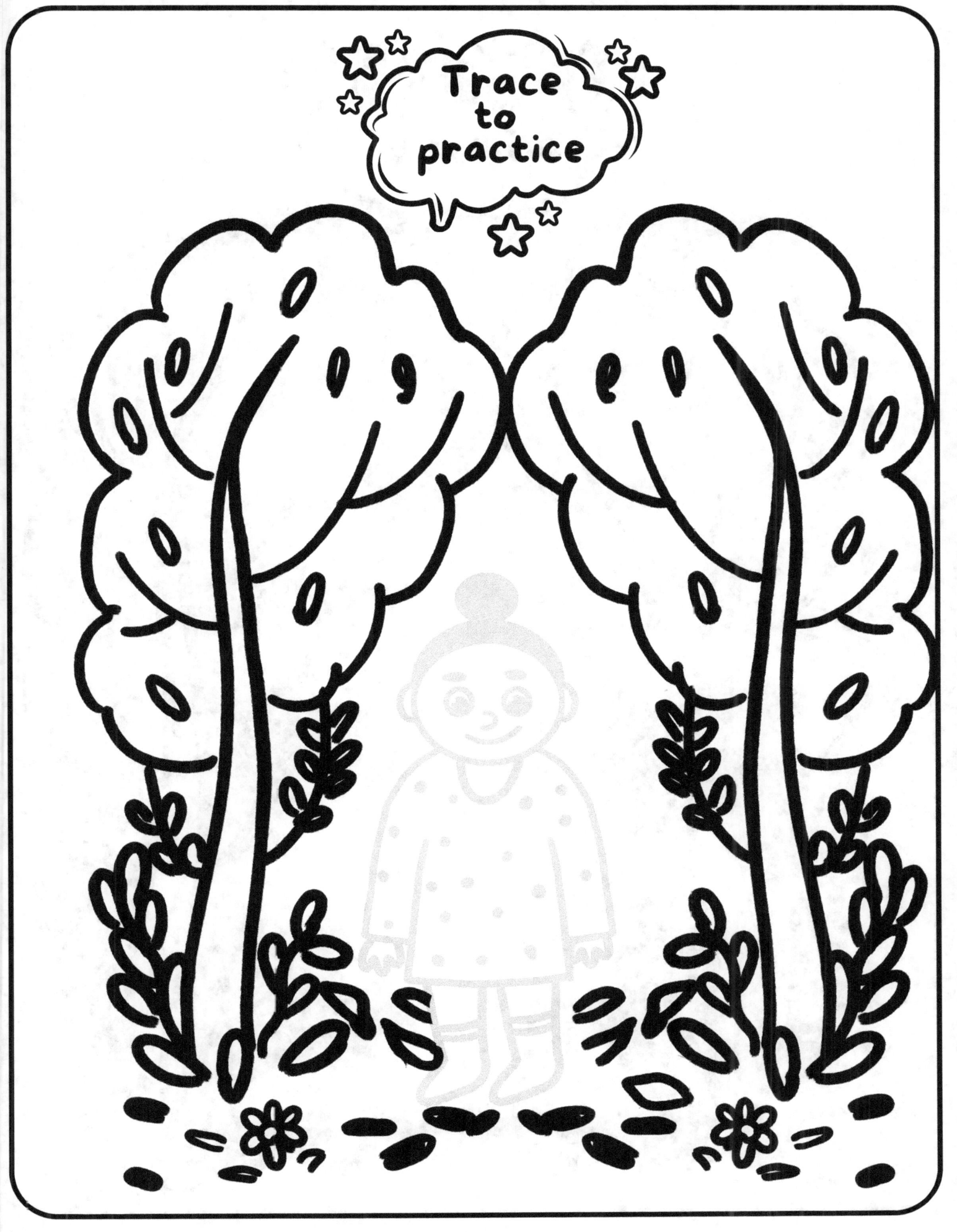

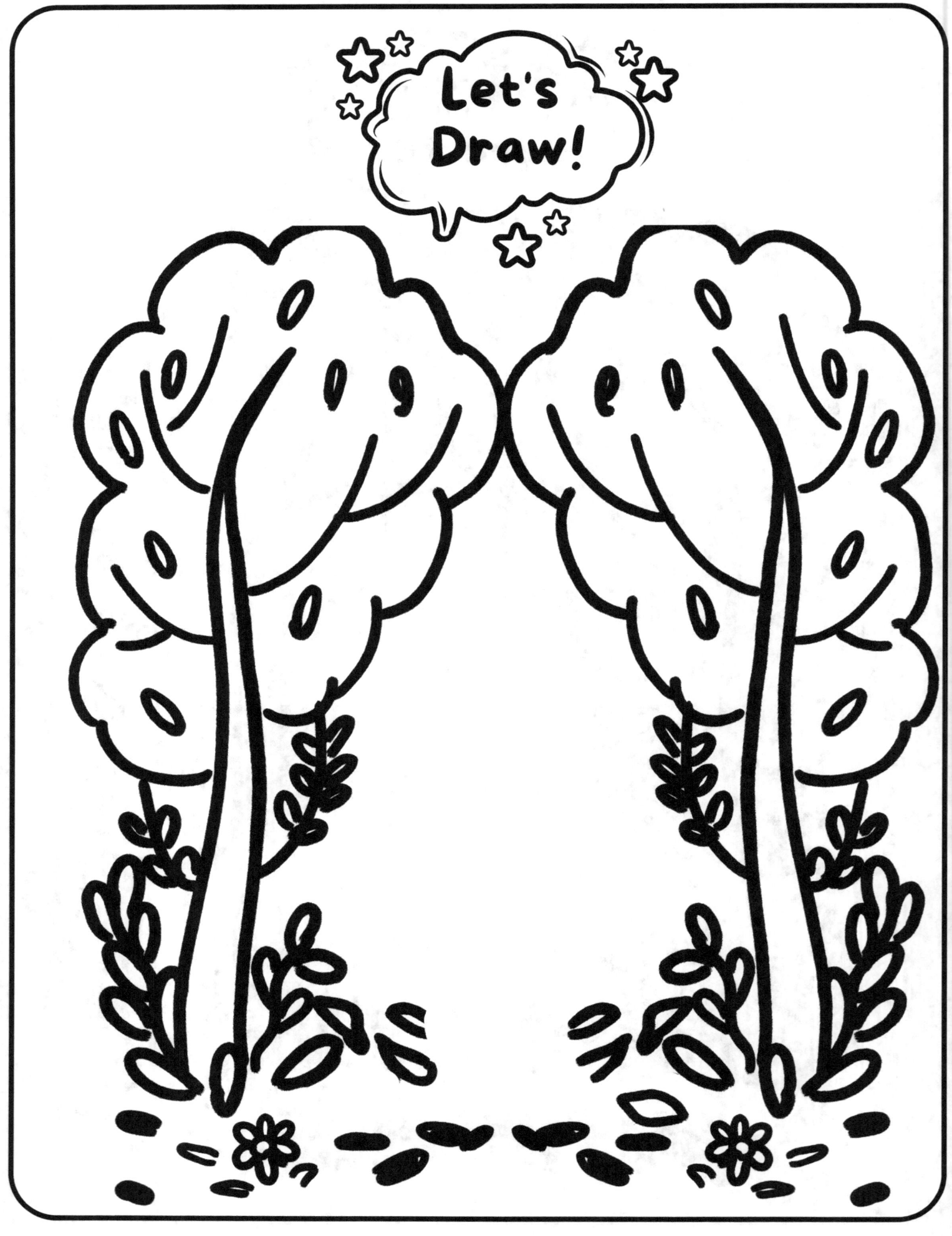

Chicken

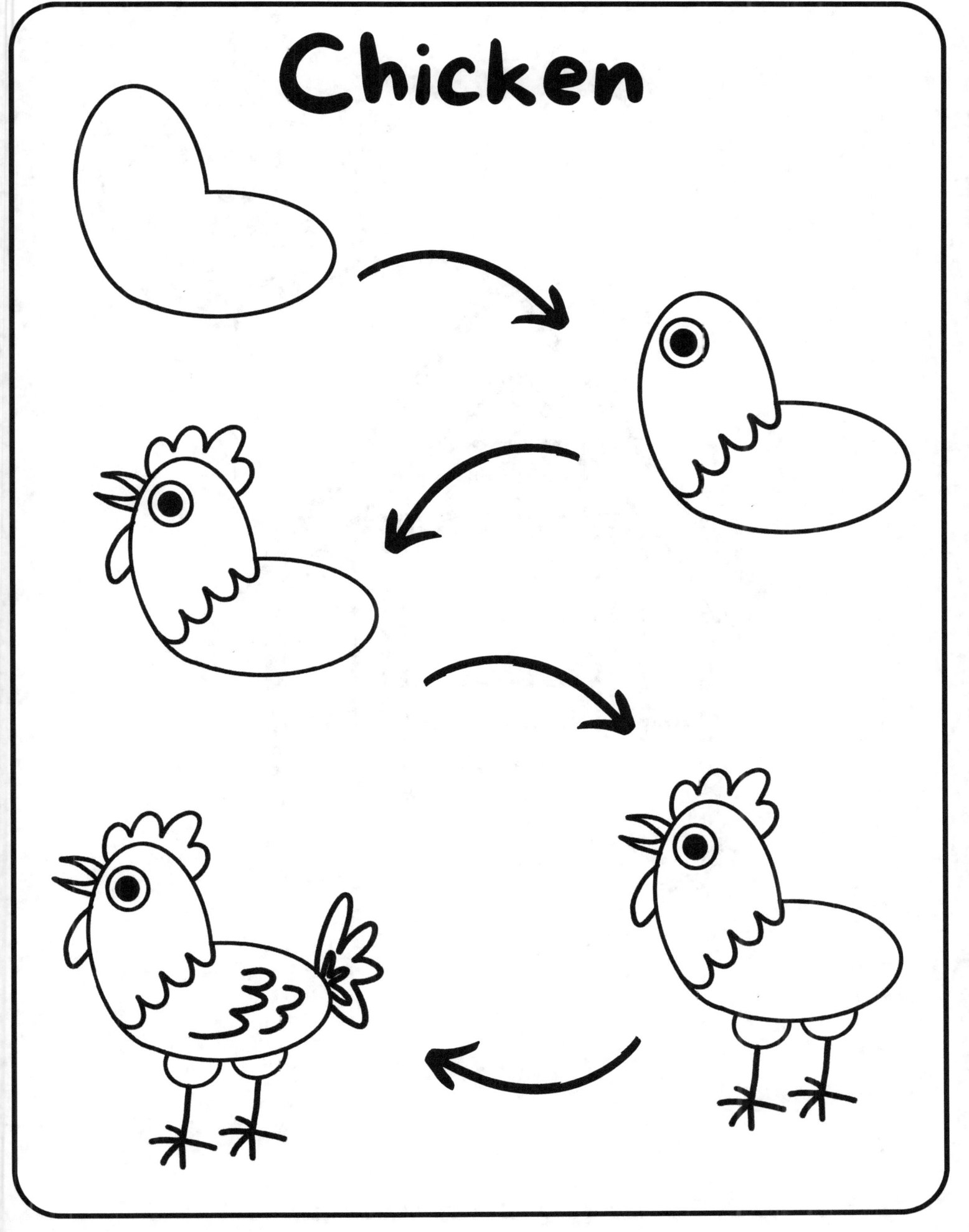

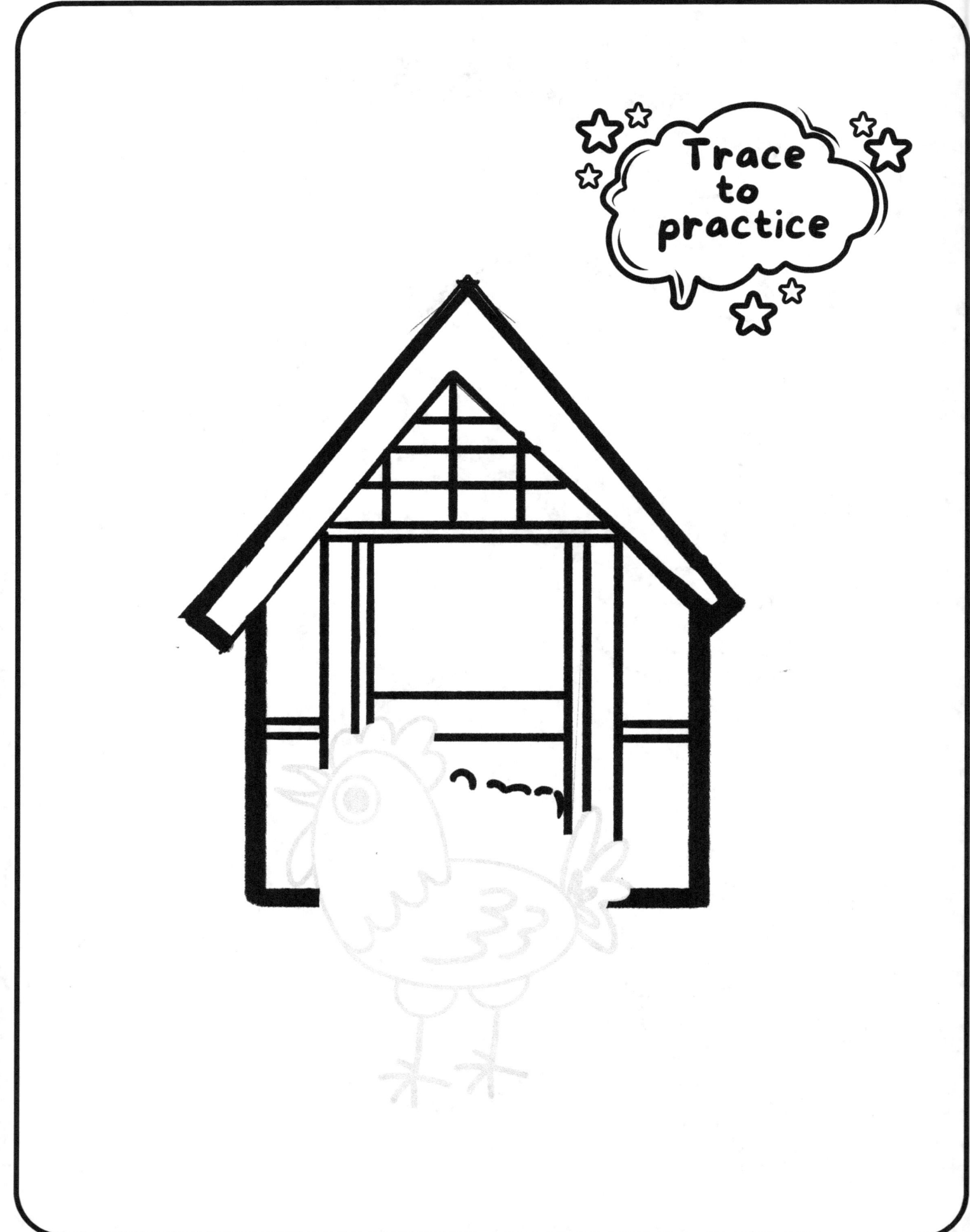

Trace
to
practice

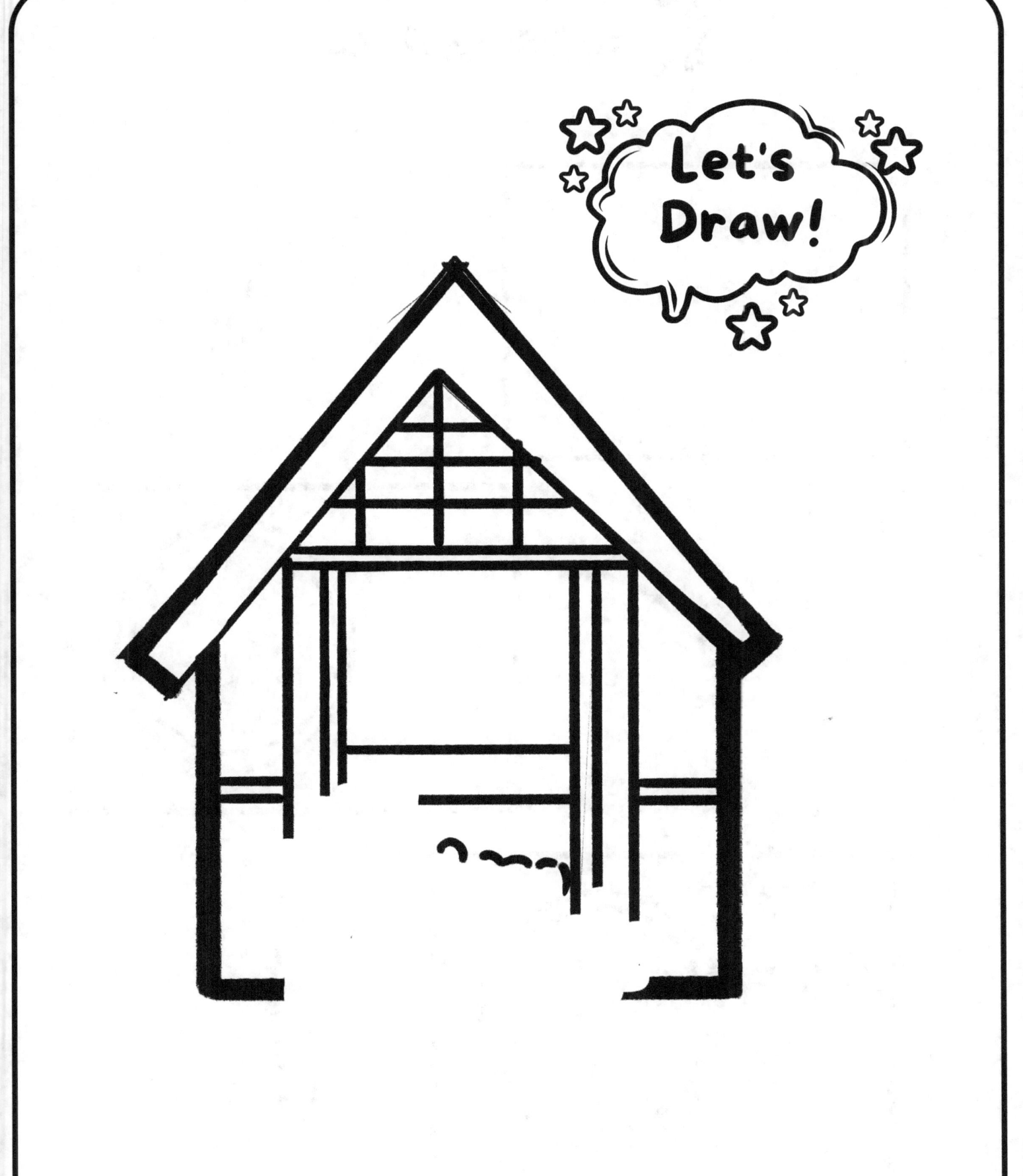

Camera

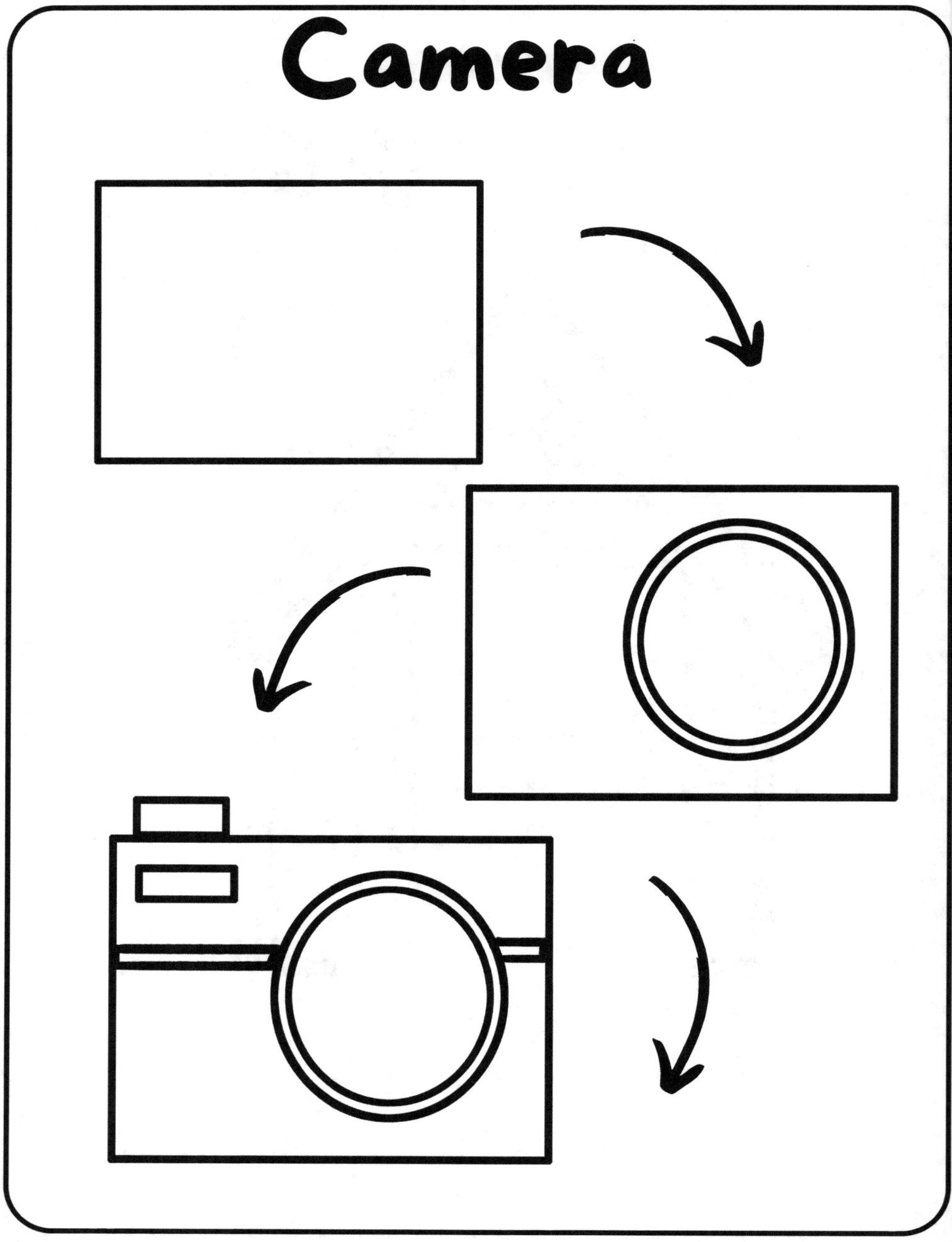

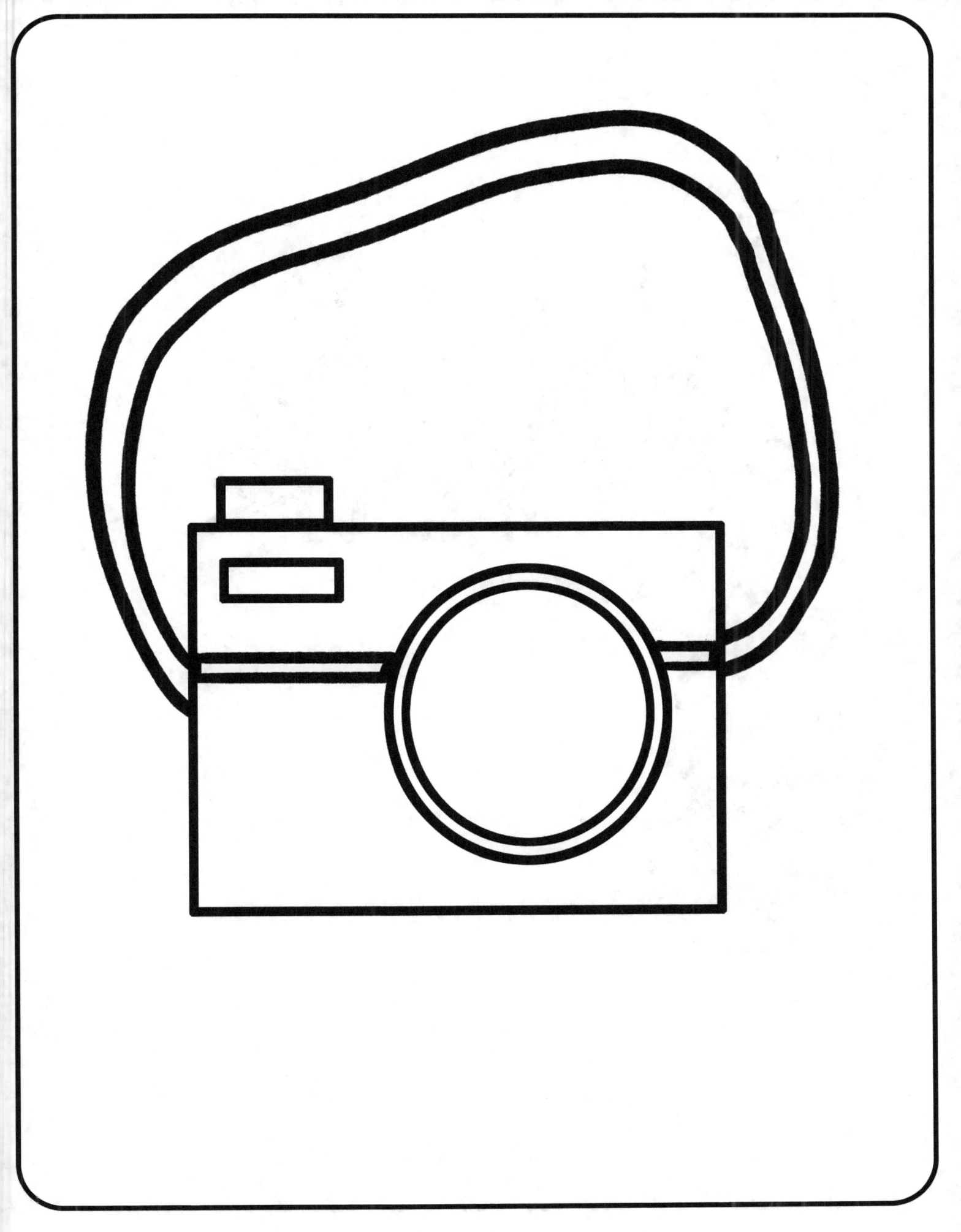

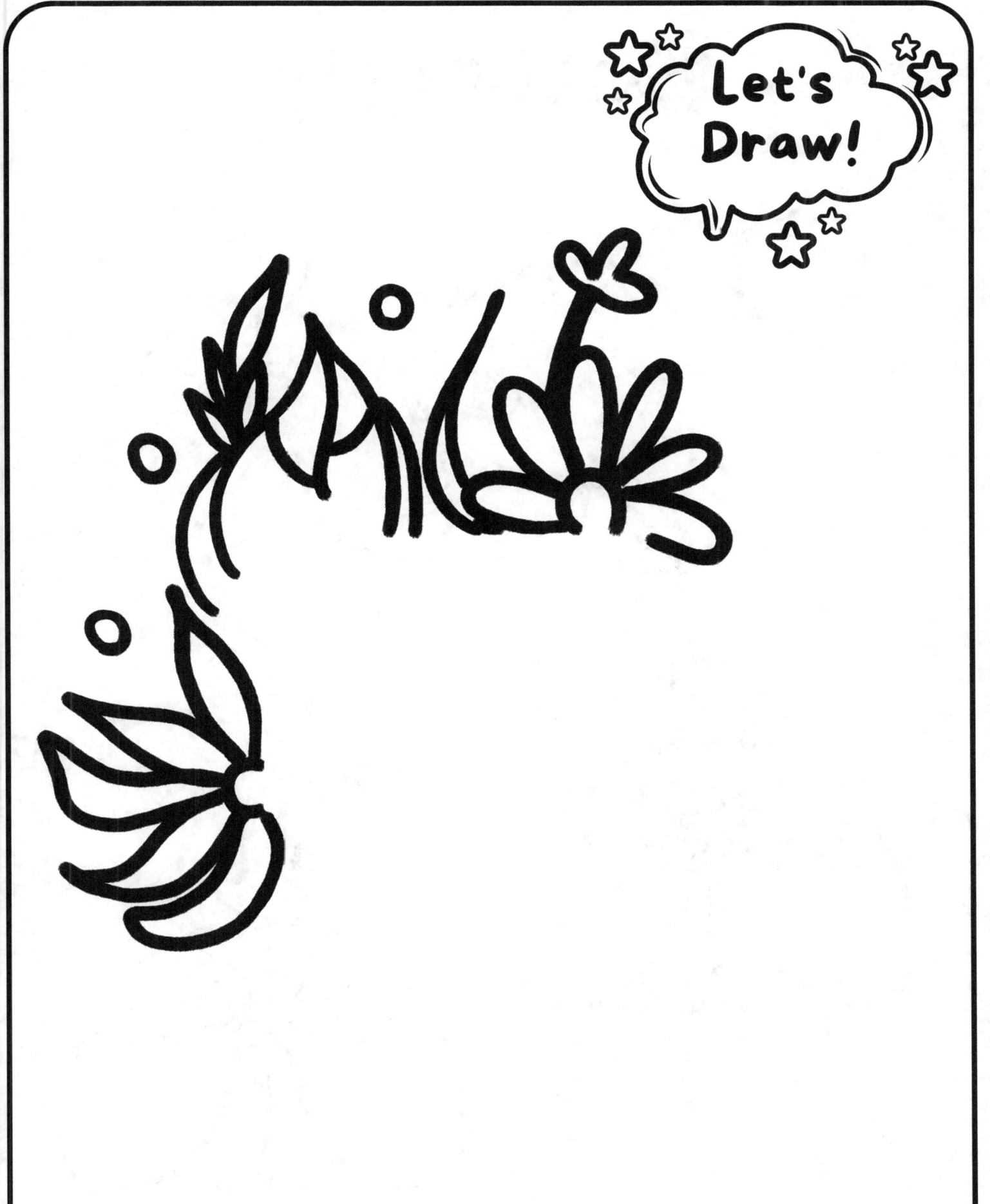

Butterfly

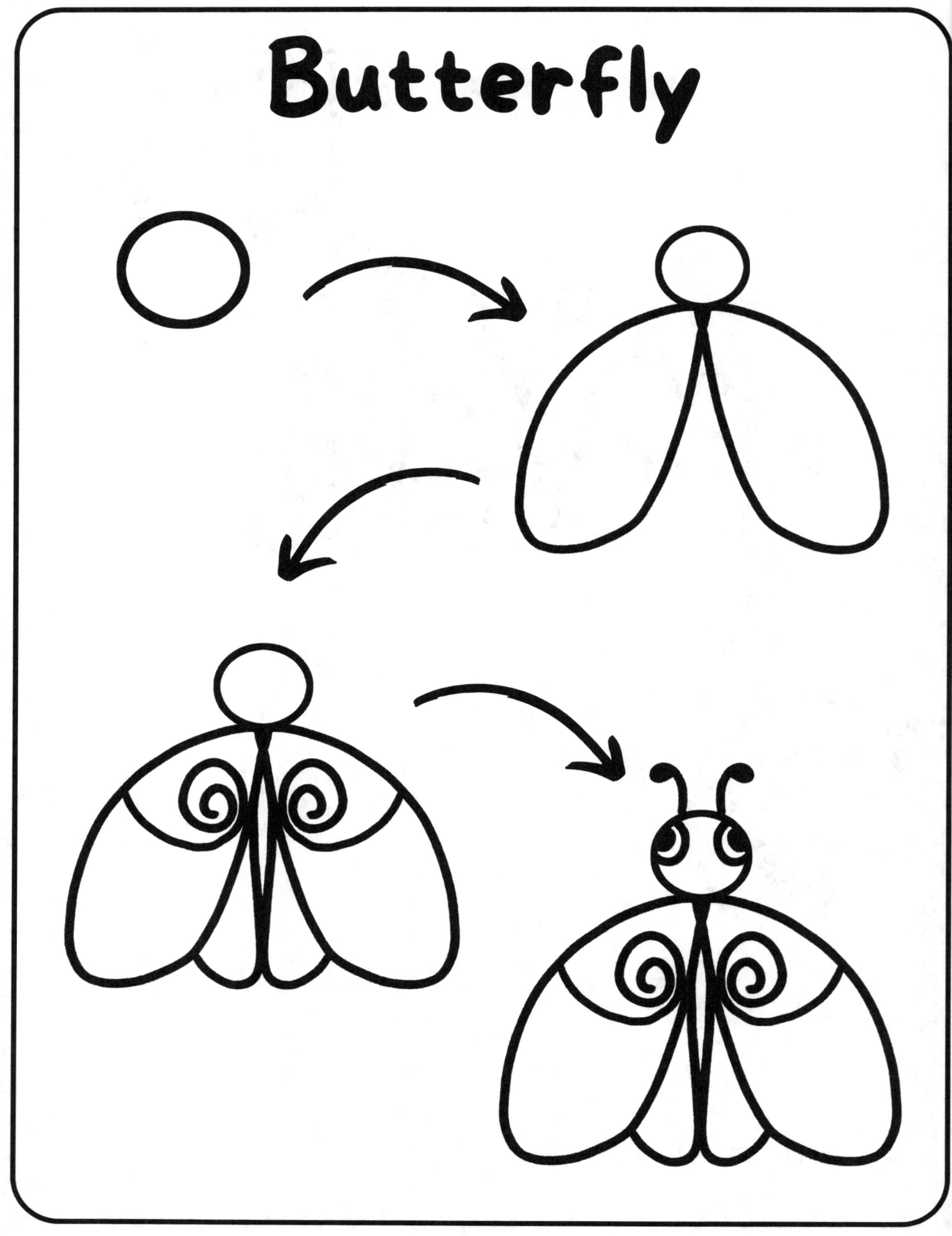

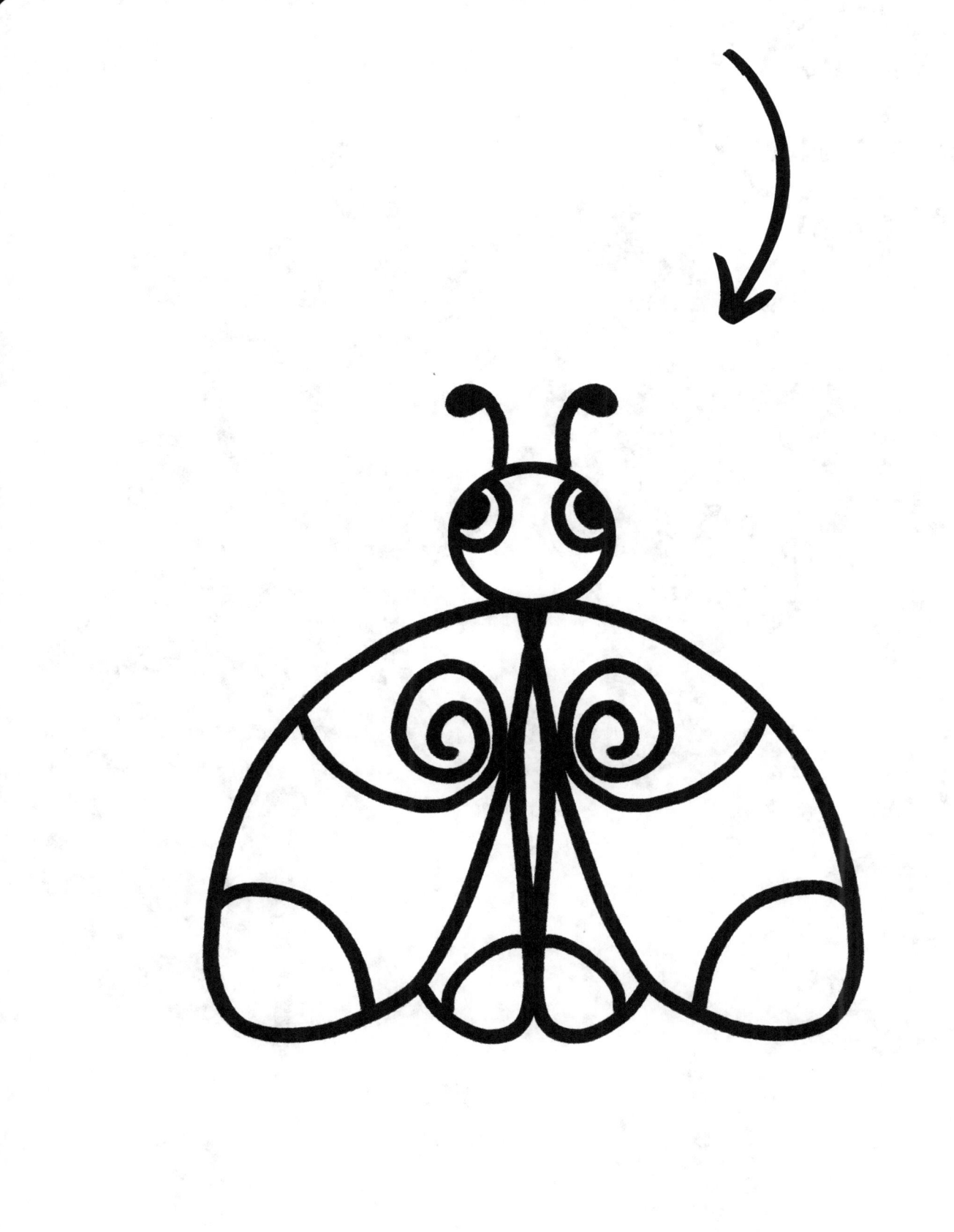

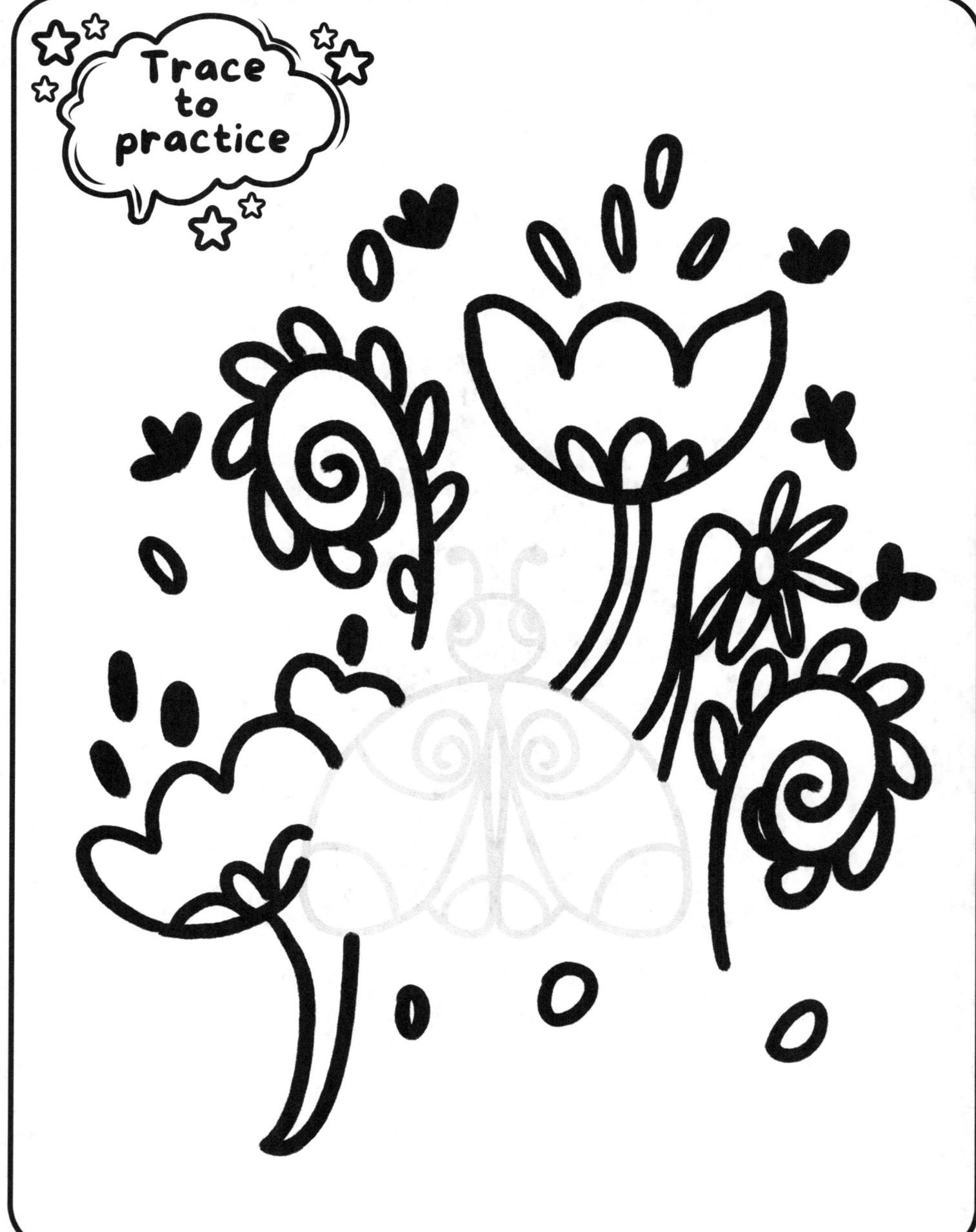

Trace to practice

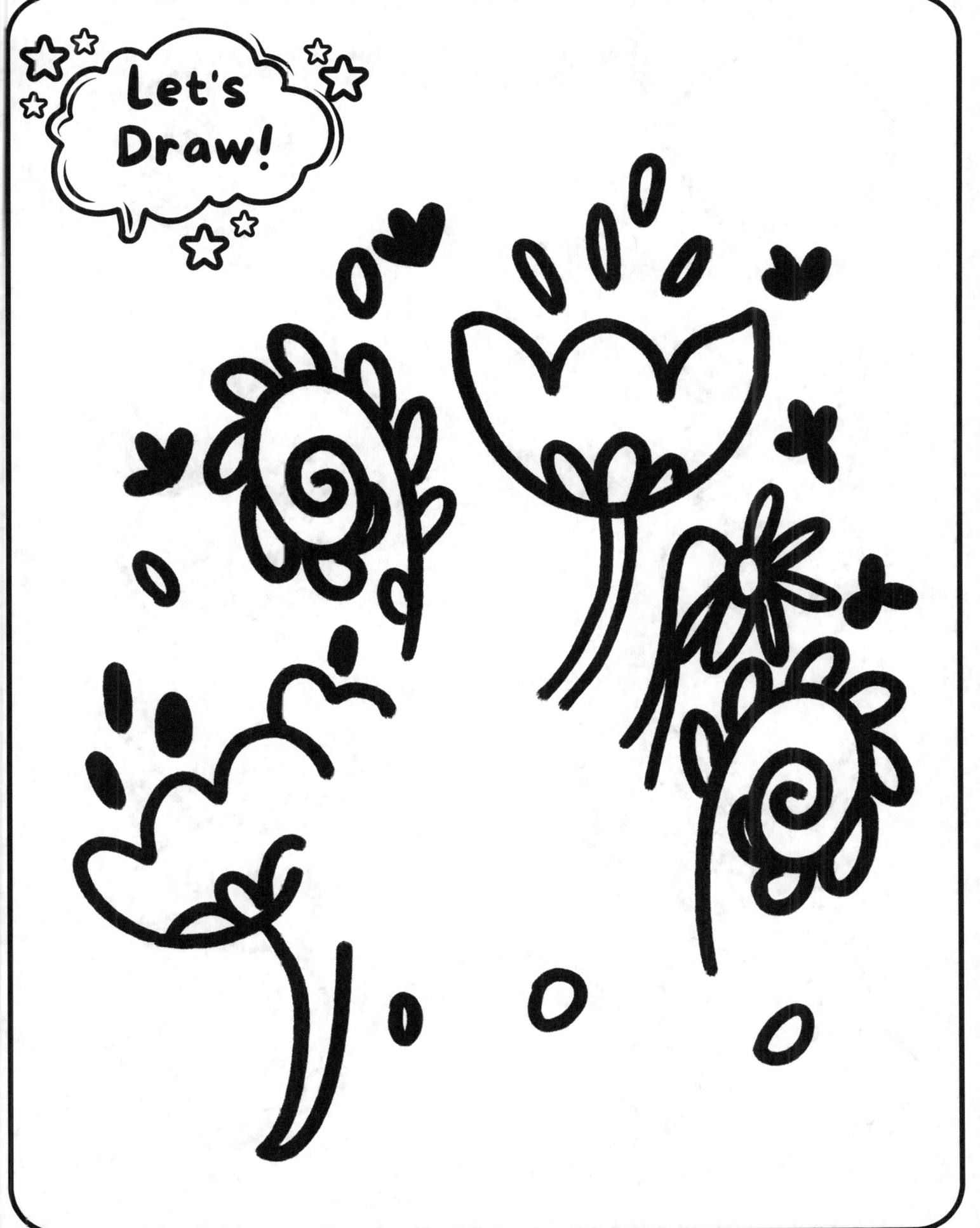

Let's Draw!

Rabbit

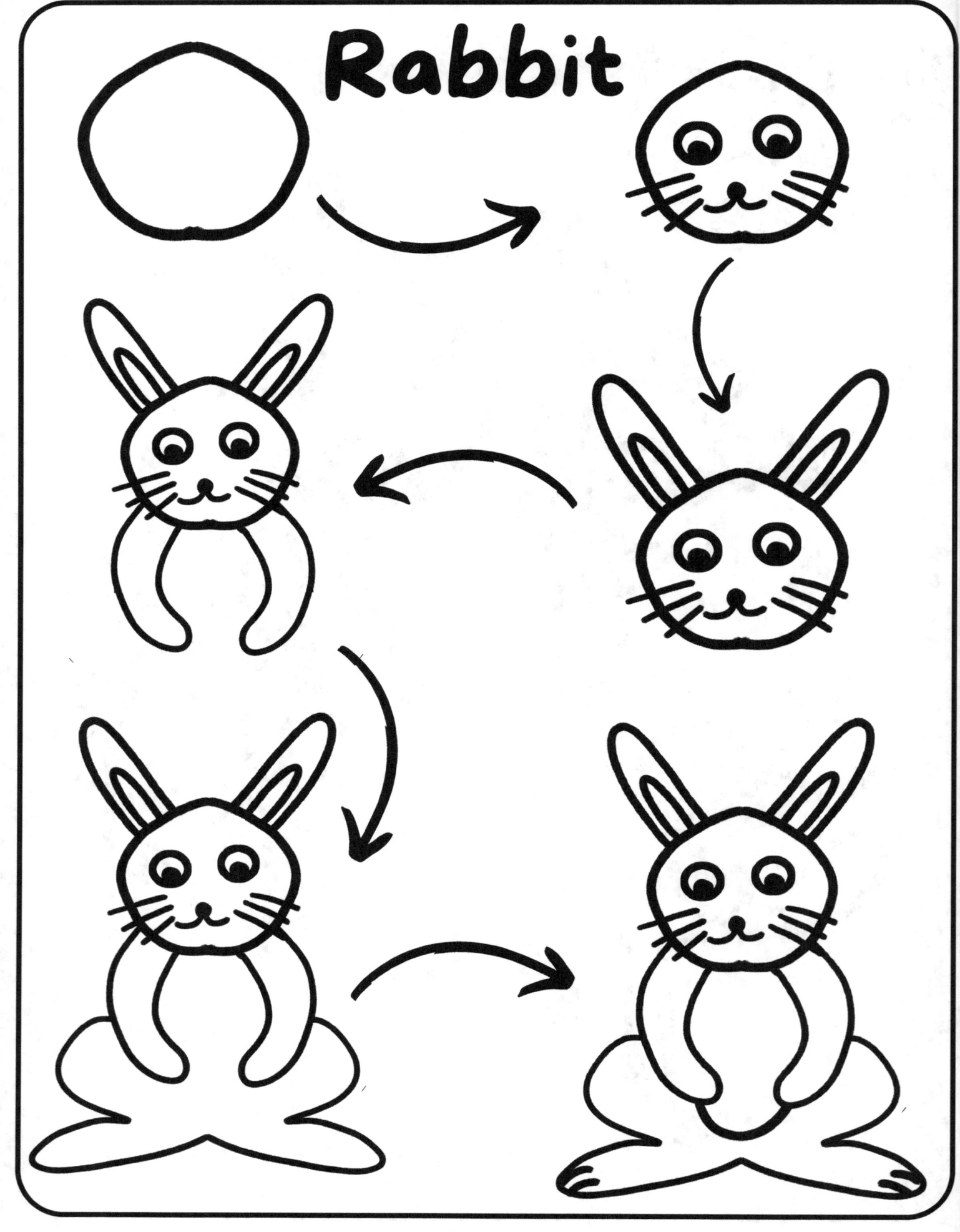

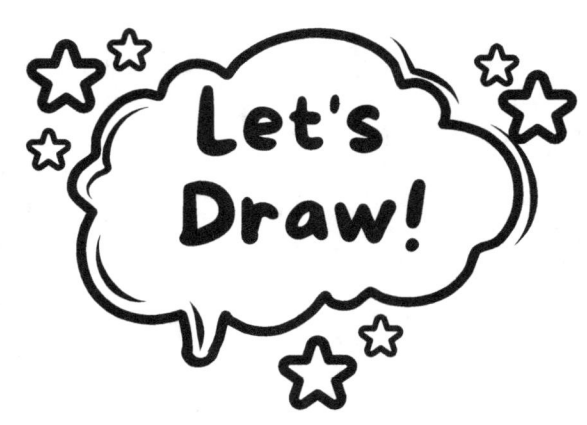

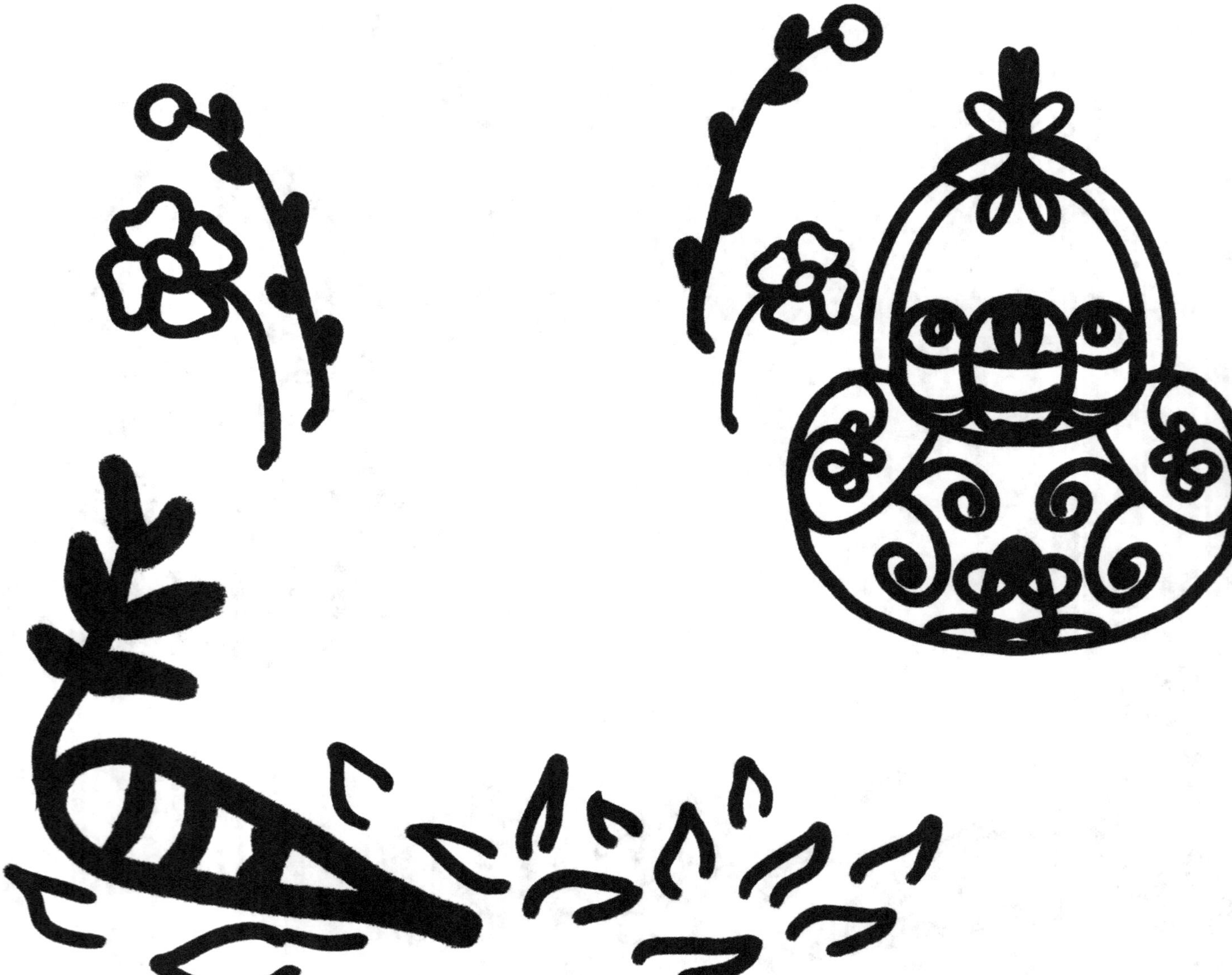

Rat

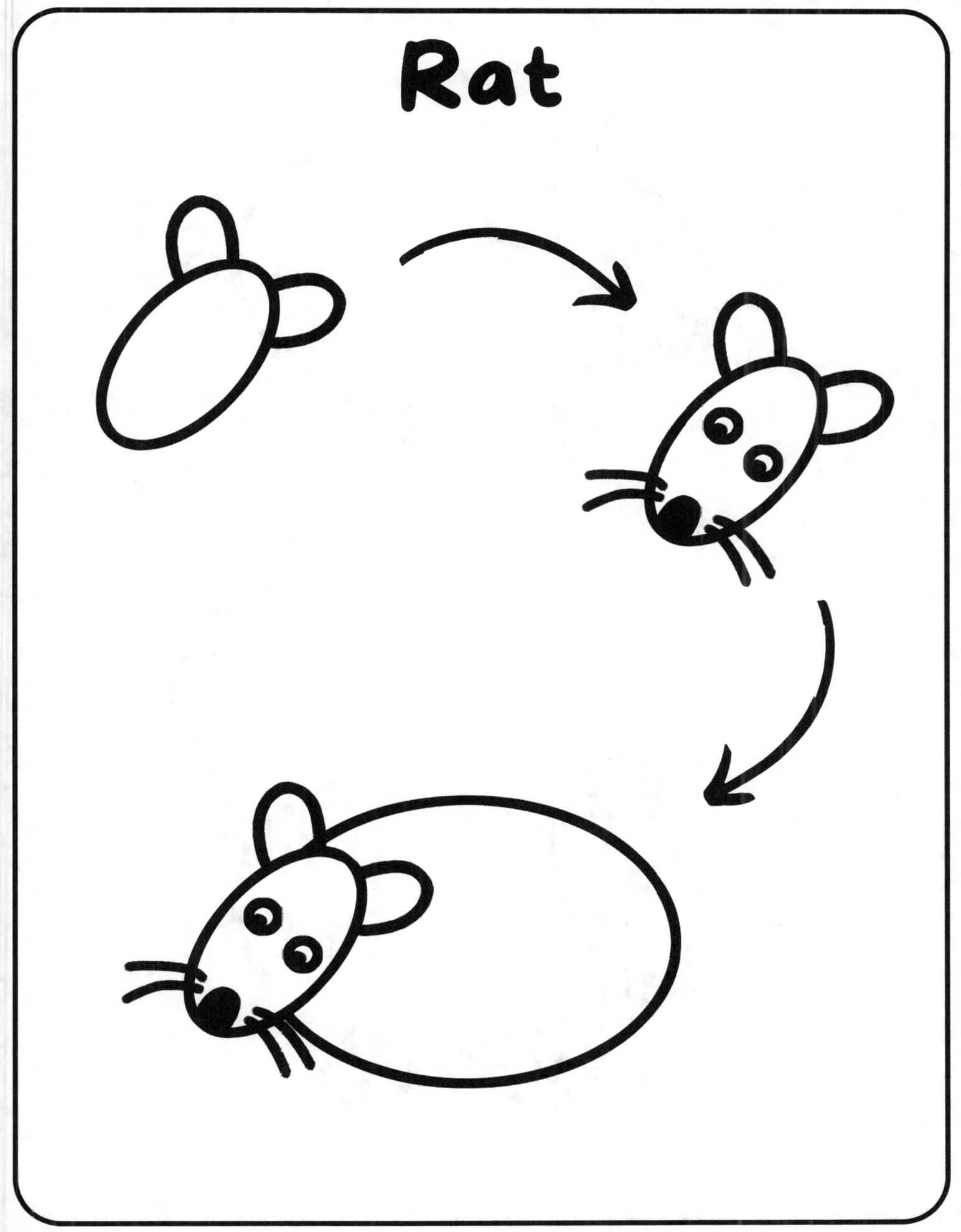

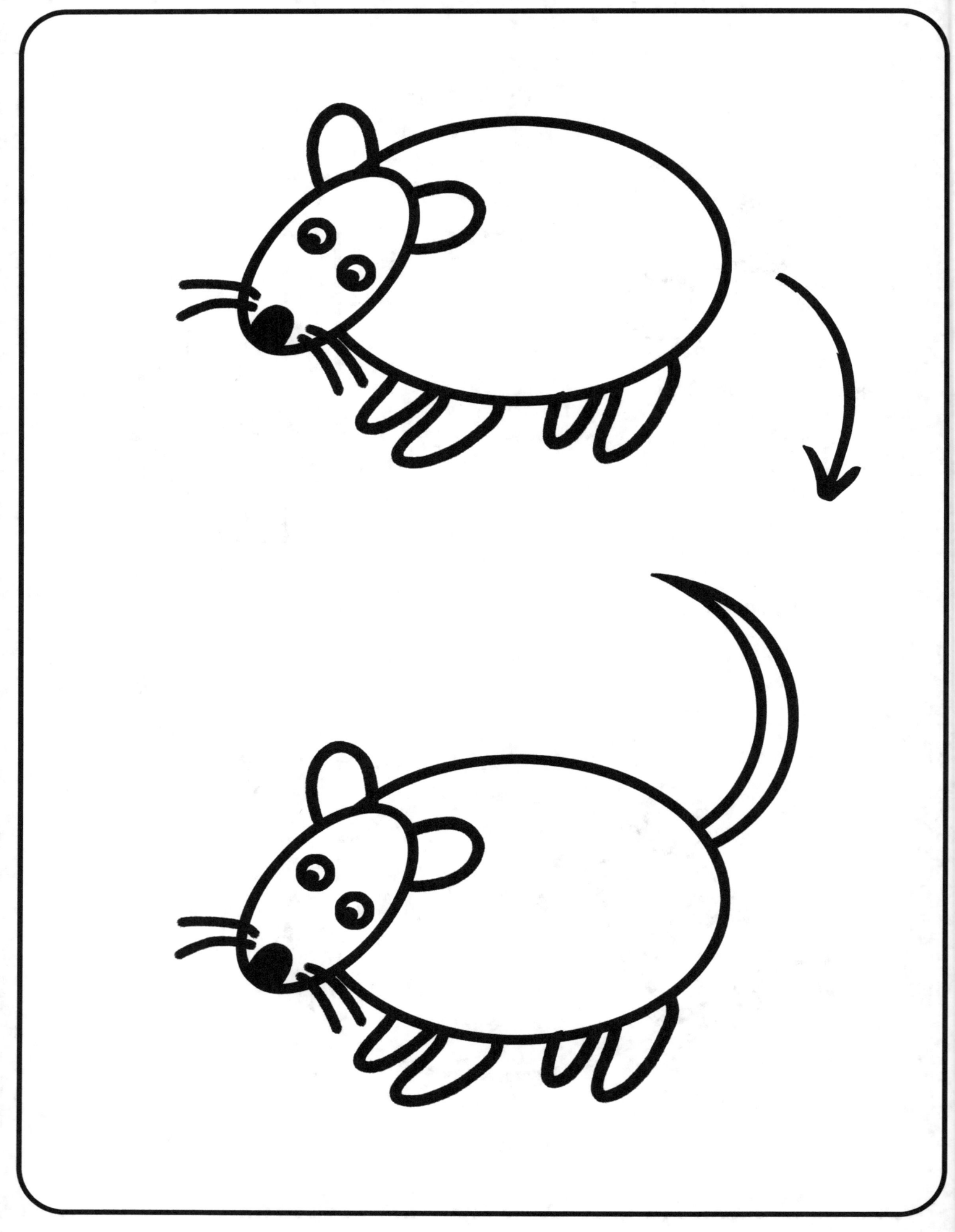

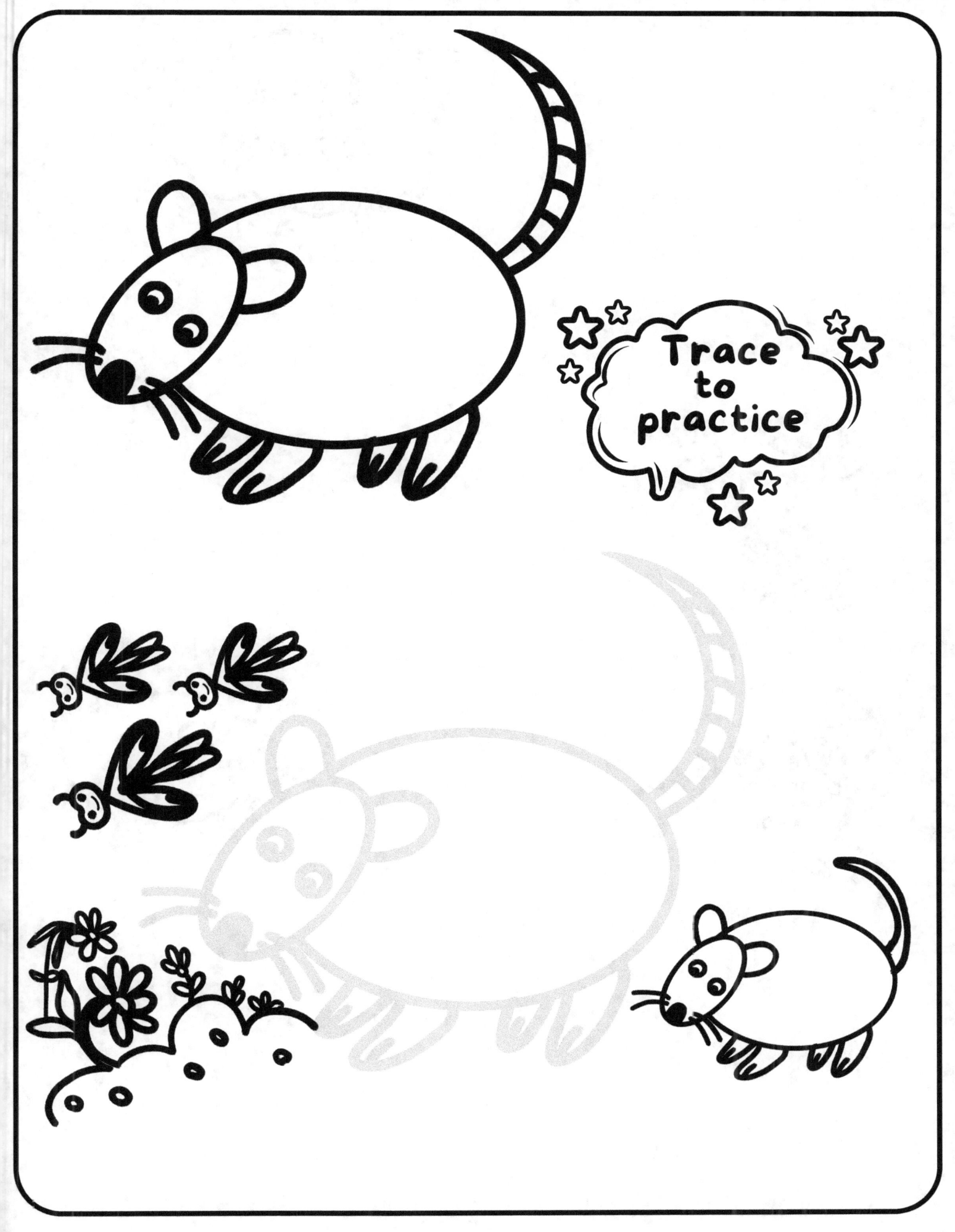

Trace
to
practice

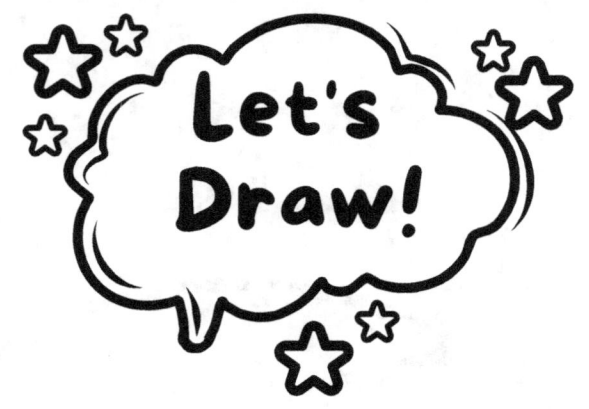

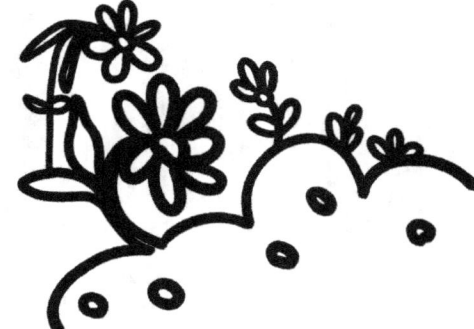

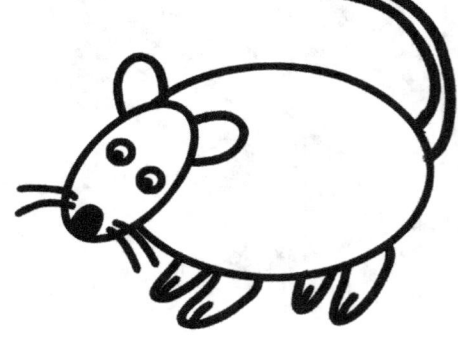

spider

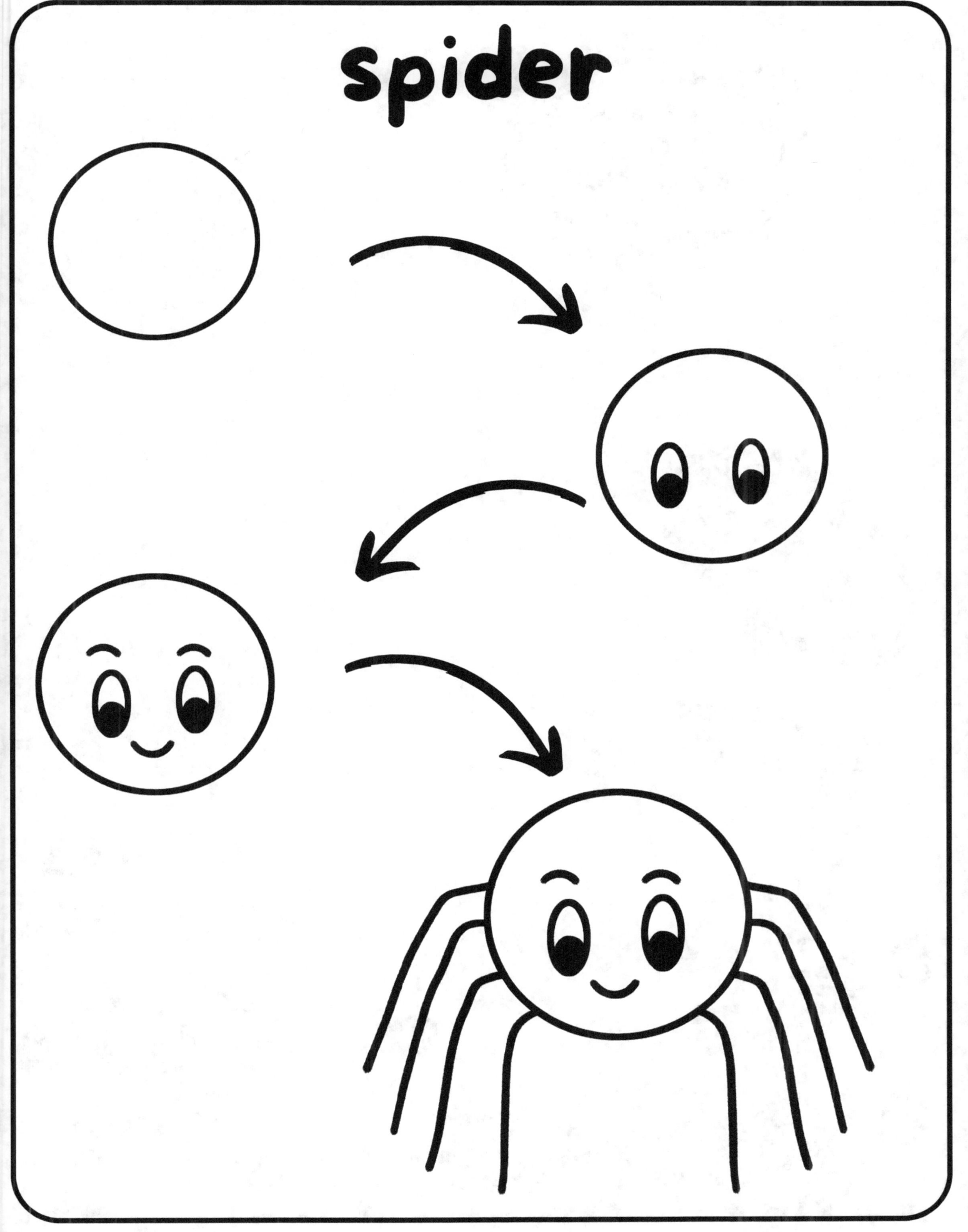

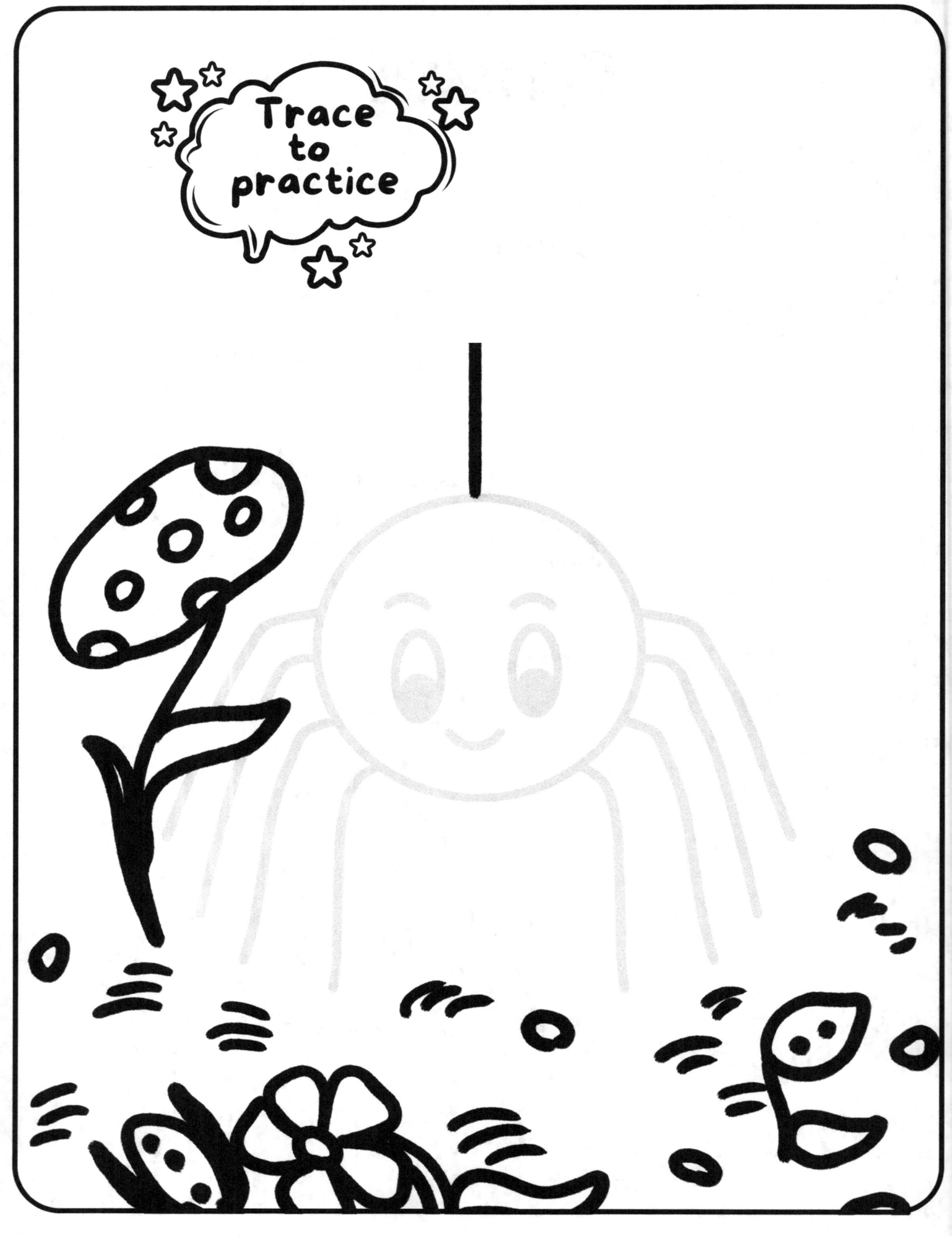

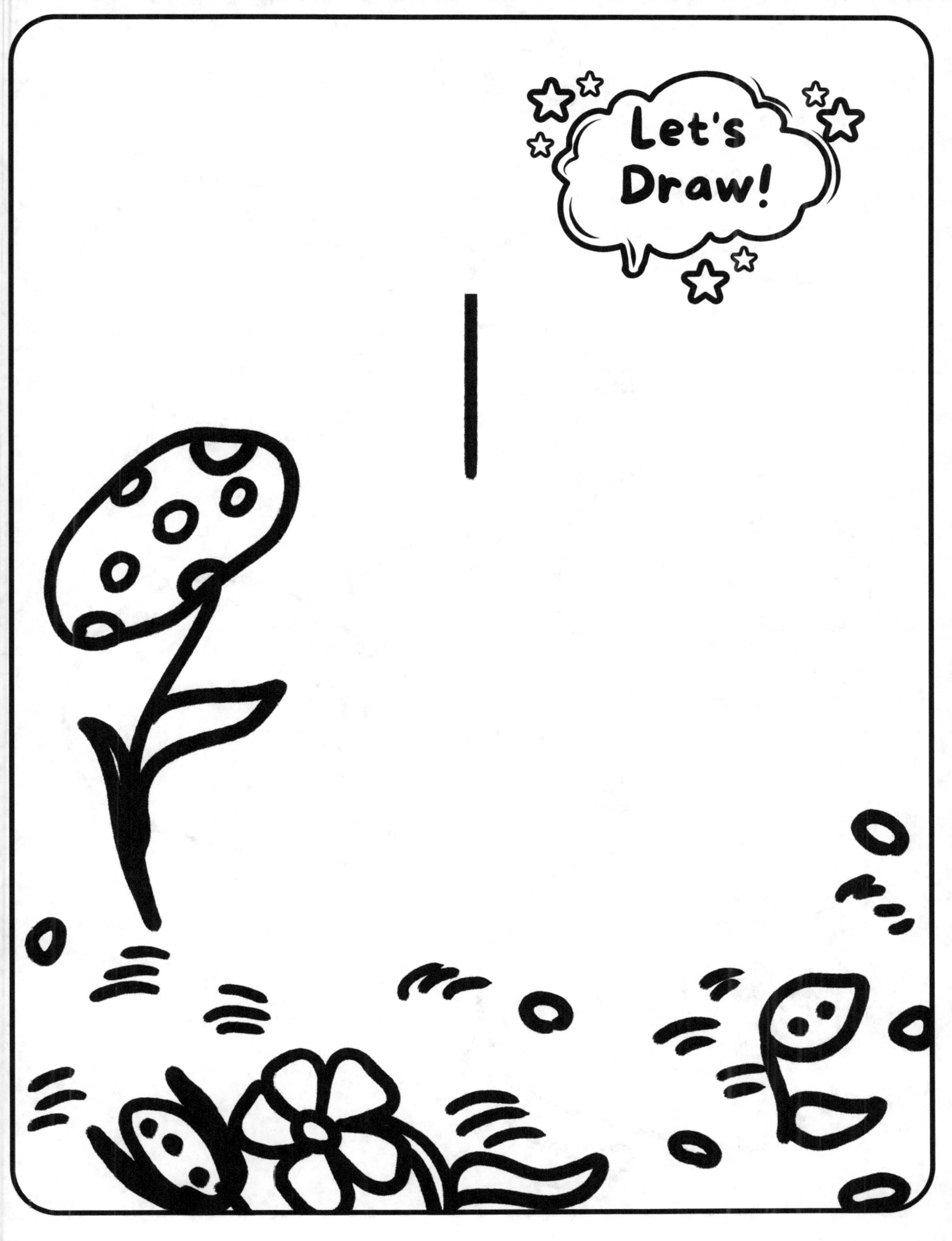

Cat

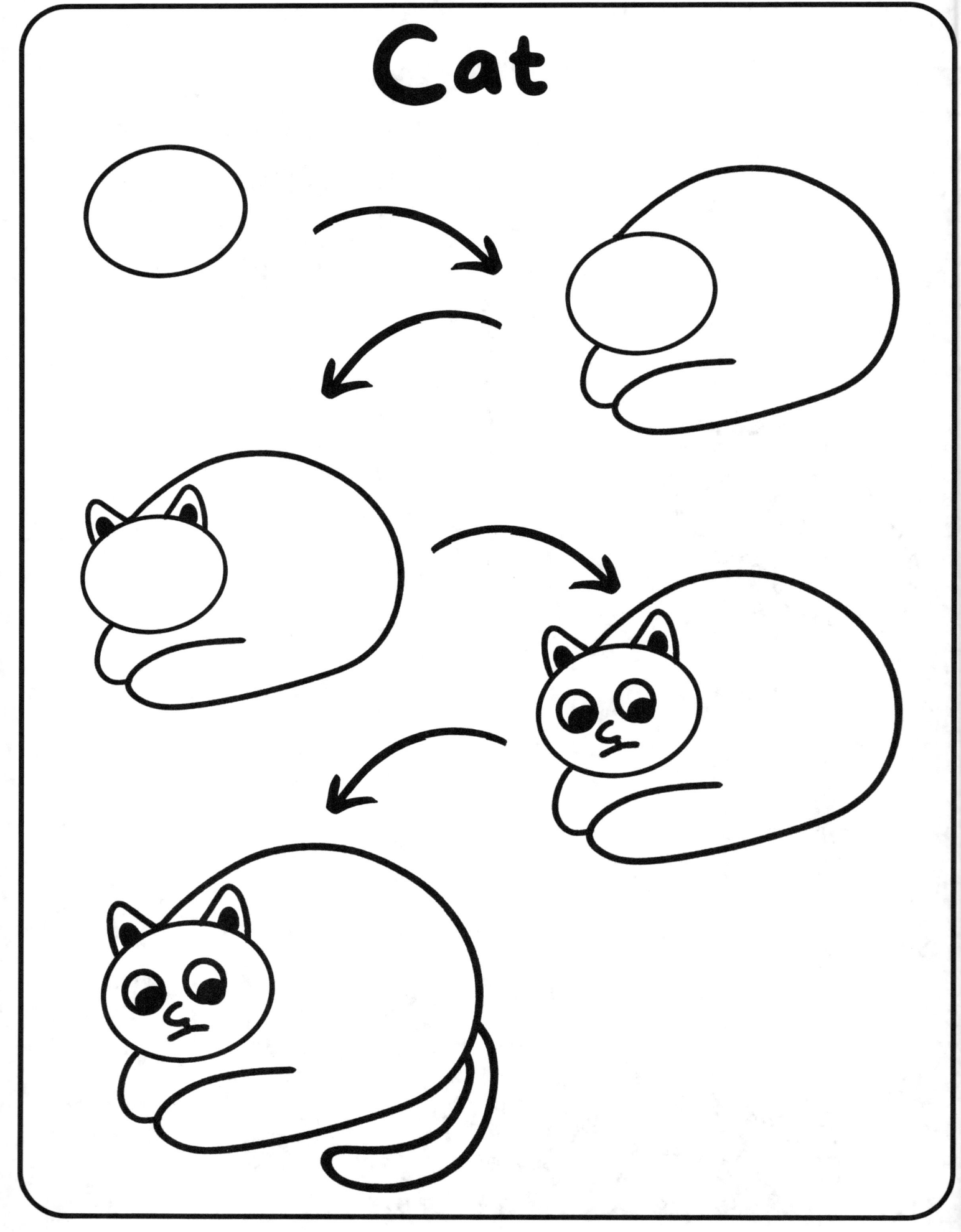

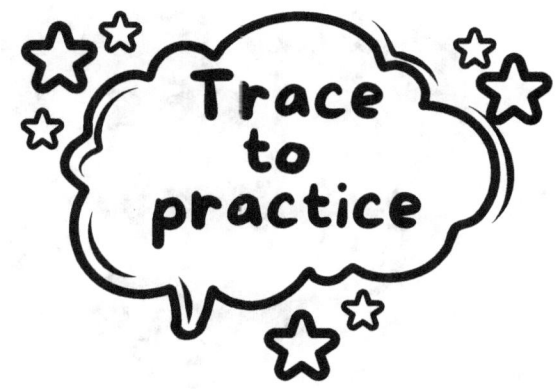

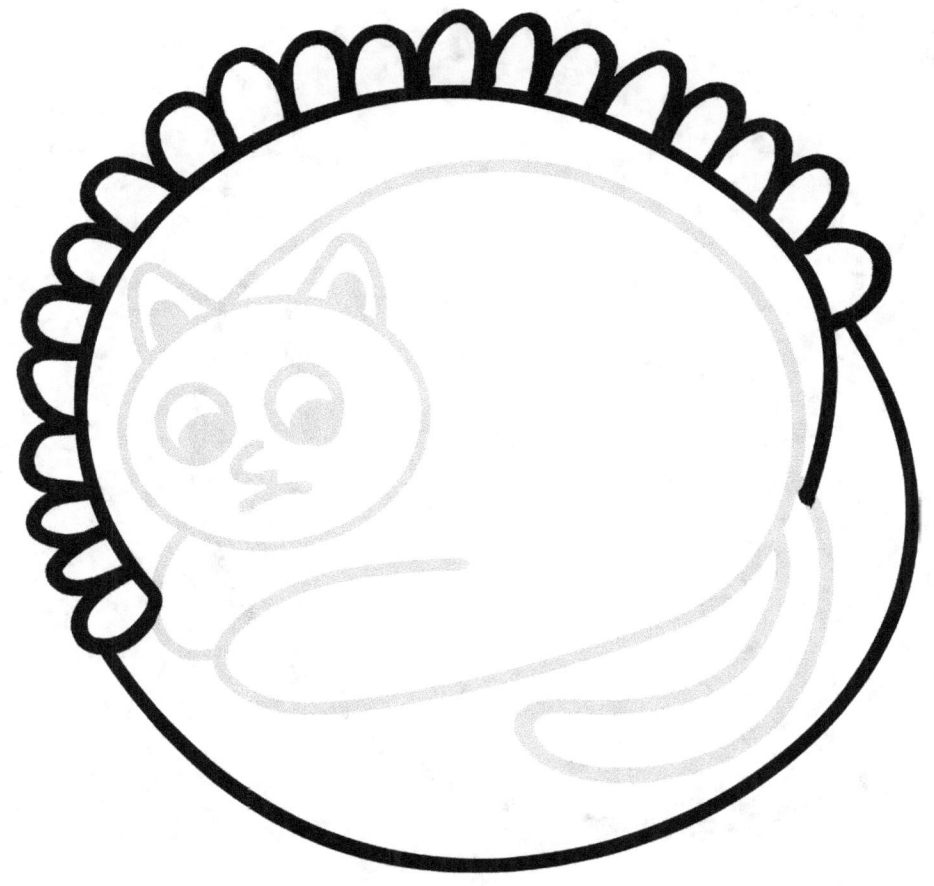

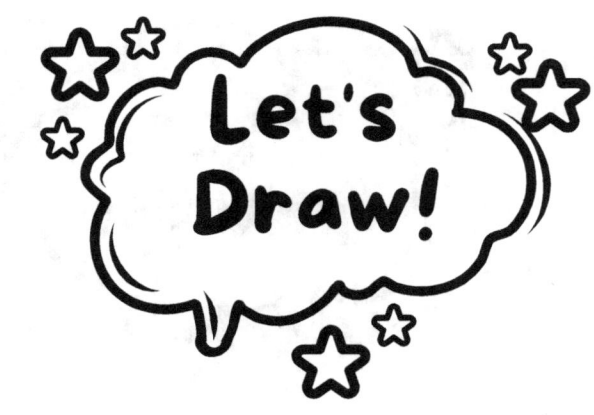

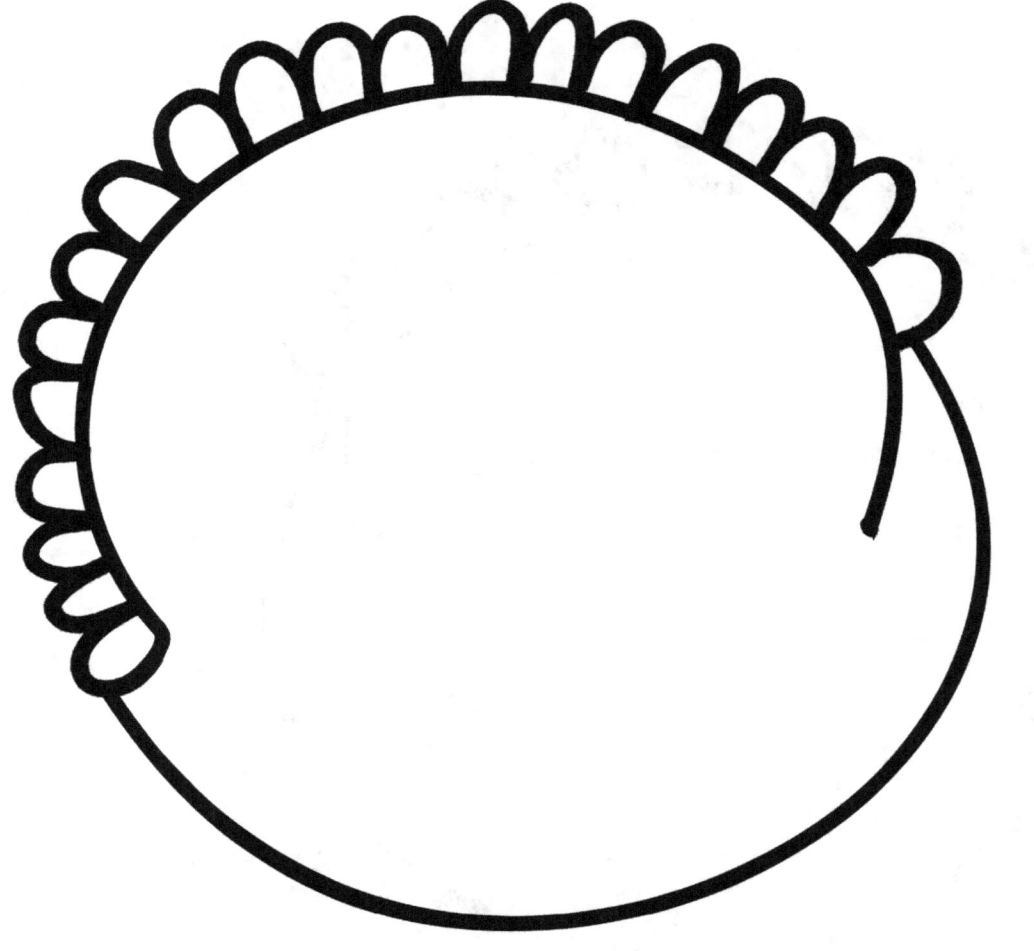

Boy

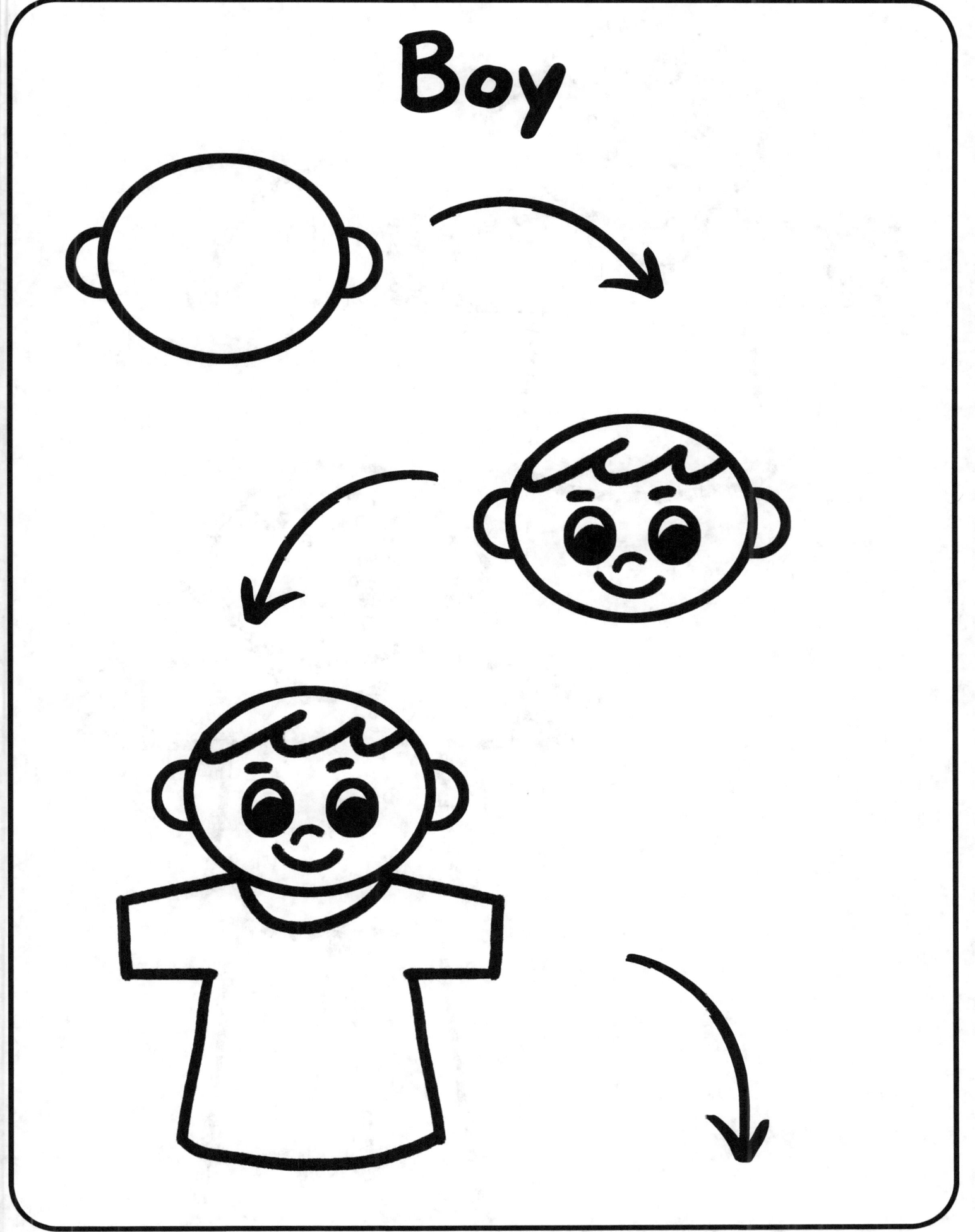

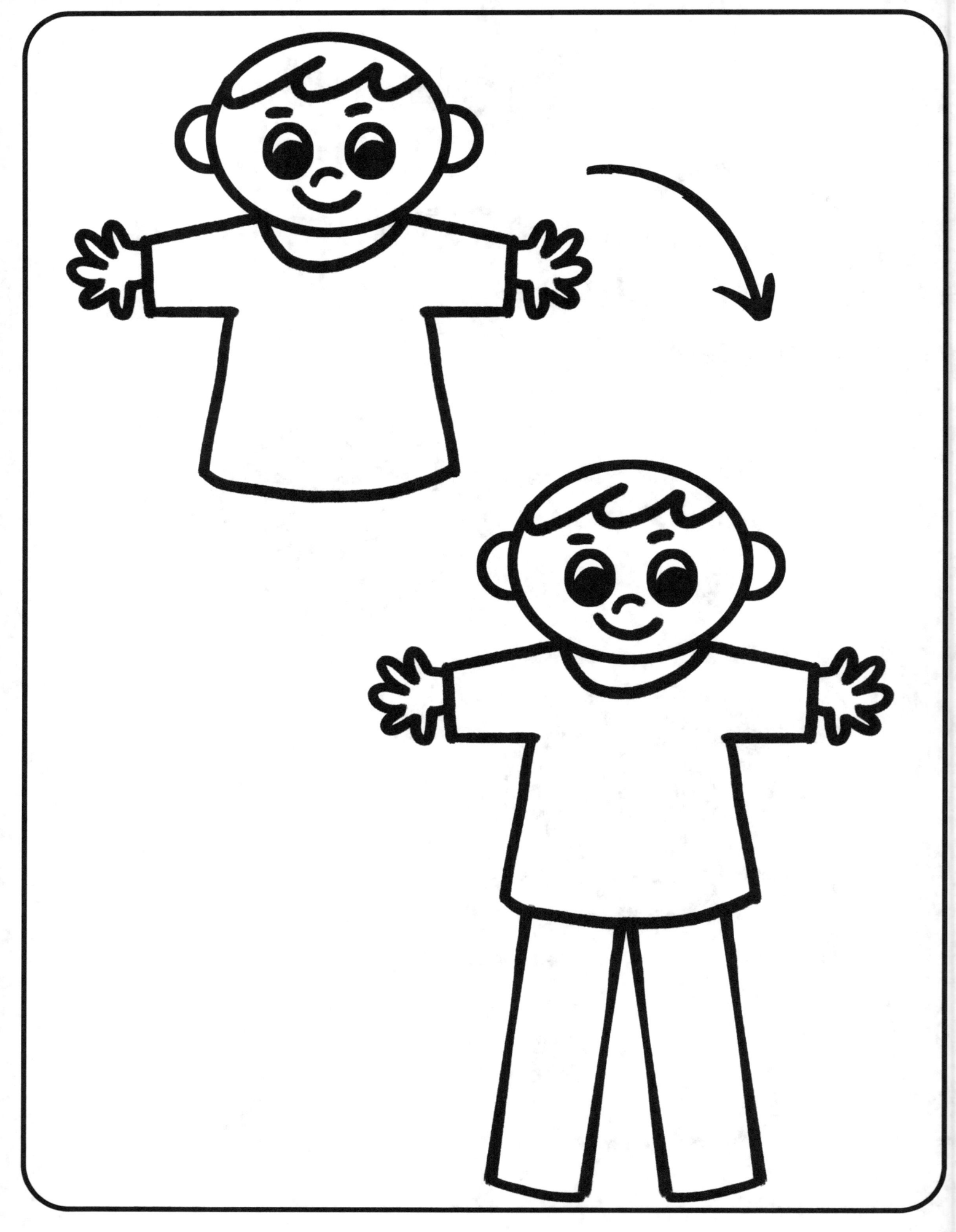

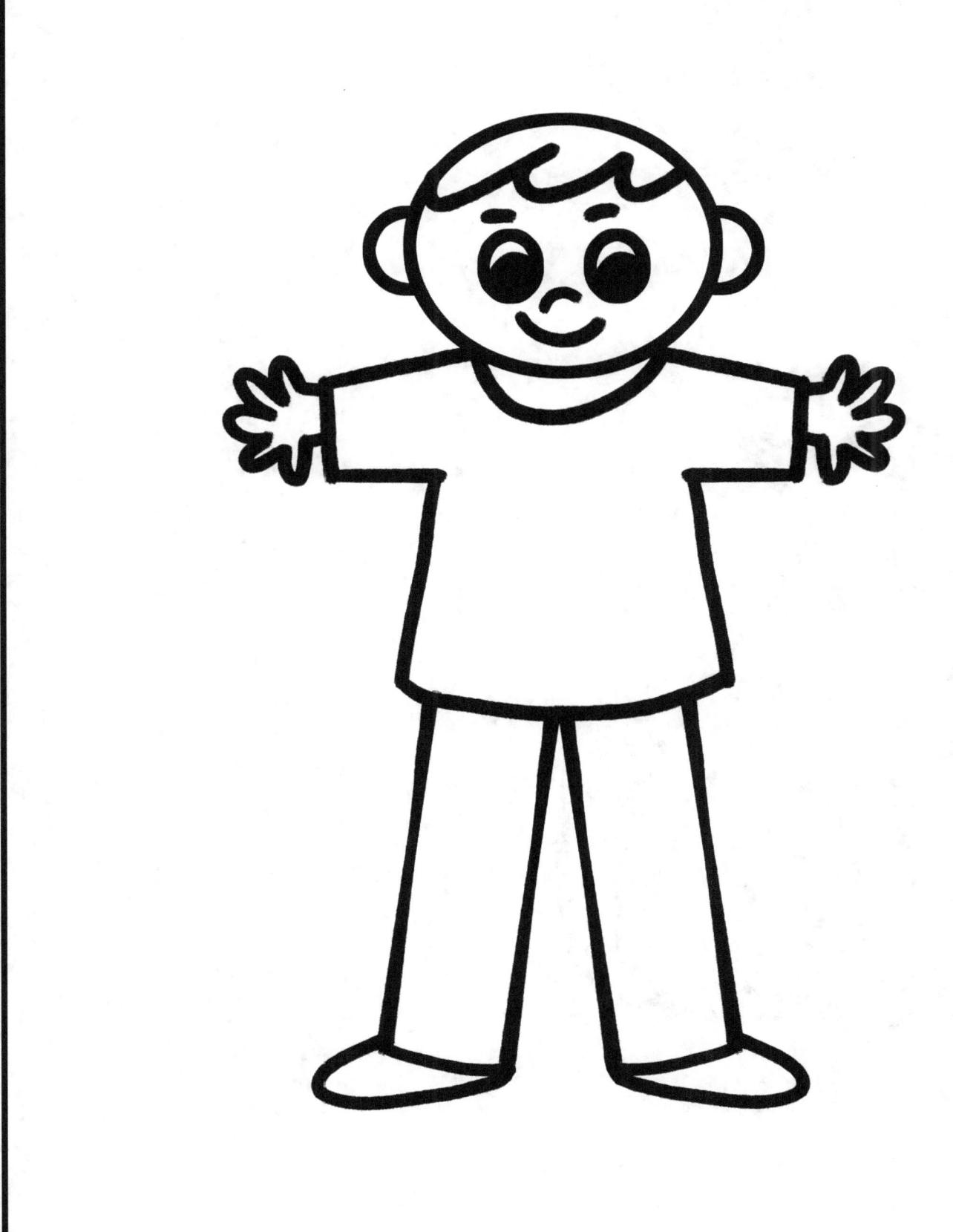

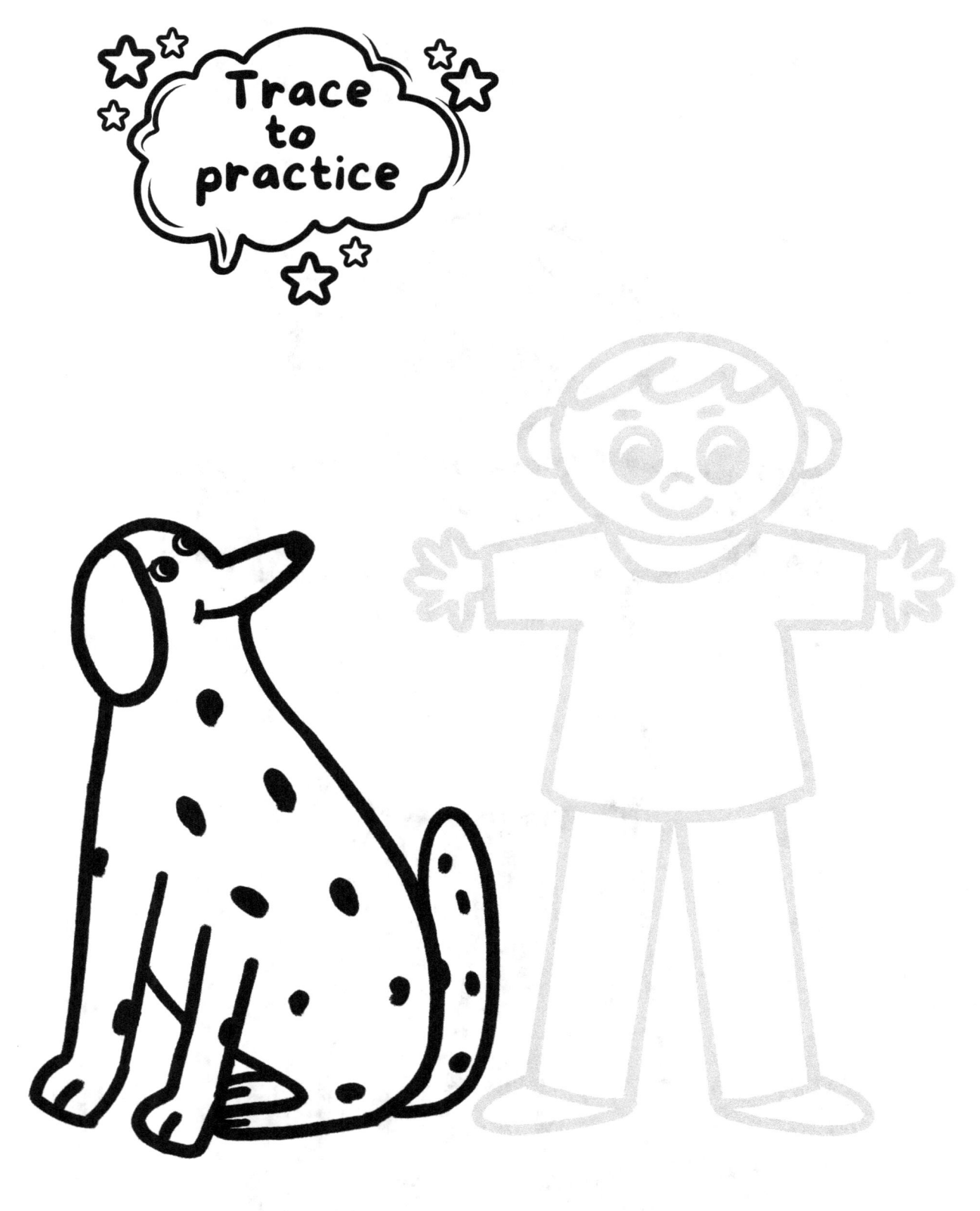

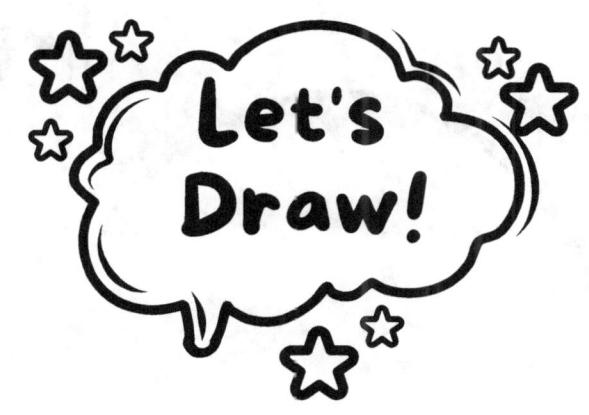

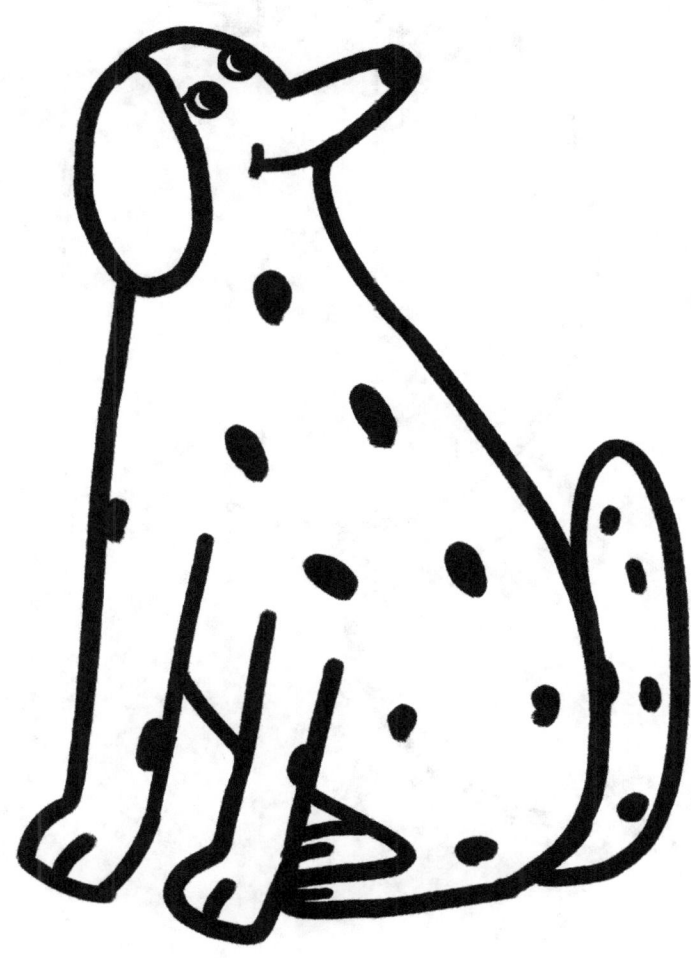

Frog

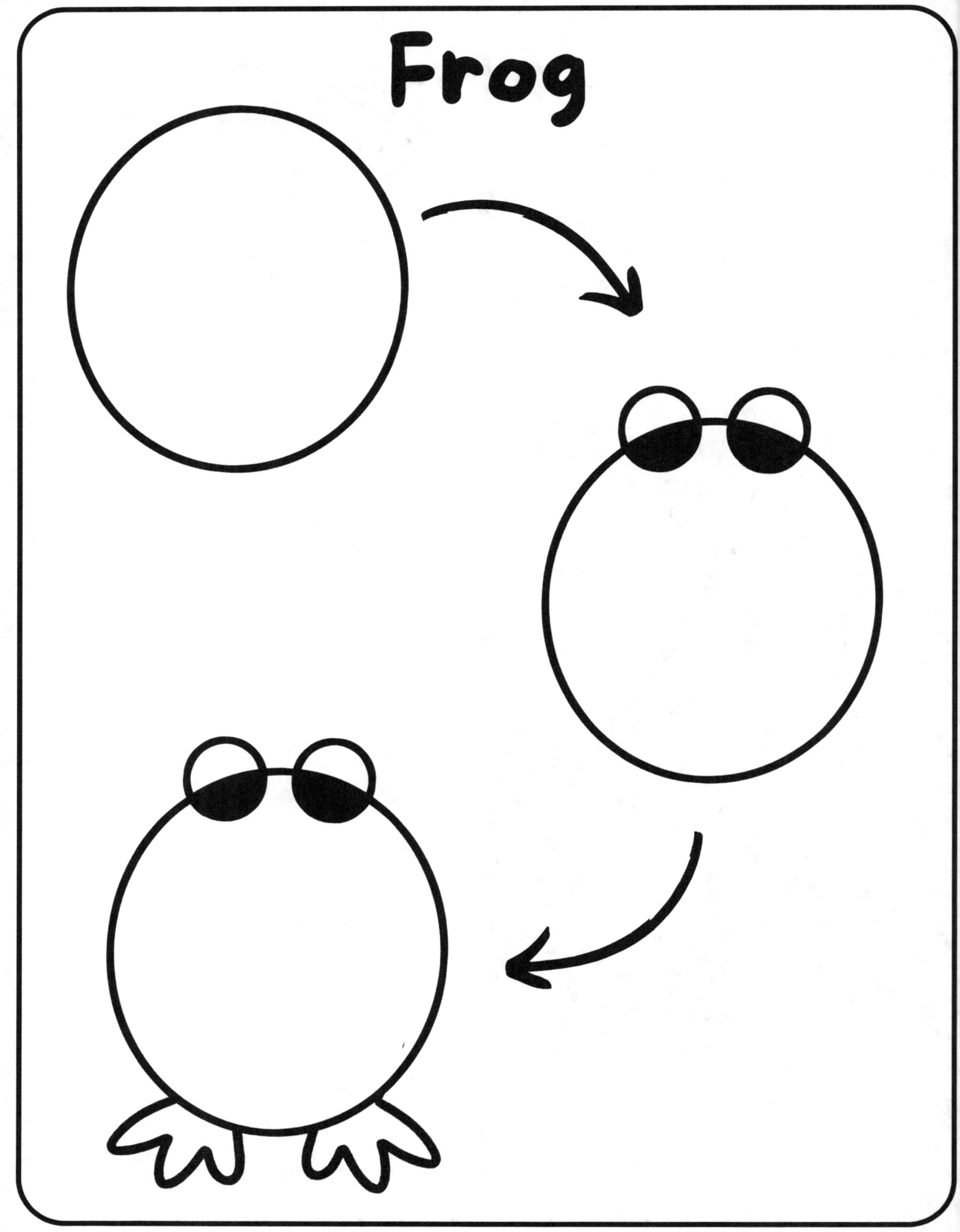

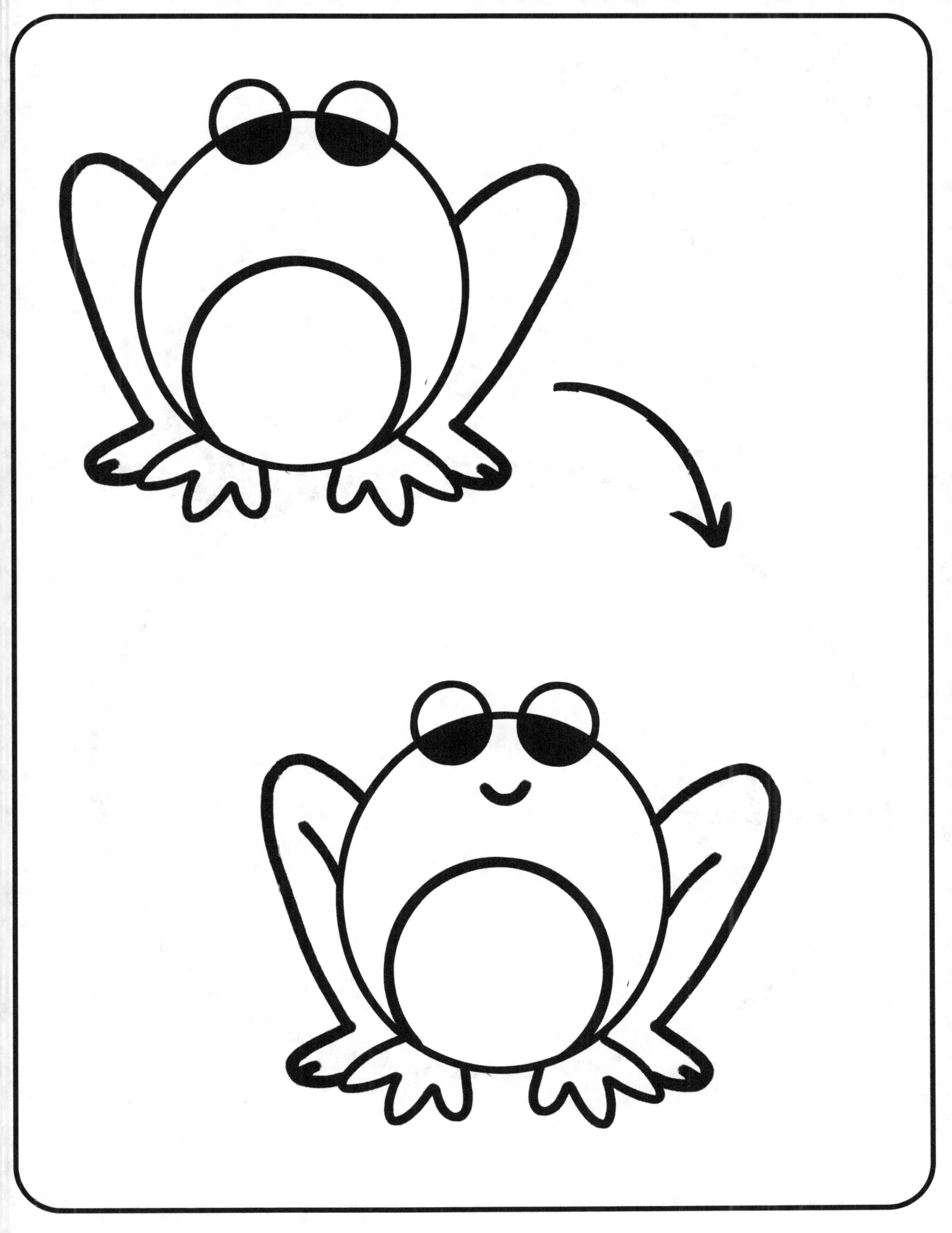

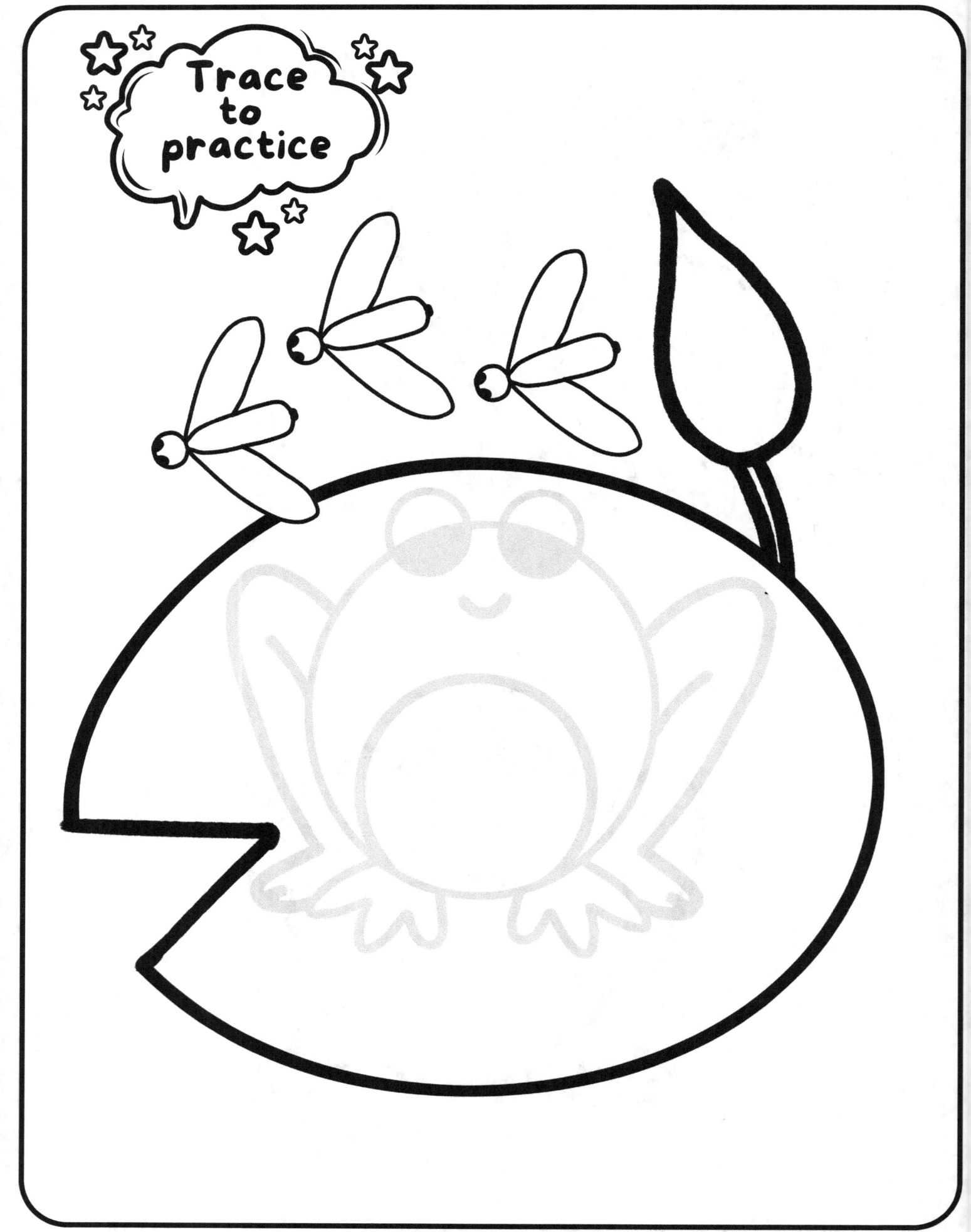

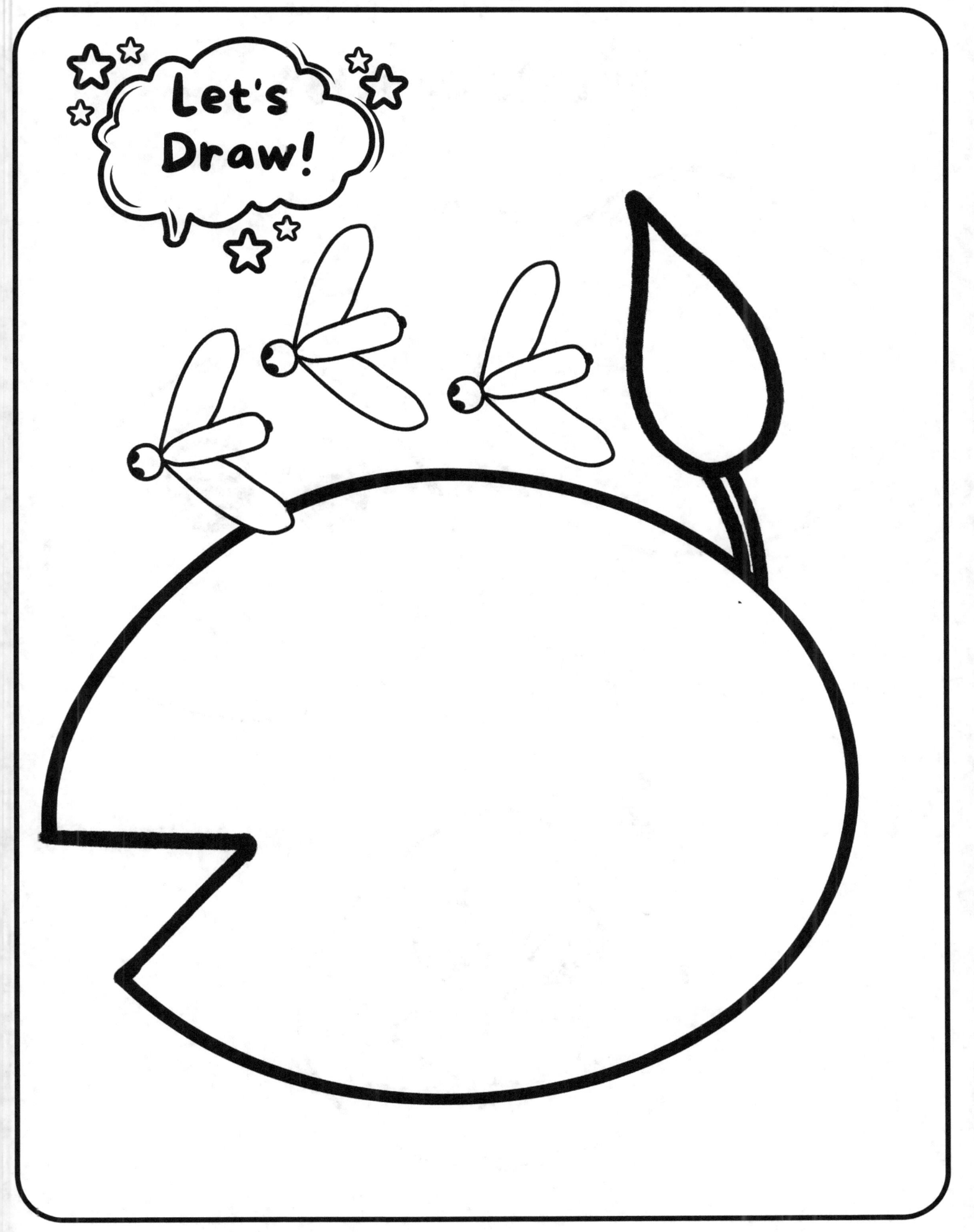

Pumpkin

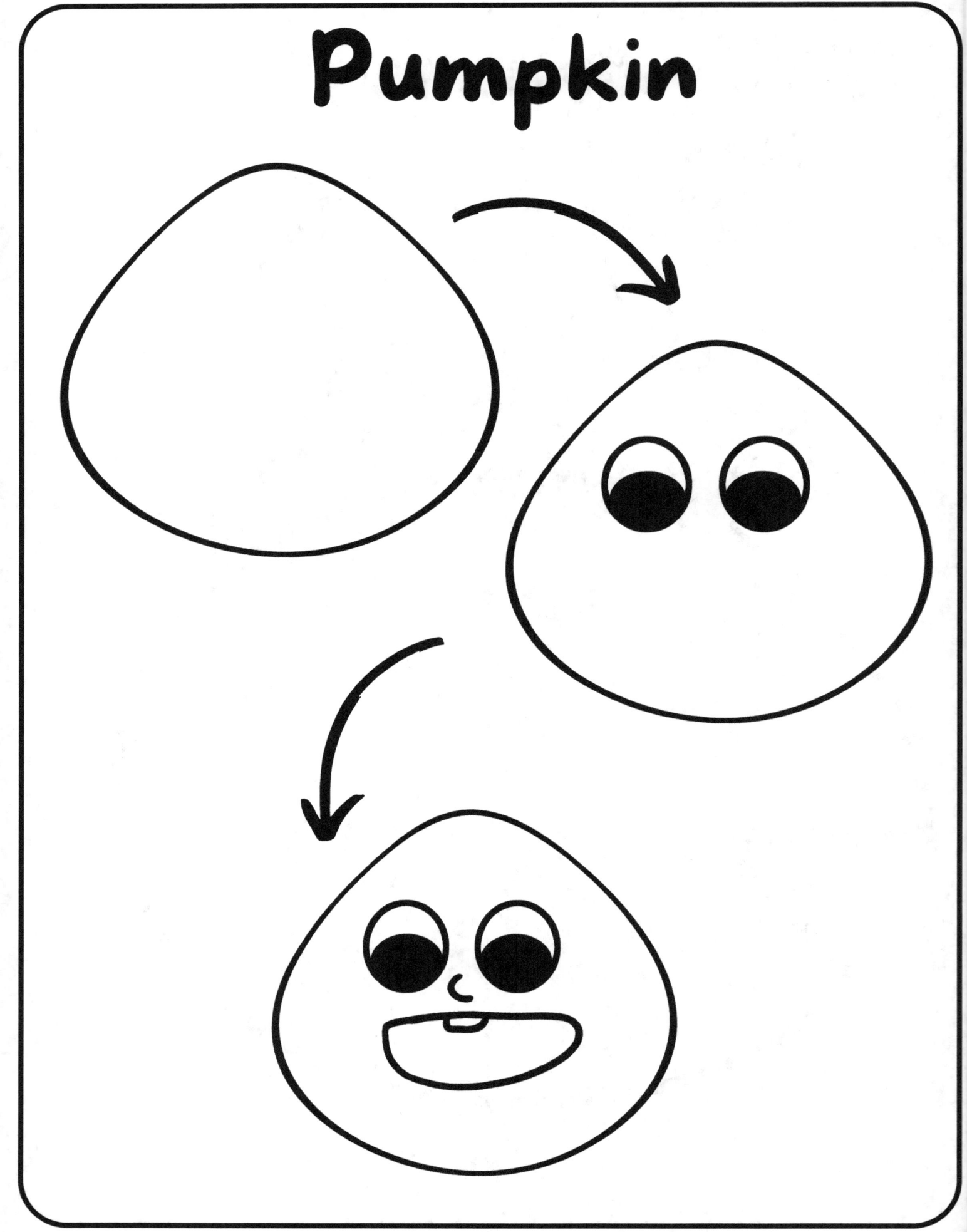

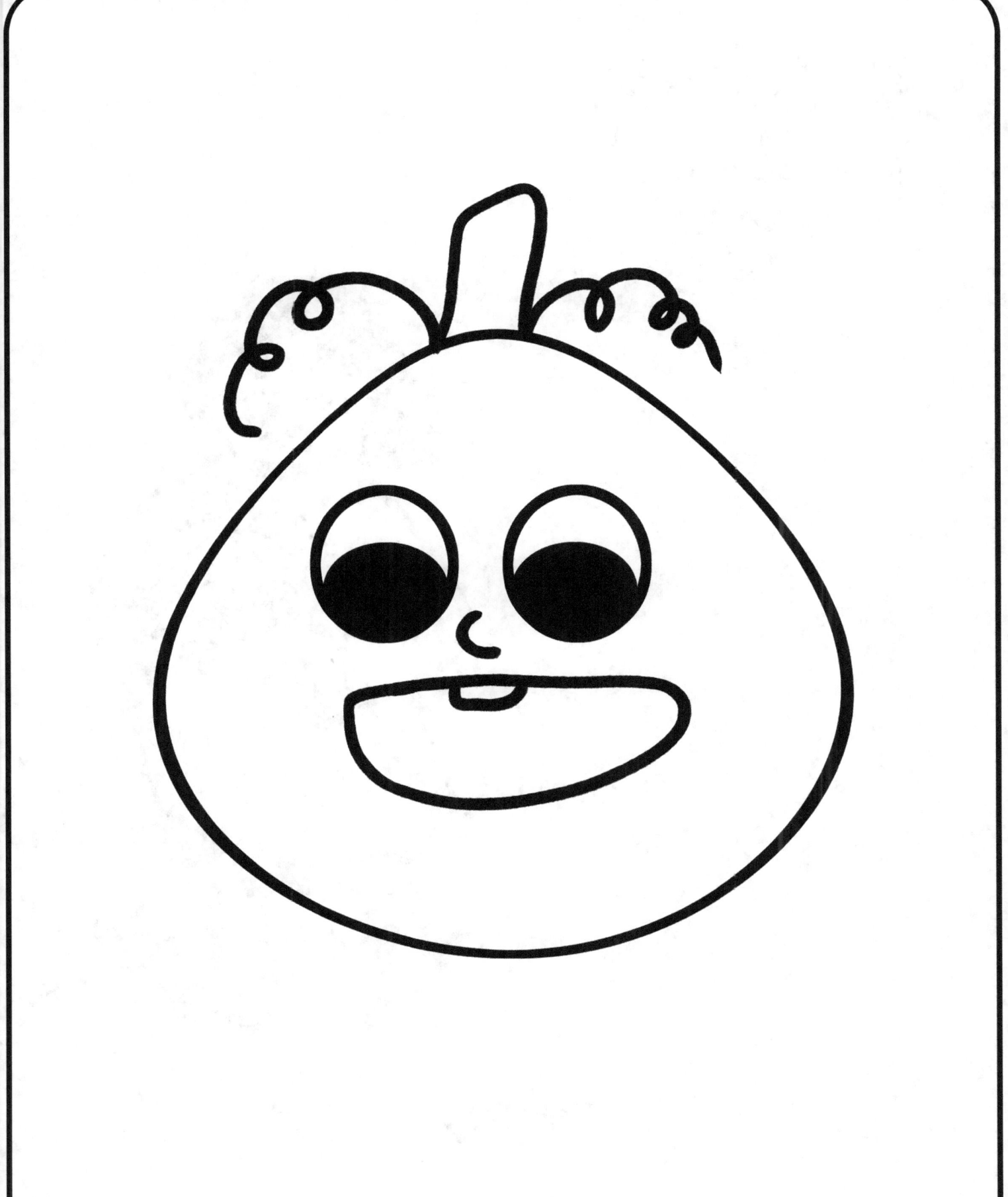

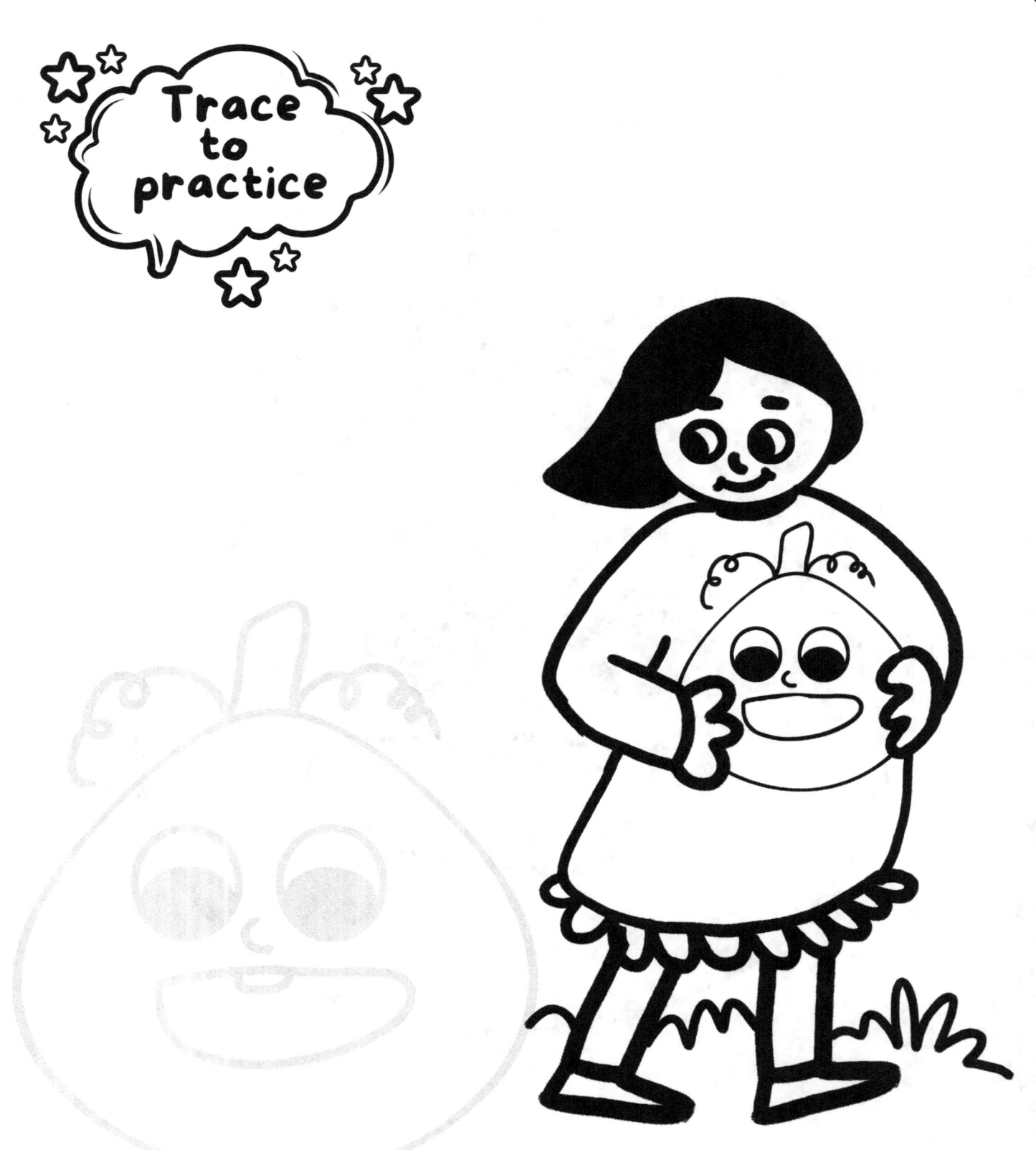

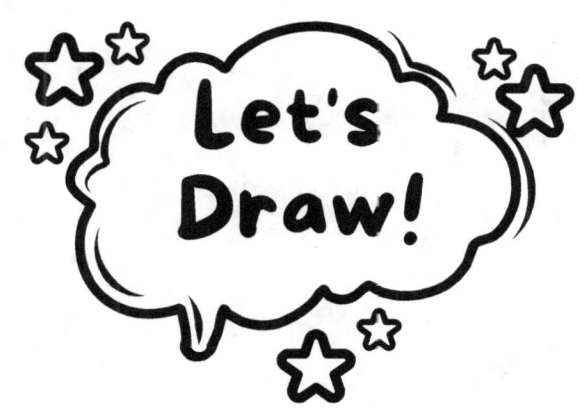

Let's Draw!

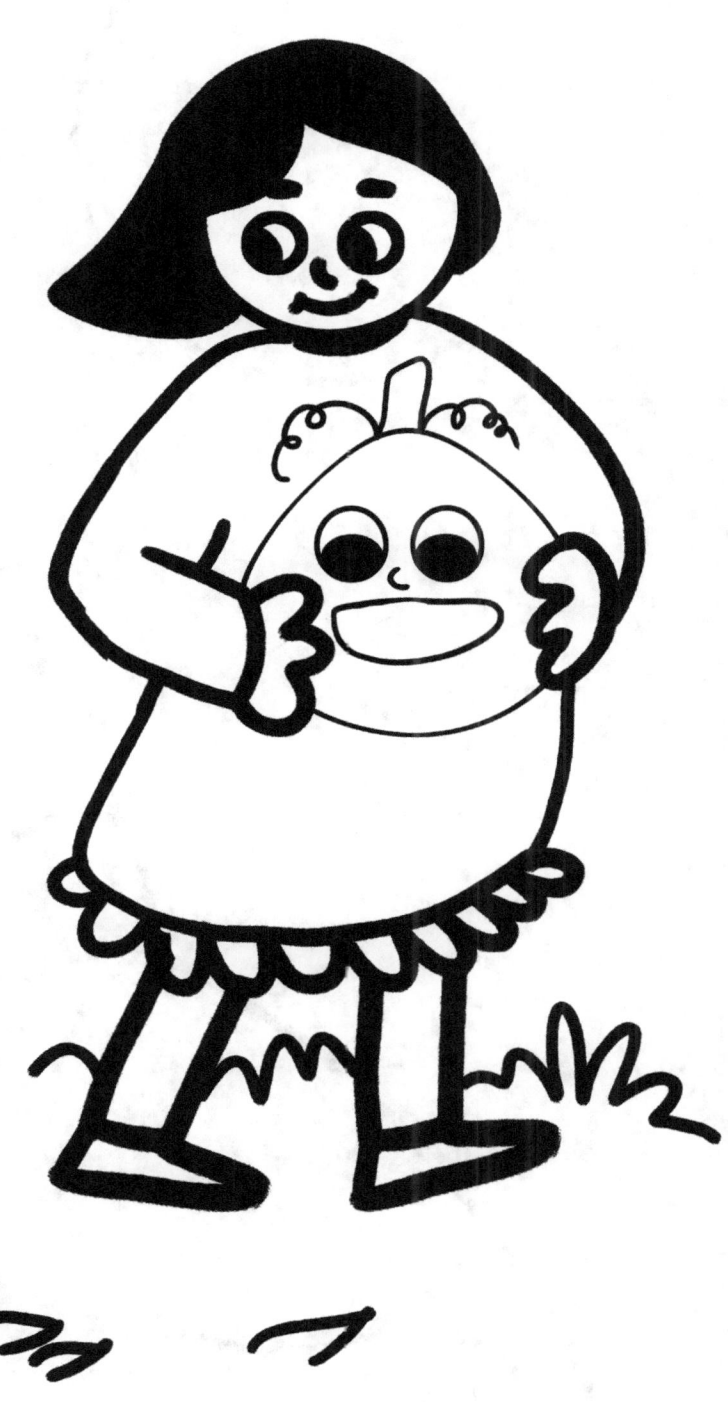

Bird

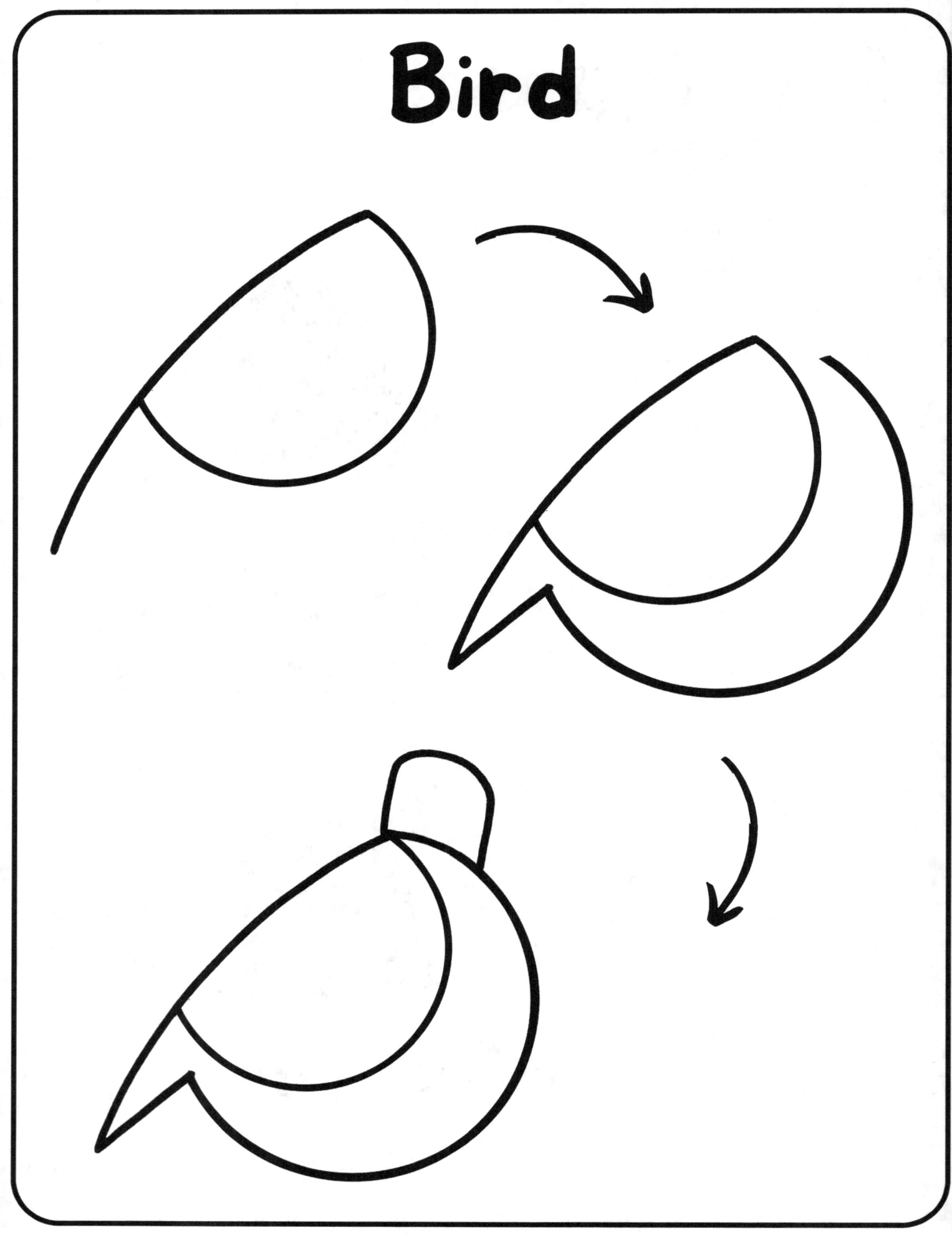

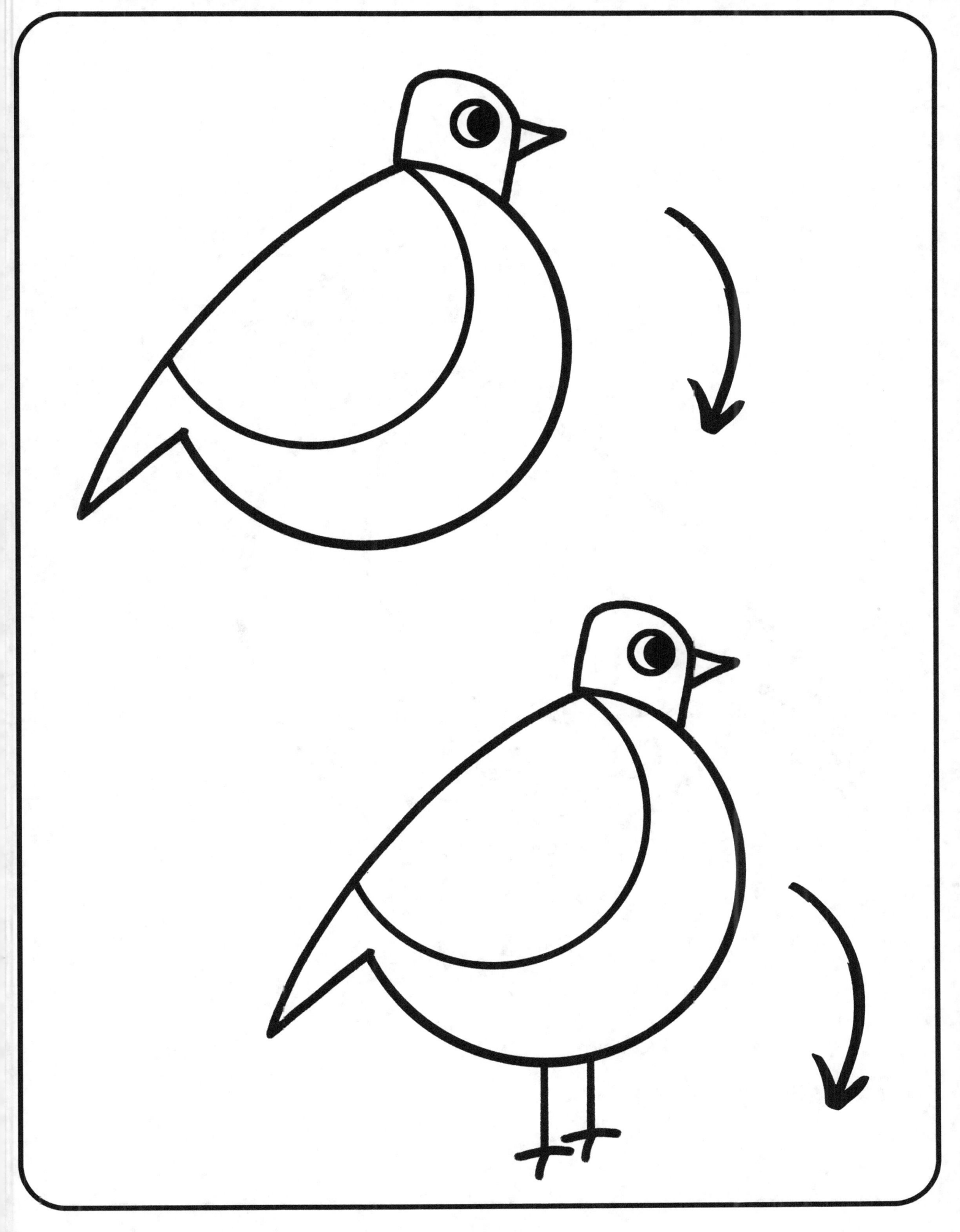

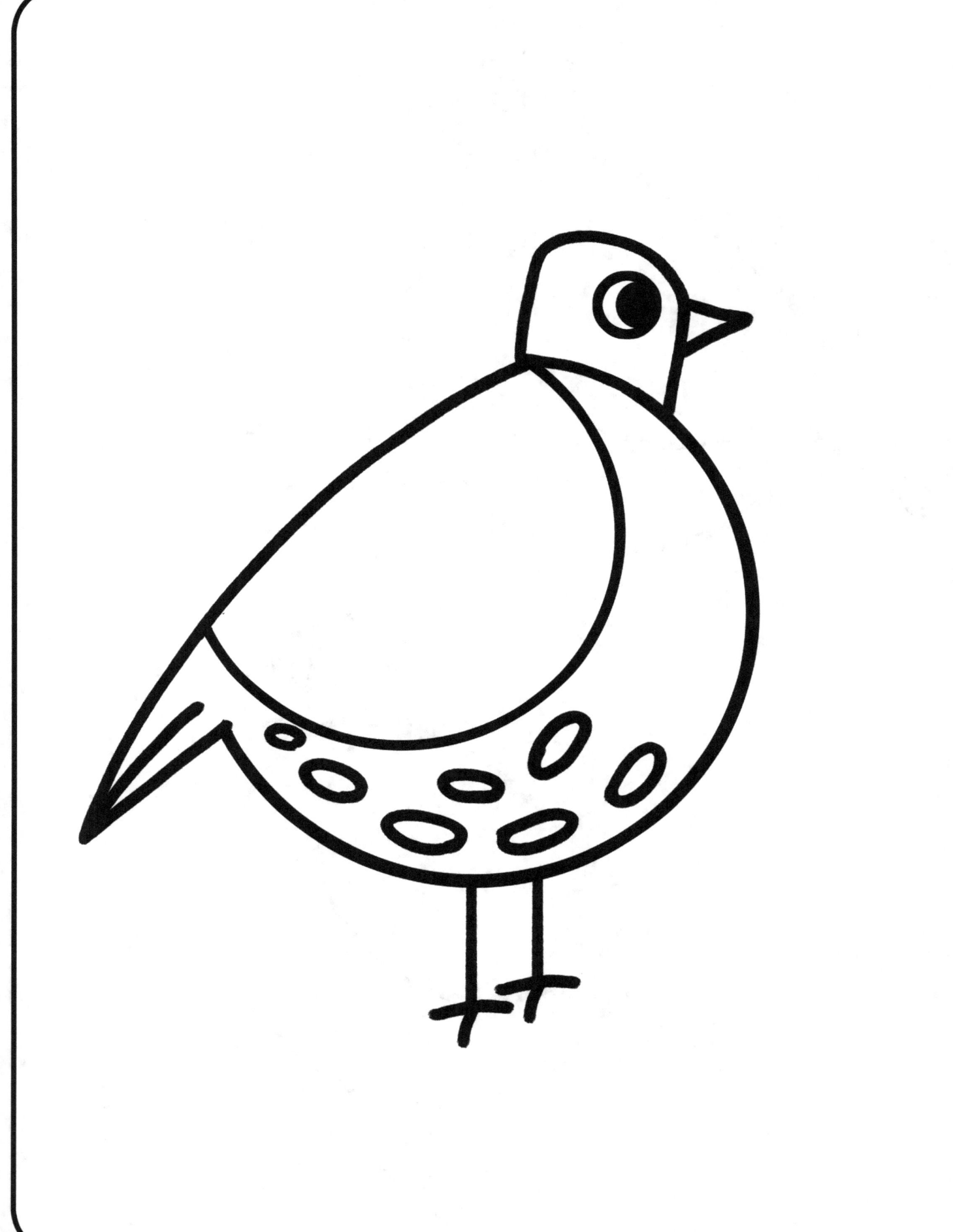

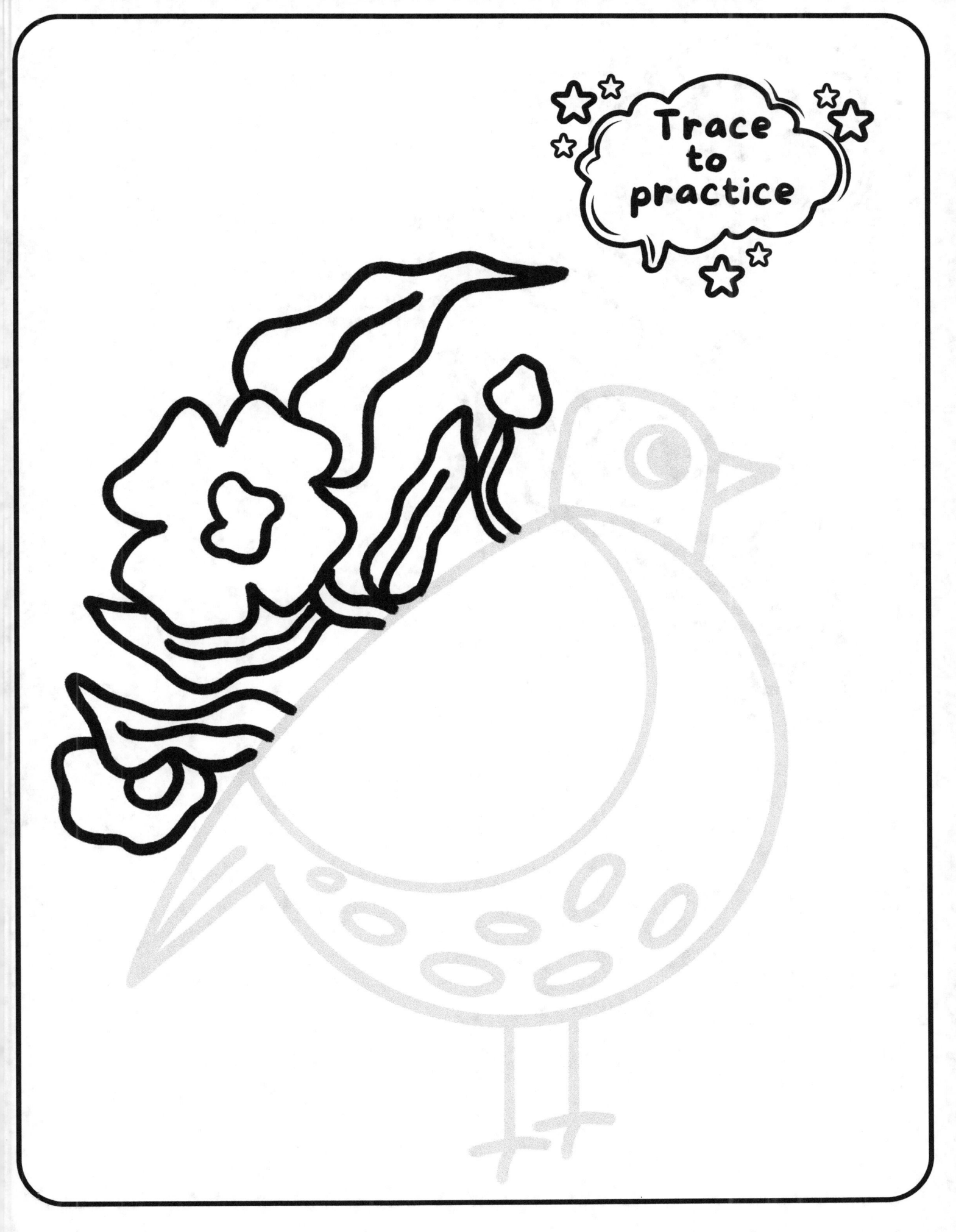

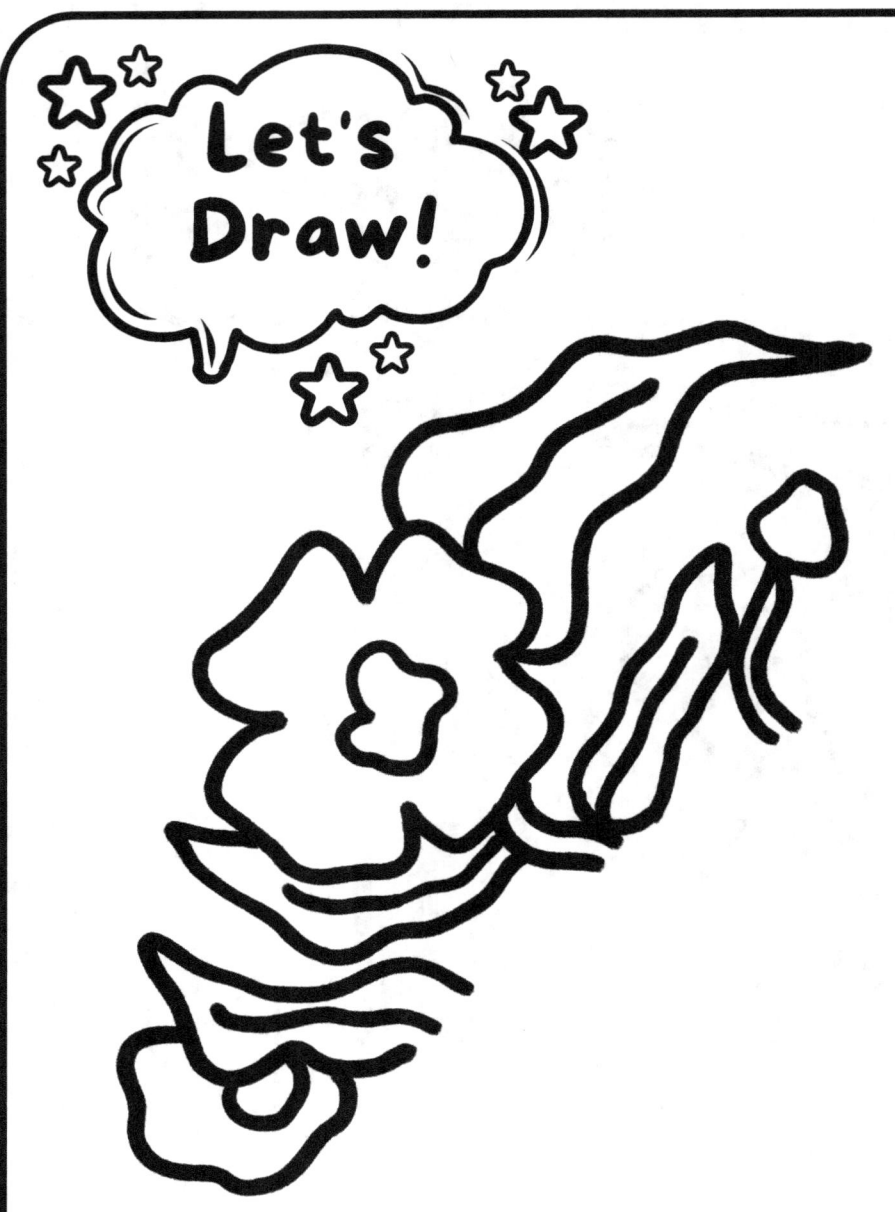

Astronaut

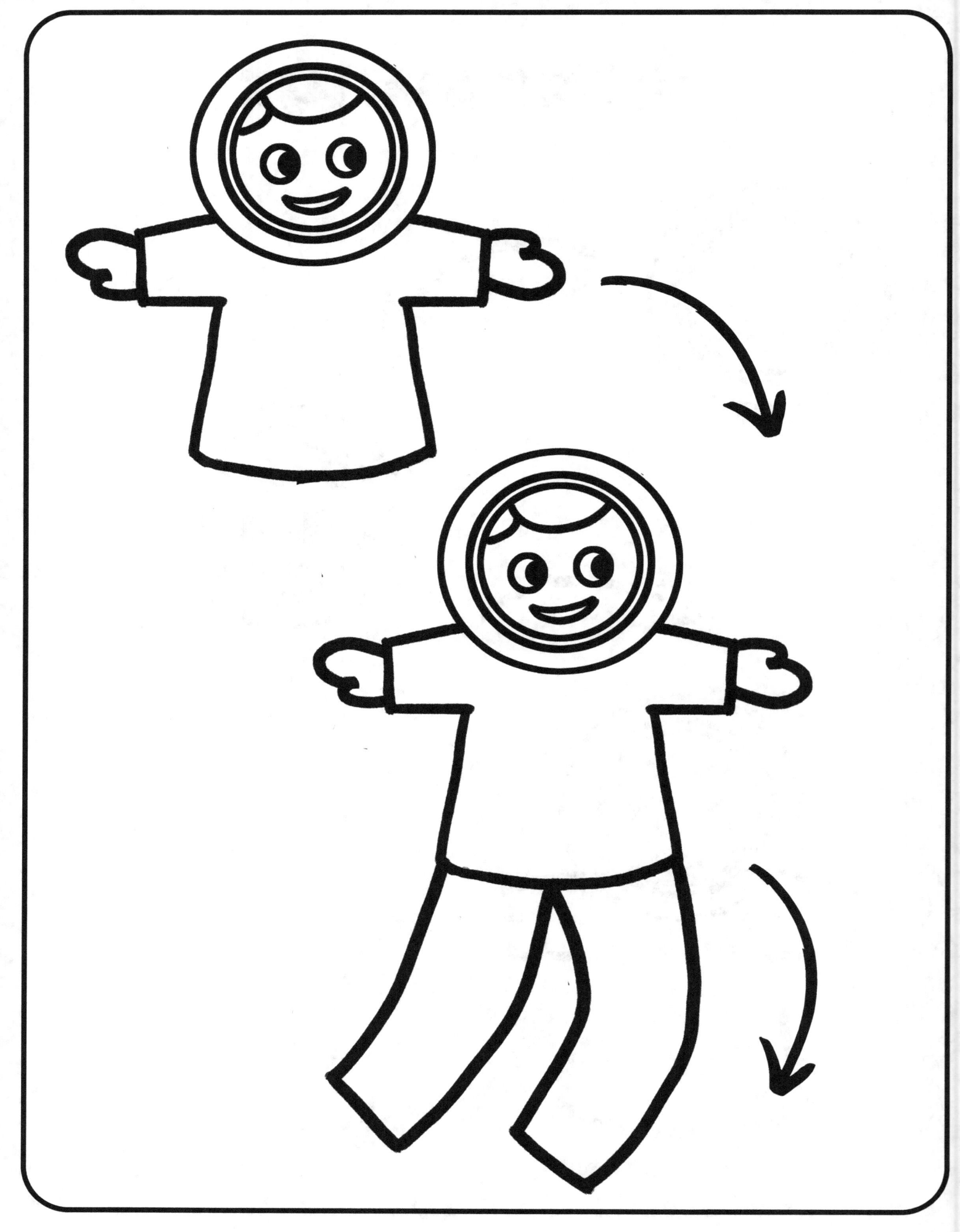

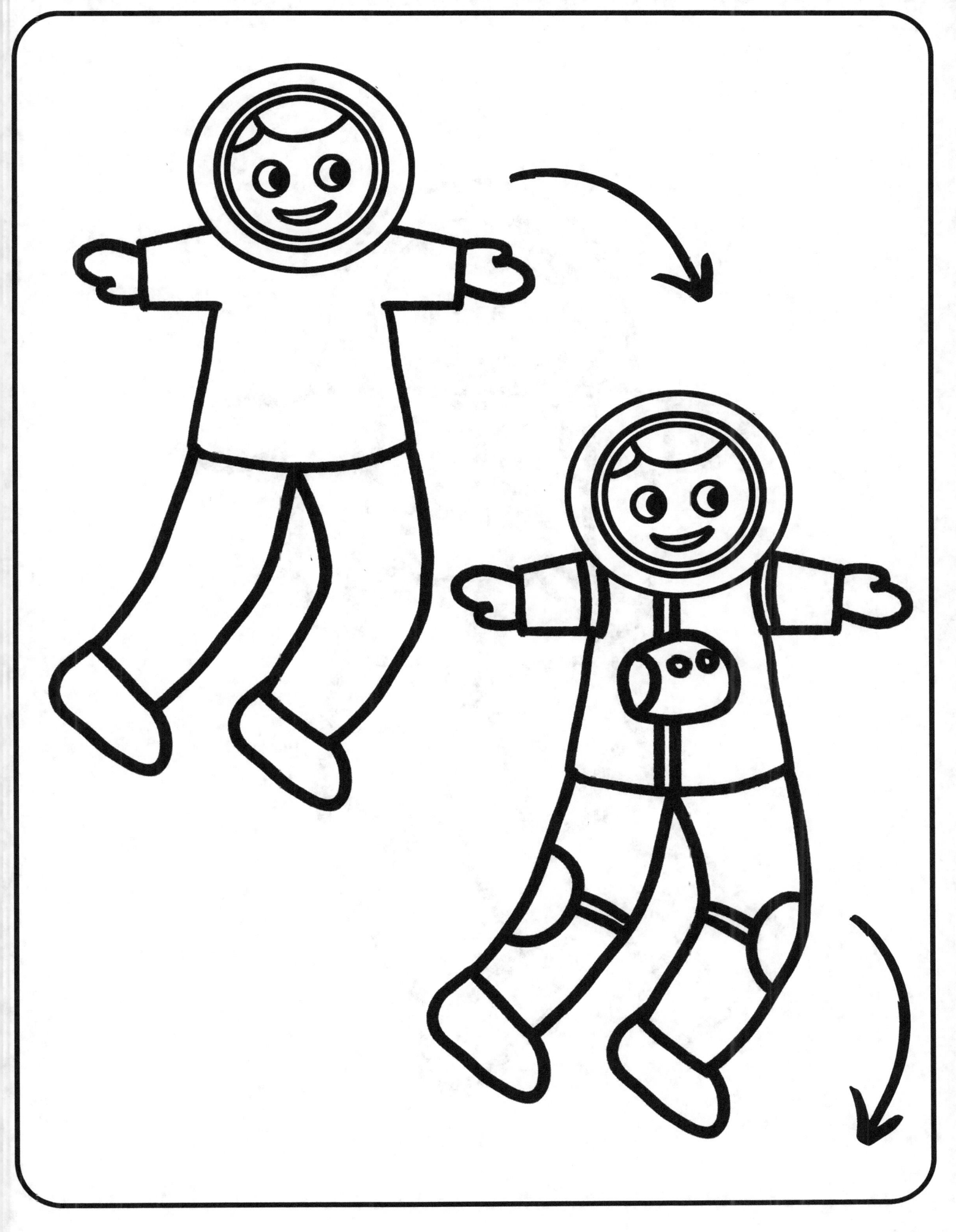

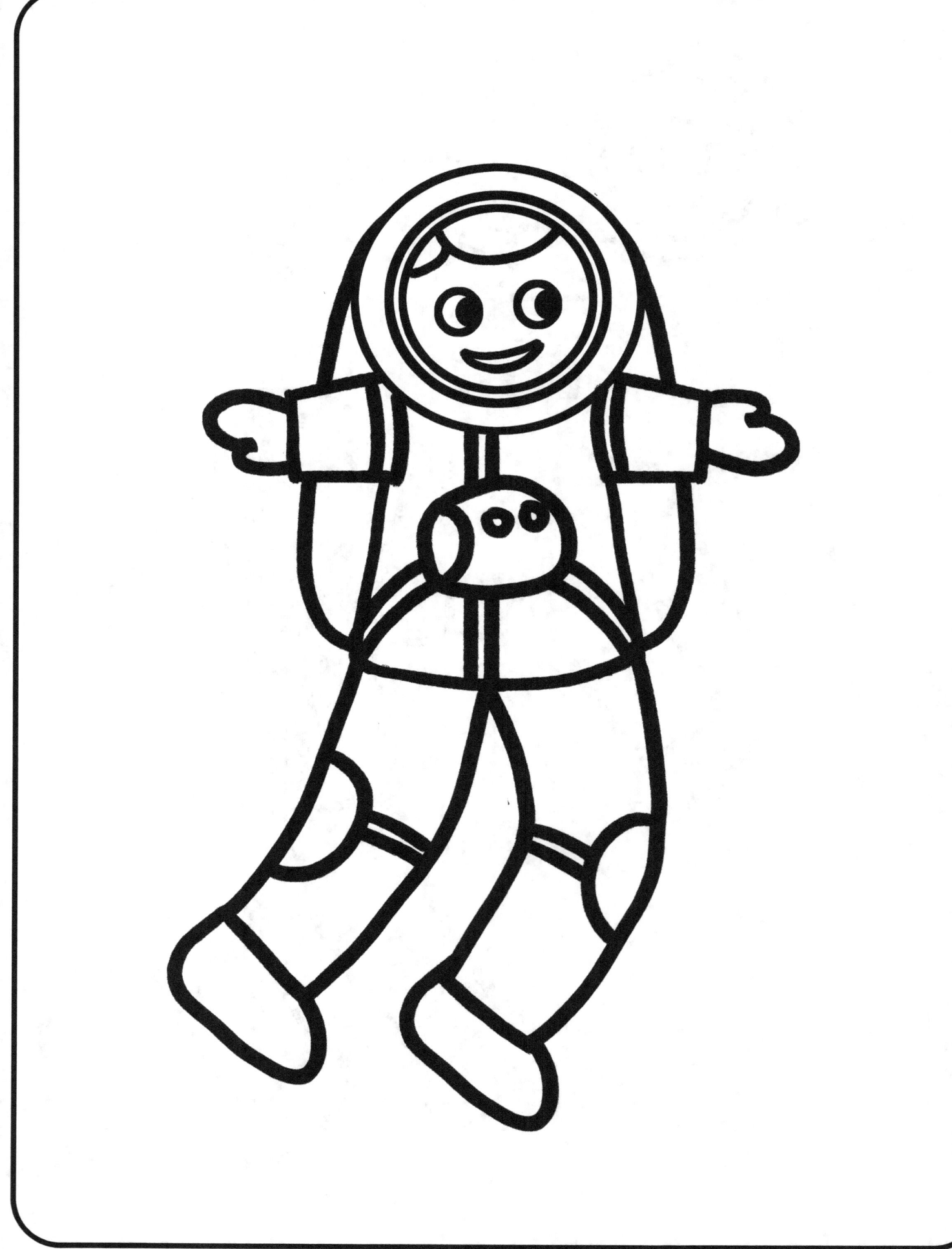

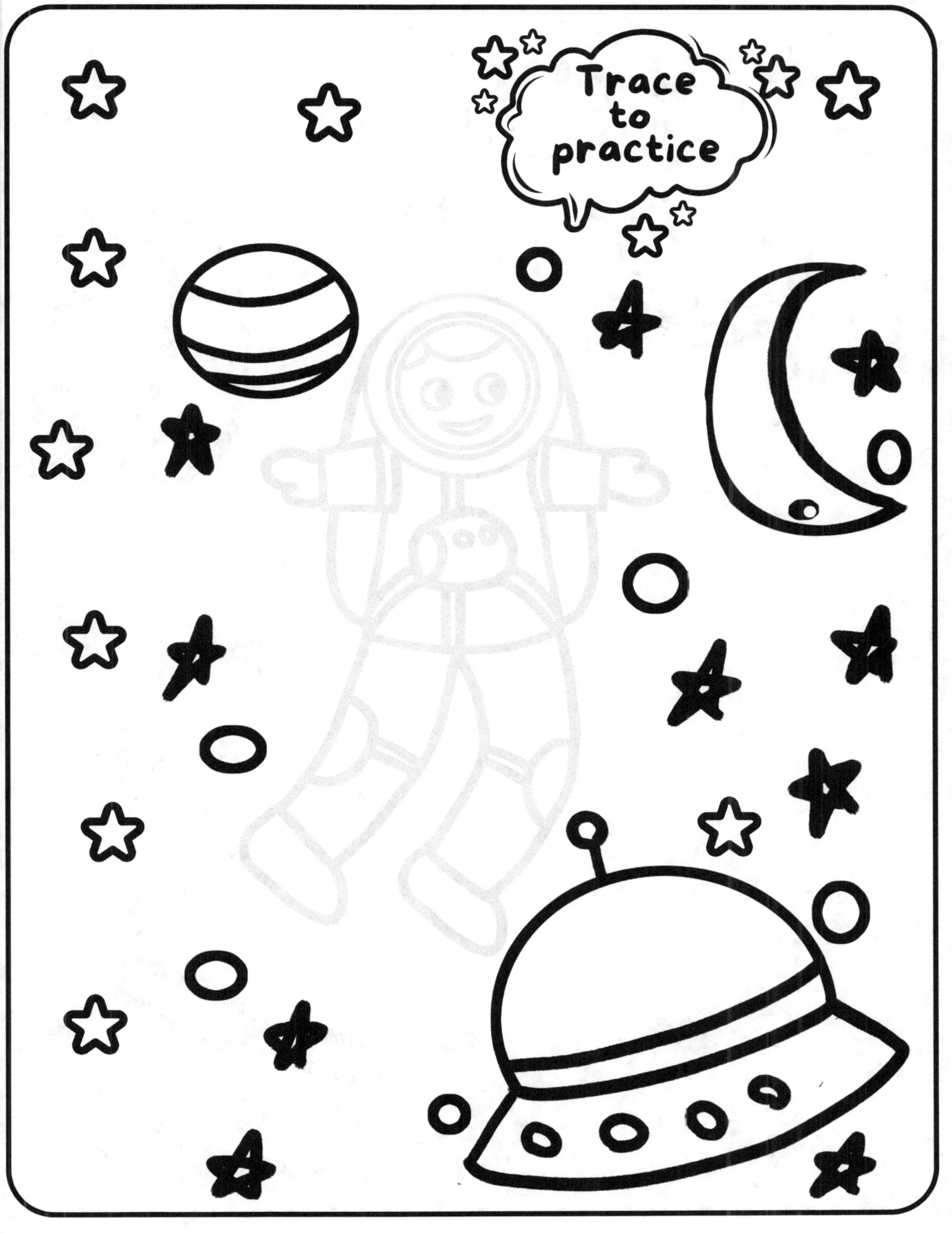

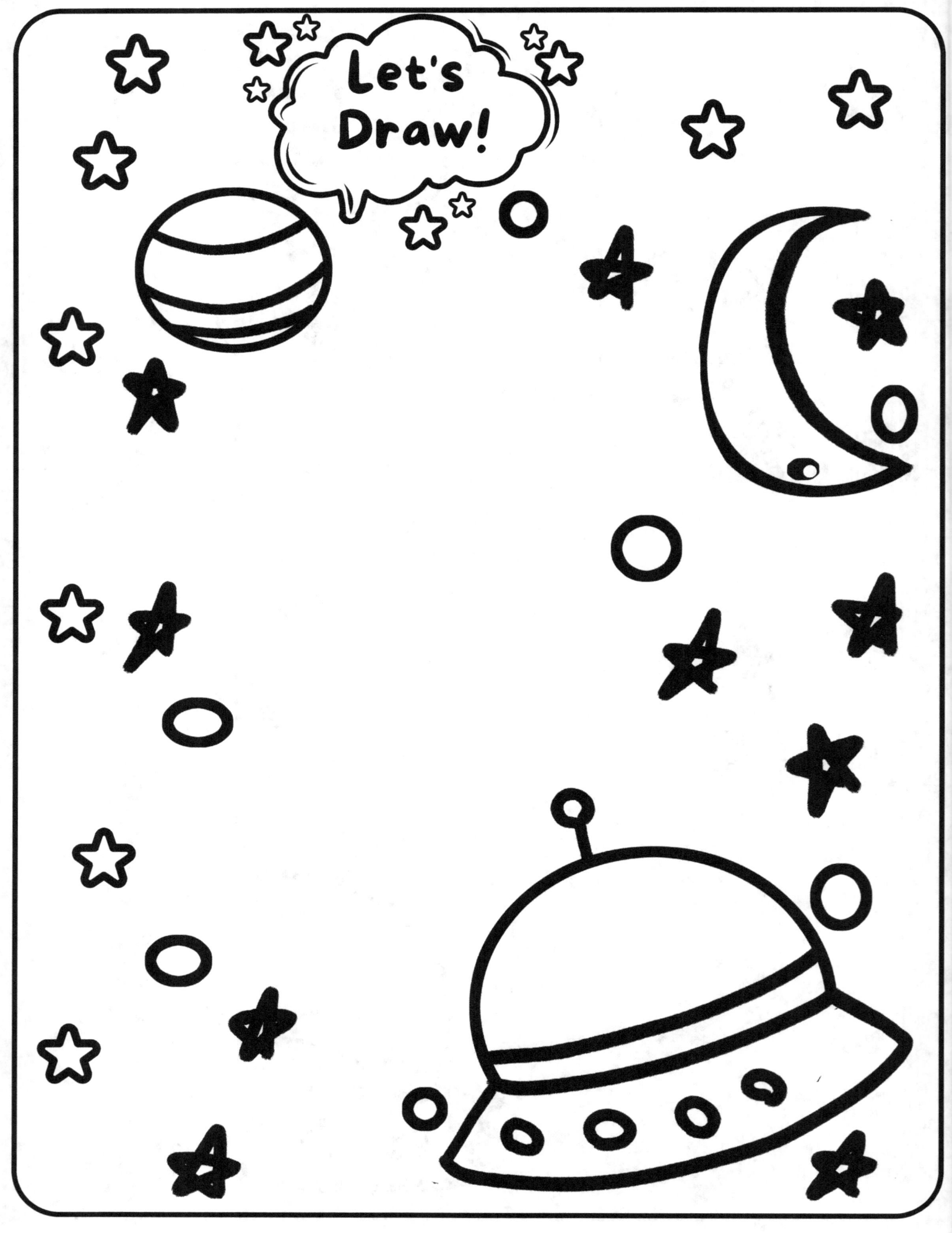

Flower Vase

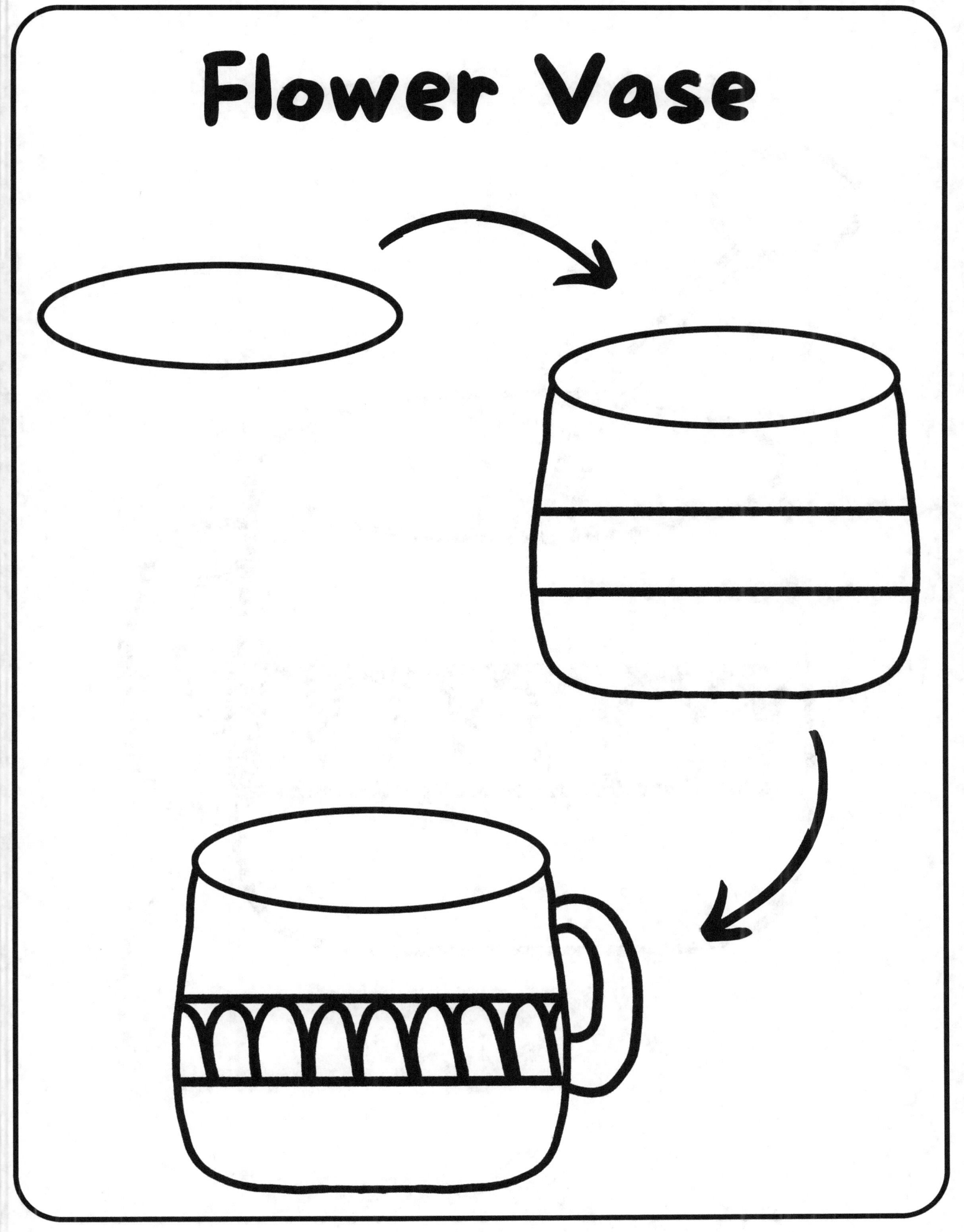

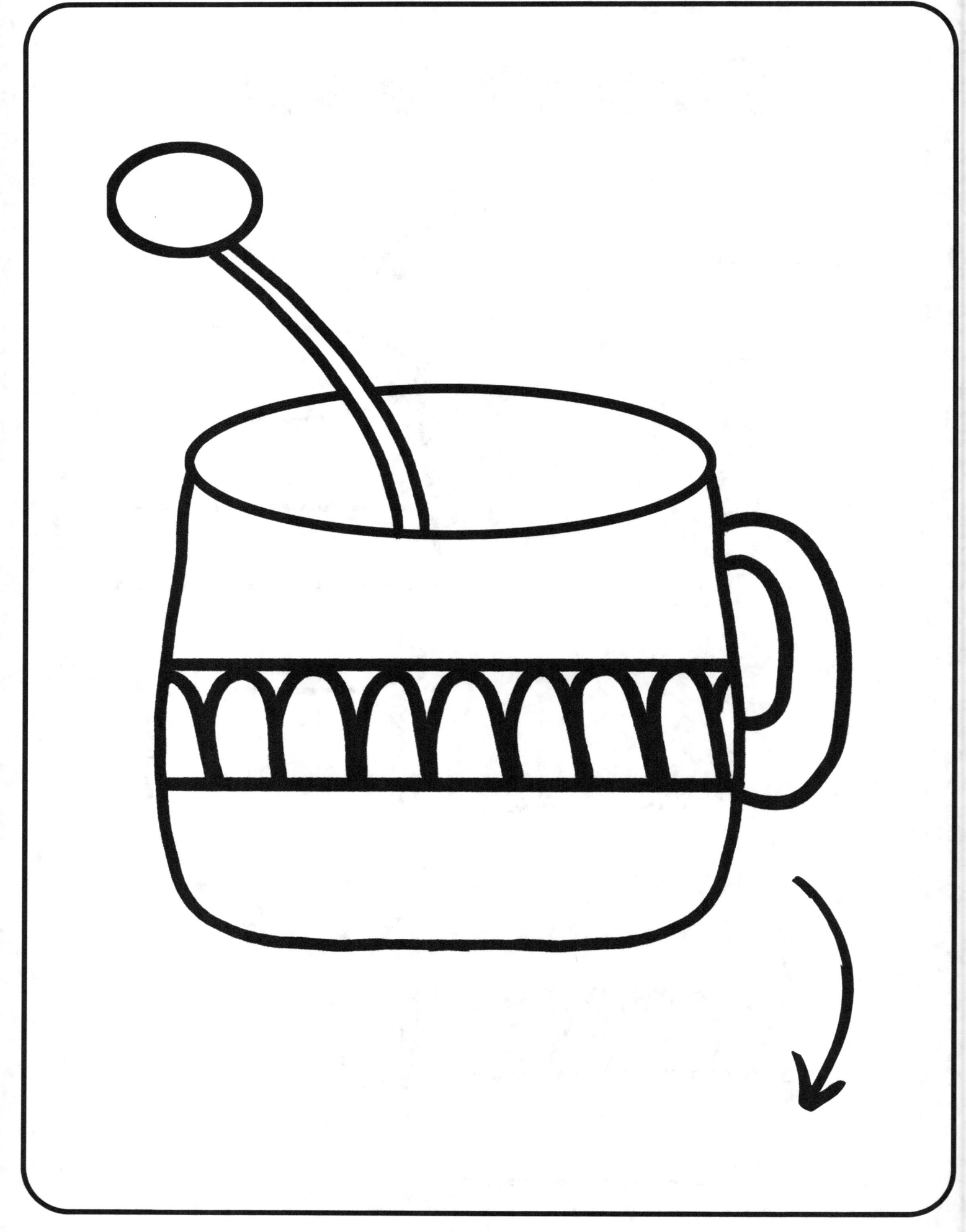

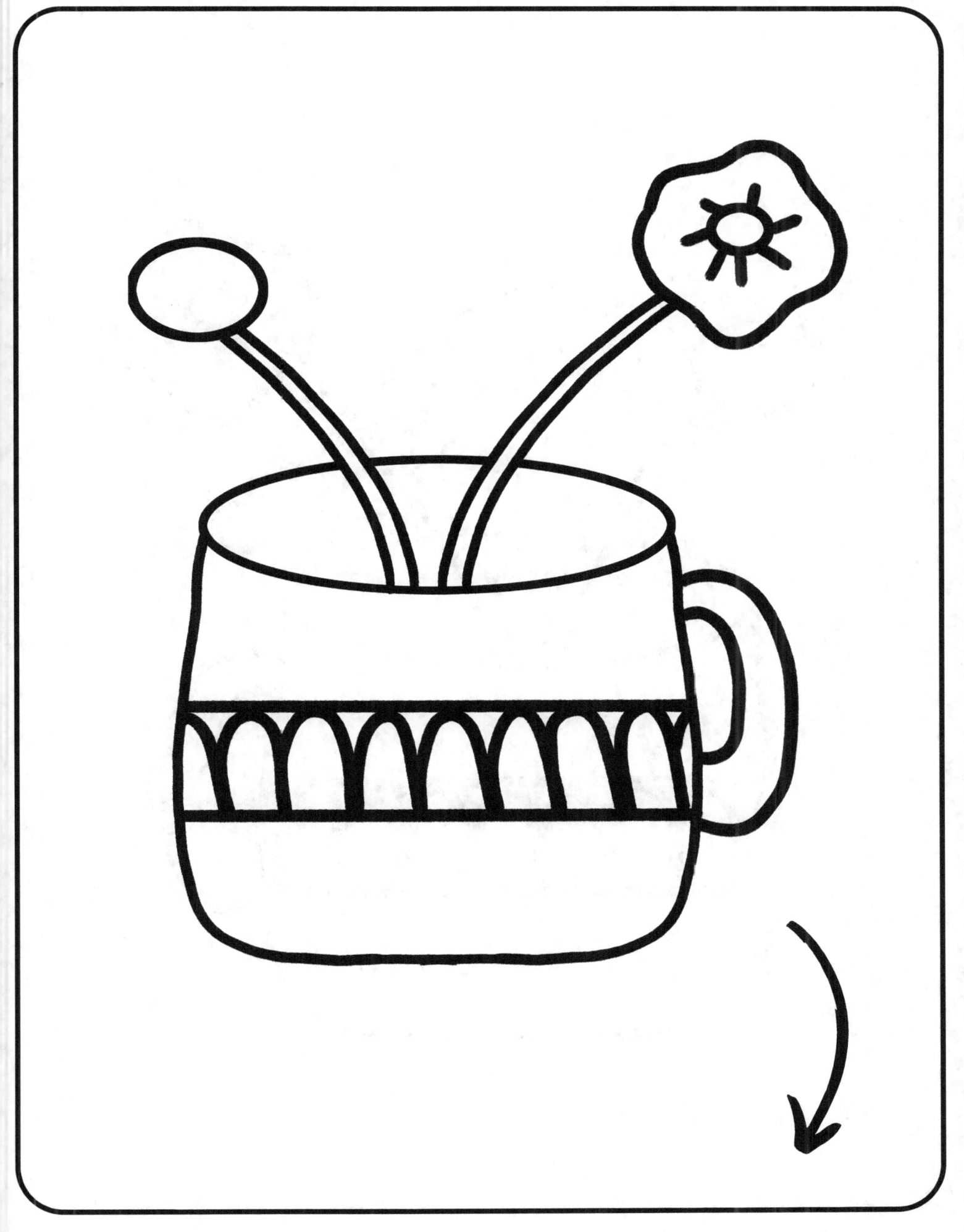

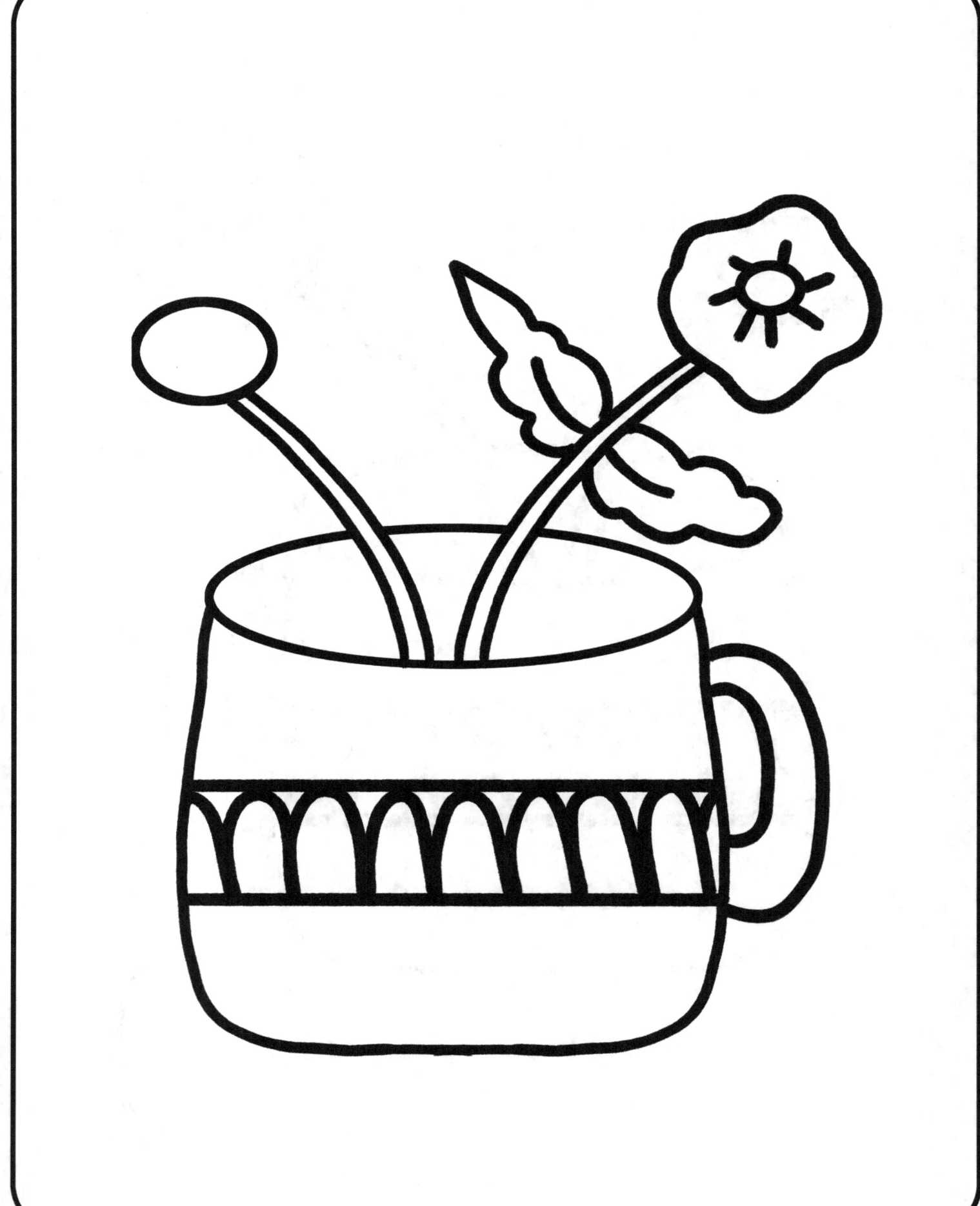

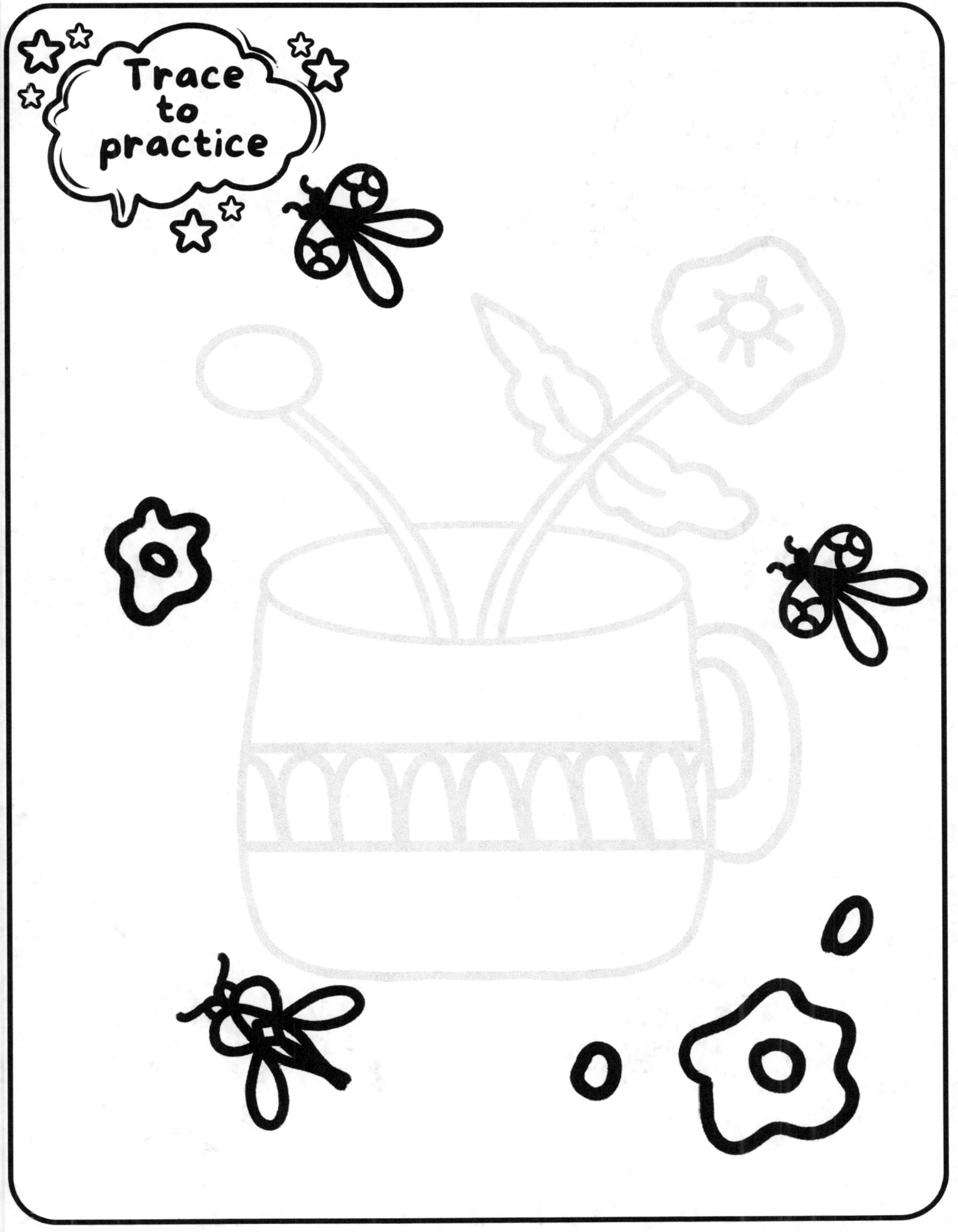

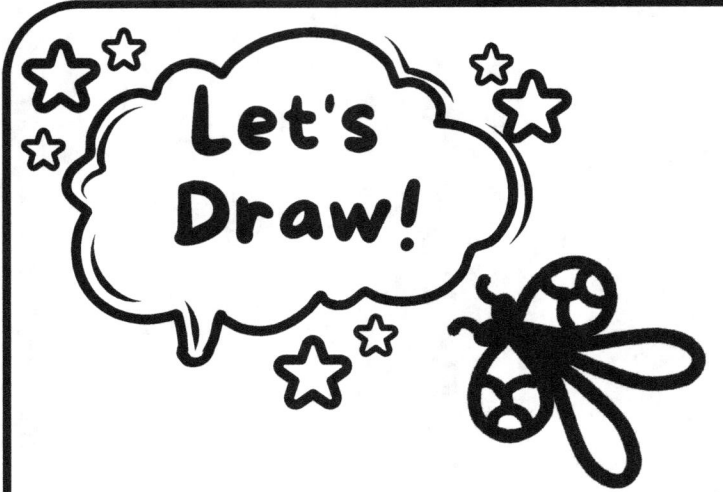

Let's Draw!

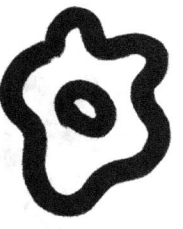
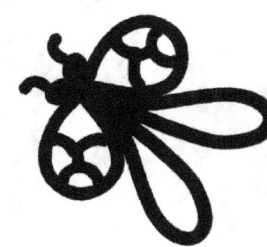
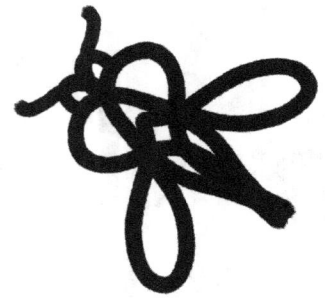
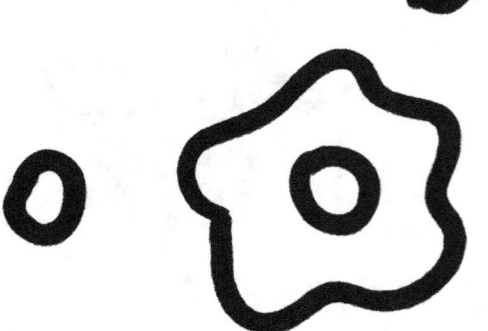

Fairy

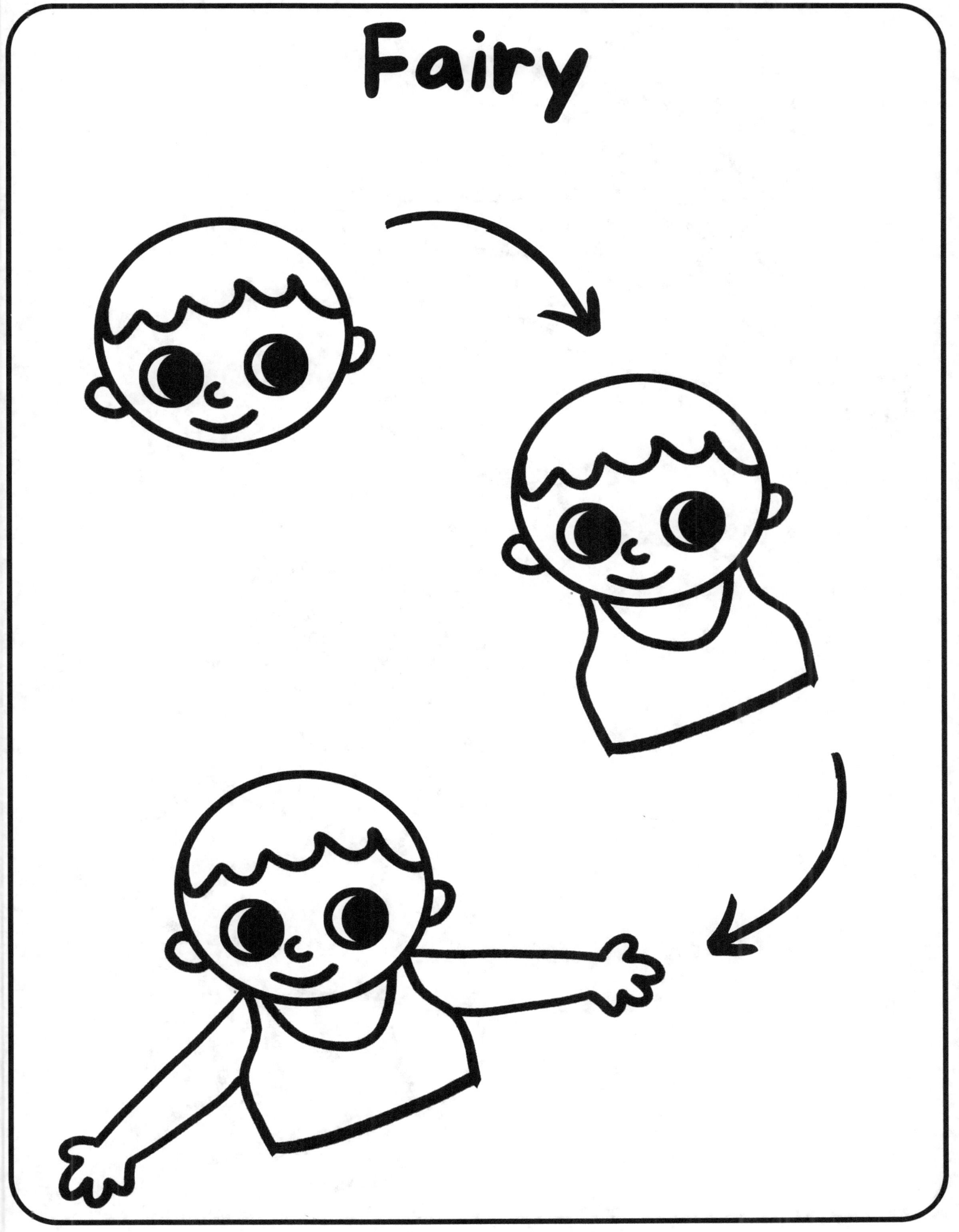

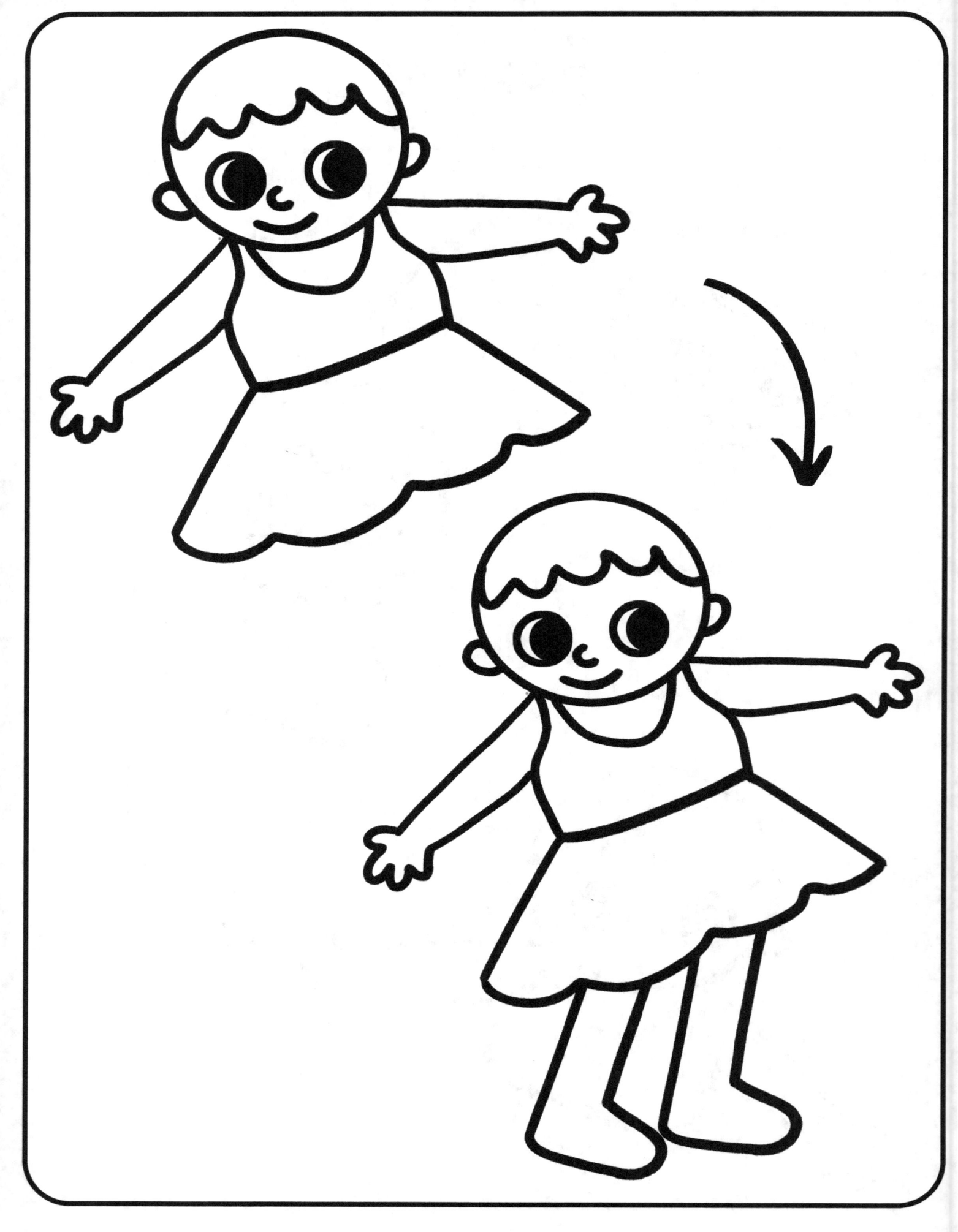

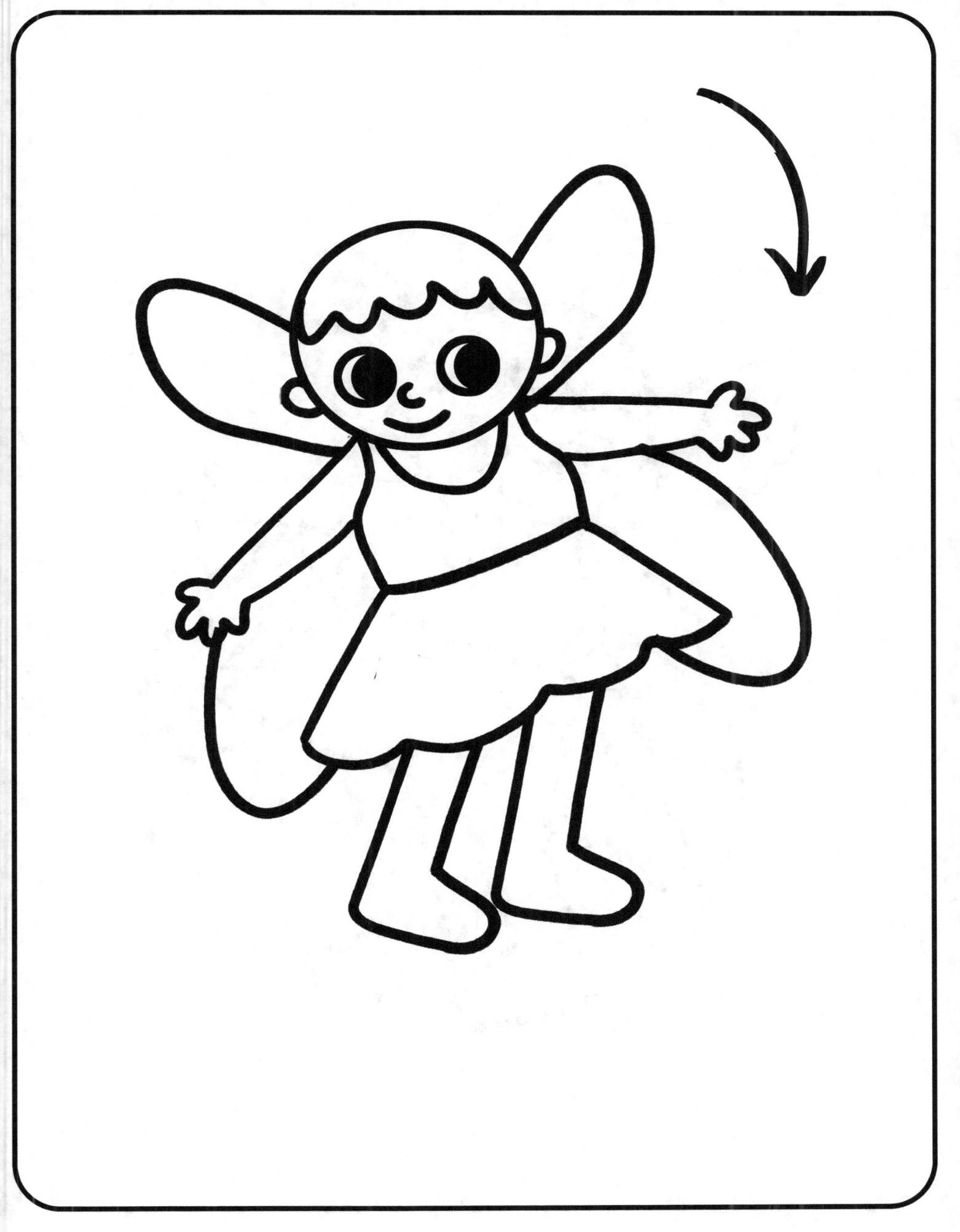

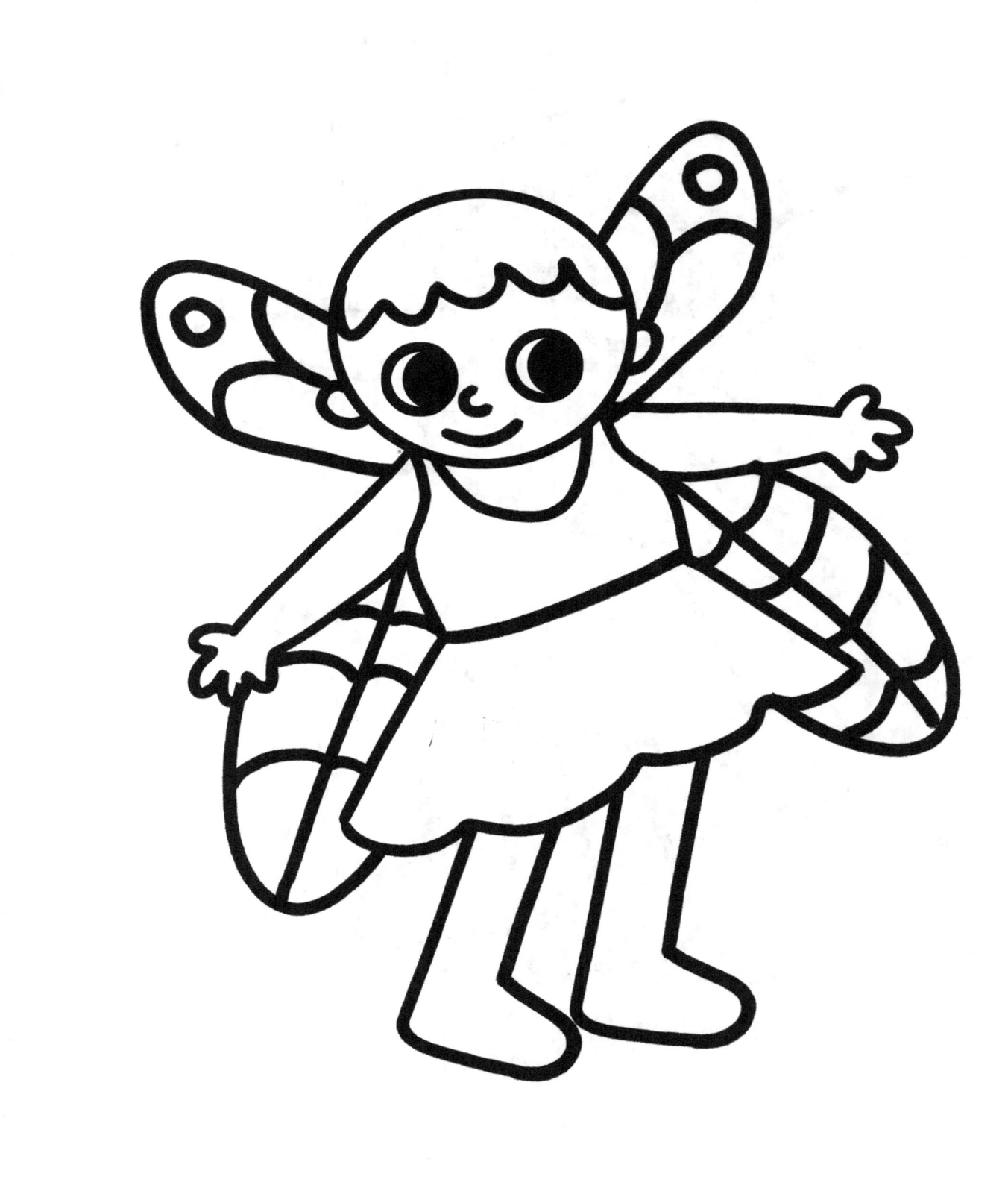

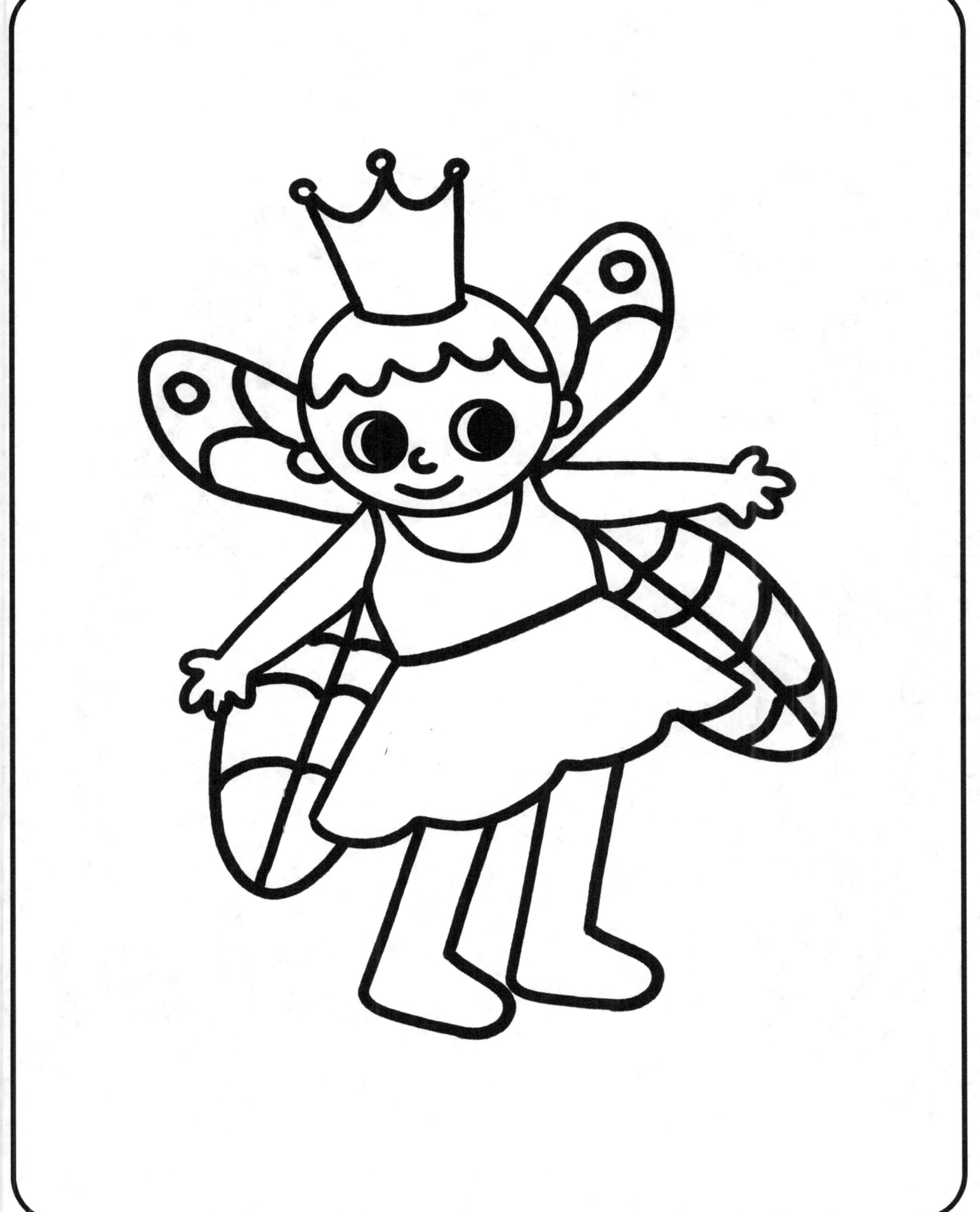

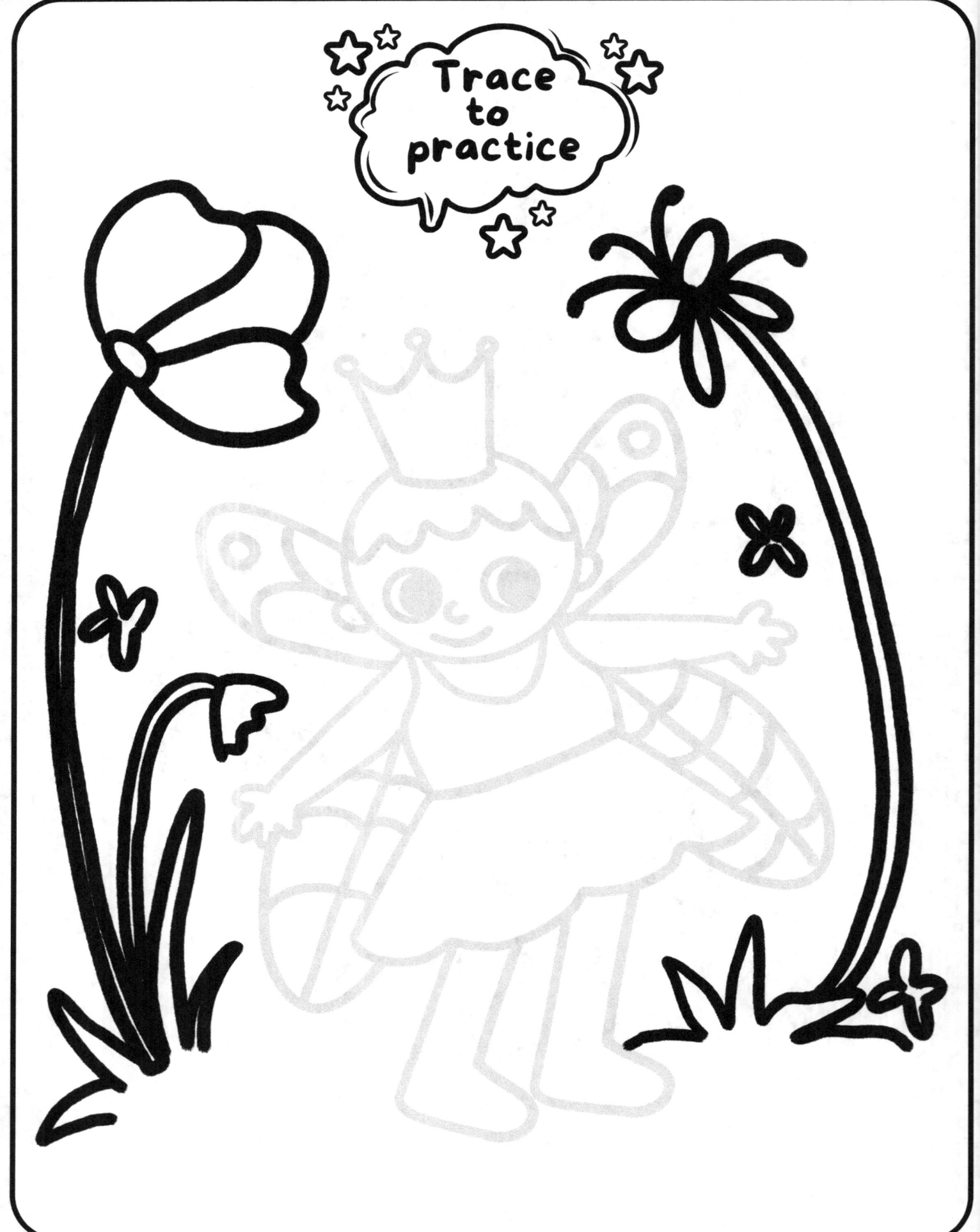

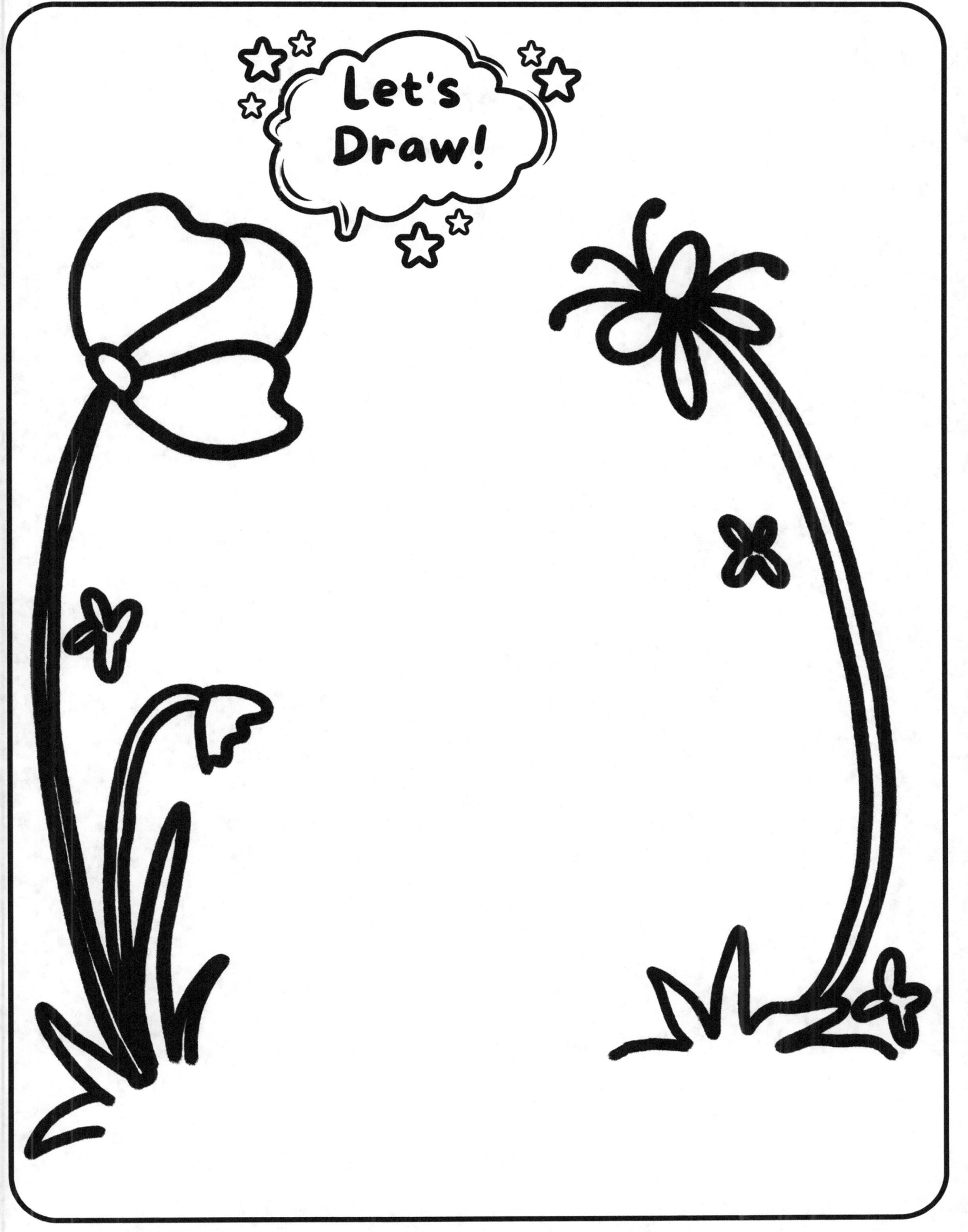